THE
KILL
BILL
DIARY

功夫

David Carradine

THE
KILL
BILL
DIARY

The Making of a Tarantino Classic as Seen Through the Eyes of a Screen Legend

HARPER

NEW YORK • LONDON • TORONTO • SYDNEY

HARPER

Designed by Nicola Ferguson

Library of Congress Cataloging-in-Publication Data
Carradine, David.
The Kill Bill diary : the making of a Tarantino classic as seen through
the eyes of a screen legend / David Carradine.
p.   cm.
ISBN-10: 0-06-082346-1
ISBN-13: 978-0-06-082346-7
New York : Harper, 2006.
1. Kill Bill, vol. 1 (Motion picture). 2. Kill Bill, vol. 2 (Motion picture).
3. Carradine, David. I. Title.
PN1997.2.K54C372006
791.43'72—dc22   2006043508

06 07 08 09 10 ❖ /rrd 10 9 8 7 6 5 4 3 2 1

For Si Litvinov, who gave me the idea,

and

*for Annie, who suffered with me through the long nights
it took to write it,*

and, of course,

*for Quentin
and
the whole Band Apart*

THE
KILL
BILL
DIARY

Prelude

This story could begin way back in 1996, when I first met QT (Quentin Tarantino, not *"Shhh"*) at the bar in the Sutton Place Hotel, during the Toronto Film Festival, or it could start on April 8, 2002, when I officially started the *Kill Bill* training. I know it was beginning to build a couple of years ago, when my little brother Mike Bowen (we have different mothers and fathers) told me on the hush-hush that Quentin was writing something for me.

More likely, the process that led me to *Kill Bill* began in earnest when I made the decision to grasp the hand of that elusive lady named Destiny myself, if only with my fingertips. That was during the summer of 2001, in Los Angeles. Days were lazy. The heat wave had passed, and from my eagle's aerie on the ninth floor of the condominium where I was temporarily residing, still smarting in the aftermath of my latest divorce, I could see palm trees waving their heads above Hollywood Boulevard, the traffic noises muted by the height. It was all very nice. Farther on, the smog took over to obscure the view, but it was all pretty benign that day.

I was trying to get up the nerve to fly to Austin, Texas, to try to hobnob with QT (the nerve and the bread). I had run into Quentin at a club about a month earlier, where we had both gone to hear Jeff Goldblum's jazz combo (Jeff plays a mean piano), and he'd rapped with me for a couple of hours, about all kinds of things, but all of it had to do with movies. Quentin doesn't care about anything else. Harvey Keitel, whom I knew from way back, when we worked together on *Mean Streets* (God, he was great!), was alongside, grinning throughout (suspiciously, I thought; as though he and Q shared some secret). Quentin makes movies featuring

ANNIE BIERMAN

cult people who can't get work. This could get interesting, I mused. He told me about this festival he runs every year where he shows a lot of movies he likes (and generally the critics hate) to cult moviegoers and other weirdos.

I decided I'd do it and the devil take the hindmost and the credit card. Go now, pay later, right? In blood, probably. I thought it might be a good way to get to know him better. I was dead-ass right. I made it there to Austin—flying coach, of course—and stretched my credit card even further staying at the best hotel in town. All this might have been one of my life's greatest decisions.

Quentin and I truly cooked together. The day I showed, he was having an all-night marathon of four revenge movies, between each of which, by sheer, happy coincidence (if there is such a thing), he was screening a 16 mm print of a *Kung Fu* episode from his collection, one from each season. I, of course, had to get up on stage with Quentin to talk about them. It turned out we were a great stand-up team. I left Austin with both of us knowing each other a lot better.

A little later, I got together with him again to show him the movie I'd made in Austin with Brother Mike Bowen, *Natural Selection,* a comedy about a serial killer, right up Quentin's alley, with me as the serial-killer hunter.

ANDREW COOPER/MIRAMAX FILMS

They've changed the name for the DVD release, to *Monster Hunter.* Don't ask me why. It makes it sound like some kind of horror flick. But that happens all the time with independent movies. They change the name from something artistic or literate to something catchy but dumb. It's happened to me a few times. *The Jade Jungle* became *Armed Response,* *Moonlight Sonata* was released as *Midnight Terror. The Silent Flute* became *Circle of Iron.* I think it's something about distributors needing to mark their territory. They have to piss on it just before they release it. If these guys had been around in 1939, *The Wizard of Oz* would have been called *Witch Hunter,* and *Gone With the Wind* would have been *The Burning of Atlanta,* or *Rhett's Revenge.*

I told Quentin I wasn't too sure about my performance. "It's kind of over the top," I said. Quentin laughed. "I've gotta see that!" He has his own screening room, decked out like a '50s movie theater. He calls it "The Church." A perfect replica of a '50s movie house.

He showed some grungy trailers before the film, and several of those cartoons advertising popcorn and soda pop, which, by the way, were available, along with a gourmet spread of sushi and fine wine.

Okay, now, fast-forward to 2002.

Volume
one

功夫

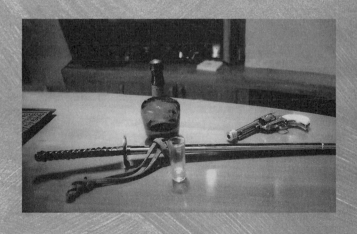

Thursday, March, 21, 2002

I'm back from across the great water. After four weeks in Alicante, Spain, making a movie called *La Bala Perdida (The Lost Bullet)*. Had the greatest time, riding my noble stallion and doing fast draws, surrounded by crazy Spaniards who hardly spoke English. Had to (get that: *HAD* to) stop in Paris on the way back. My wife, Annie, and I spent one glorious romantic night there, and then took the Eurostar, the train that goes under the English Channel, to jolly old London to close a deal to do a play there next year. We walked the streets, saw a play, and took the train back to Paris for one more day. It turned out our flight was cancelled—something to do with terrorists—so we were "forced" to stay an extra two days in Paris. Poor us.

Our hotel was a sweet little bed-and-breakfast right around the corner from the Arc de Triomphe. We visited the Sacre Coeur, a beautiful church on a hill that overlooks all of Paris, above the Place Pigale, where all the strippers hang out. A visit there has been an *always* tradition of mine since around '75. We spent an afternoon on the Ile St. Louis, an island in the middle of the Seine, and crossed the bridge to the Ile de la Cité, where Notre Dame Cathedral is, the place where Quasimodo the hunchback rang those bells. Then, that night, I took Annie for an extra treat: the Crazy Horse Saloon, for the classiest strip show on earth. She was almost the only female there, except for the ones on stage. Annie loved it. My kind of girl. After the show, the owner made us get on stage with the girls for a picture.

We walked back to our little hotel on a rare balmy Paris night, and kissed on the sidewalk, something we try to do on every sidewalk we're

A day in Paris

on. So far, we've done that in seven cities on three continents, plus a few small towns, and a temple or two.

When we got back home to L.A., there were three messages from Quentin Tarantino. Something about a documentary he was doing; interviews connected with the DVD releases of Quentin's movie *Jackie Brown*. There was also a message from my agent. I called him first, and was told I was up for a movie called *Kill Bill*, directed by Tarantino and starring Warren Beatty. I called Quentin and we set it up to meet at a Thai restaurant on Sunset Boulevard the next day, Friday. I was jumping! "I'm going to be in a Warren Beatty film!"

Friday, March 22

The next morning, I dressed myself in the cool clothes Annie had impelled me to buy in Alicante, Spain, and hopped into my '82 Maserati Quatro Porte. The place was hard to find. There were three Thai restaurants within two blocks, none of them with the name I remembered Quentin giving me. On the third try, I finally walked into a dark chamber with '50's rock & roll posters on the walls. I knew this must be the place. Quentin was already eating. I didn't recognize anything on the menu, so I ordered something more or less at random, which turned out to be a huge pile of noodles. Quentin talked pleasantly about this and that.

He said, "That's a great jacket."

"Yeah," I said. "Annie got this for me in Spain. I don't pay any attention to clothes. I usually just wear stuff from the movies I make."

This is not strictly true, but Quentin said, "Yeah! Me too!" Then he said, "Do you remember when we met, in a bar someplace in Toronto, during some festival?"

"Yeah," I said, "the Toronto Film Festival."

"There was this song you were playing on the piano. It was over the titles in *Sonny Boy*." (This is a cult movie I made in New Mexico, in which I wore a dress—kind of *Bonnie and Clyde,* with me as Bonnie.)

"Yeah," I said. "'Paint'; it's called 'Paint.'"

"Yeah," he said. *"Maybe* it's 'Paint,' right?" Quentin has an incredible memory. "I like that song."

What the hell! Did he come here to talk about my music?

Then, finally, he got down to it. "You said a psychic had told you to meet me."

"Well, yeah. My wife . . . *ex*-wife . . . was . . . uh . . . I know it sounds weird . . ."

"No," he said. "It doesn't. What you said was this psychic told you we were supposed to *work* together." He put a big emphasis on "work."

DAVID CARRADINE

"Uh, yeah. That's what he said."

"Well," Quentin said, "now's the time."

Cool!

"And," he said, "it's come about in a really organic way."

I said, "Isn't just about everything you do done in an organic way?"

"Well, yeah. It's kind of my *métier."* He laughed. Quentin laughs big. He does everything big. "Do you know anything about *Kill Bill?"*

Well, I knew a lot about it by now, but I just said, "Only that it's a movie you're making with Uma Thurman."

Okay, then he began this long story about his "love affair" with Warren Beatty, and how that had sort of soured.

"So, we had this meeting," he said. "And, sometimes I was thinking, It's okay, we can make it happen. And sometimes it was like, No way! This is just not going to work. I was beginning to think Warren just didn't *get* it, you know?

"Then, Warren suddenly blurted out, 'Look, I don't give a shit about Chinese kung fu movies, and I hate spaghetti Westerns, though I like Clint personally, and I wouldn't go to a Japanese samurai movie if you paid me.'

"Now," Quentin said, "he was saying that for effect, you know. And, well, it *HAD* its effect, you know? It just wasn't romantic! The relationship [I don't think Quentin really said "relationship"] between a director and his star has to have a little romance to it!

"And Warren was saying now, 'Hey, how long is this really going to take? How much time do I really have to put in? Do I really need to do all that training?' So, I'm thinking, You know I was really writing this character for you . . . about you, all the time . . . and I'm thinking, *Shit!* And we had another meeting, to try to put it back together—I mean Warren had been part of the film for a year—and I was saying how I wanted him to act . . . to be . . . sort of like David Carradine in this movie, and Warren said suddenly, 'Why don't you offer it to David?' Well, that gave me my out! Sooo . . ."

Suddenly I was getting it. This movie was no longer a Warren Beatty film. He was talking about me playing Bill. I was not stunned—no; nothing stuns me—but flipped out for sure. Quentin knew the effect he was having. He was really digging it. Beaming, he handed me a thick, I mean *thick,* script and told me to read it and get back to him and we'd meet Sunday and talk about it. He said he wanted to make sure I *got* it. If I did "get it," apparently the part was mine.

I walked out of there on some kind of cloud, almost bumping into things. Somehow I found my Maserati.

I looked at the cover of the script, almost two inches thick, with the title in hand-printing with a Magic Marker, which looked pretty childish. It said:

The 4th film by

Quentin
Tarantino

UMA
THURMAN

is going to

KiLL
BiLL

written
&
directed
by

Quentin Tarantino

Based on the character
of "the bride", created by

Q&U

. . . Only much funkier.

Saturday, March 23

Now, I'm thinking, Who knows what a script by Tarantino is going to be like? It could be toilet paper. I mean, his movies look as though they were improvised, don't they? Well, not *Jackie Brown*, for the most part. Still, I had no idea what to expect. On the first page, it identified the script as owned by a company called "Supércool Manchu" with a French *acute accent* on the "e"! Okay, let's see.

Well, with four kids all over me, it was really hard to get the chance to read the thing. I knew I couldn't skim it. I had to be ready with a smart answer for anything Quentin was going to ask about it. Anyway, once I got alone and started on it in earnest, there was no way to skip a single word. This script was hot! It was late Saturday afternoon when I finished. It turned out what was inside was actual literature. Beautiful, gripping stuff, worked out to the last detail. And funny! Two hundred pages of it. Just brilliant.

And, he essentially wrote it for me!

Actually, scratch the "essentially." According to Quentin, he wrote it for me and about me, thinking at every page, What would Carradine say, how would he react? Not the guy in *Kung Fu* so much as the guy in *Americana*, the film that won me the People's Prize at the Directors' Fortnight at the Cannes Film Festival, which he's watched on video several times. He'd rather see movies in their original real movie format, which in the case of *Americana* would be wide-screen 35 mm, with four-track magnetic surround sound; but a print is hard to find. Make that *impossible*. And the guy in *The Long Riders*, for sure. And the guy in *Shane*; he has 16 mm prints of that. Because of his fascination, you could say his obsession, with cheap movies, bloody movies, revenge movies, actually *any* movies, but particularly ones that are near the bottom of the industry's barrel, the ones that almost don't get a release, he has also consumed an almost fatal dose of my seventy-five independent, largely exploitation films, most of which went straight to video. He knows about the eleven Shakespearean plays I was in, too. This guy does his research.

And then there's the guy in my personal public figure, and, yeah, my mystique, I guess you have to call it. I think he was more . . . not impressed by, but simpatico to the iconoclastic madness of my life story than anything. He loves that shit. It's him, or the *Him* that he dreams of himself. Like Hunter Thompson. I think it might have been Tom Wolfe (if it wasn't, my apologies, Tom, and my apologies to whoever it was) who said in print once, "David Carradine lives the life that Hunter Thompson only writes about." And that's Quentin: able to get inside the heads of people who've experienced things which only a madman would wish on himself for real.

So, he wrote *Kill Bill* about me, or about what, with the help of my movies and the stories about me, he imagined I was like. He, of course, couldn't make the deal with me in the role, the Hollywood outsider and near pariah. (Which was, like I said, one of his reasons for digging me. His company, after all, *is* called "A Band Apart.") So, Warren Beatty was hired. A great choice, if you're stuck with someone on the A list. Warren is Royalty.

Destiny prevailed, however, when Uma Thurman got pregnant. A year of keeping it on hold gave the project enough clout so that it didn't really need Warren anymore to fly, and then he and Quentin sort of fell out of love. Then, during one of their frustrating last meetings about it, like the date you have with a girl after you've broken up, when you almost put it back together, and then somebody says something that scatters the little house of cards you're building, Warren himself pitched me for the part. Just busted out with it, I'm told. "Why don't you offer it to David?" Quentin shook hands with him, I guess with a little tear in his eye, and started those wheels turning. Harvey Weinstein himself told me that he asked Quentin, "Is he crazy?" Quentin said, "No, he's not crazy!" Harvey said, "Well, okay, you're the boss." And they went for it.

So, it's late Saturday afternoon, and I call Quentin. He later did an imitation for the amusement of the cast of my call. A great . . . no, a perfect imitation of Quentin Tarantino imitating David Carradine is what he did.

He said, "So, I'm waiting. It's Saturday morning. He doesn't call. Saturday afternoon. Still no call. I'm thinking, What the fuck! Finally later—a lot later—the phone rings."

"Hi." He pauses in his narrative, for the effect. "It's . . . David"—Talking very slowly.

"'Oh. Yeah. Hi,' I say," he says.

"So . . ." Pause. He says, "I've read the script."

"Yeah?"

"Yeah." Pause . . . *Long* pause. "I . . . like it." Long pause. "Sooo . . ." Pause. "I . . . guess we should get together," Another long pause, then: "Aw hell! I fucking *LOVE* the script!"

Pretty much how it went, except I think some of those long pauses were more what he'd seen me do as Kwai Chang Caine on TV than how I was actually talking that day. No matter; Quentin gets to play around if he wants to.

He makes a date for Sunday afternoon. That would be Academy Awards Sunday. I have to go to Norby Walters' "Night of a Hundred Stars" at the Beverly Hills Hotel that night. I need to make it back and get into a tuxedo in time to get picked up by the limo and walk the red carpet. I'd managed to reserve the lone Cadillac sedan the limo company owned, in spite of the Oscars rush they were having. I hate Lincolns. A prejudice, I know, but I nurture it. Bob Dylan once identified the Lincoln as "A good car to drive after a war" and I've never been able to ditch the image of the owner (or passenger) of one as a fat war profiteer, sitting in the back, smoking a fat Cuban cigar. Not that I have anything against Cuban cigars, just fat war profiteers.

I don't sleep much that night, my head full of what I'm going to say to Quentin. I wish I could think of a way to act like my regular self when we meet, but I know that's impossible.

Sunday, March 24

I can't believe Quentin has time to take off on Oscar Sunday to meet with me. Well, yeah, I can believe it. The guy's his own man (A Band Apart, remember?) and this is about casting the lead in his movie, his great epic film.

So I put on some jeans, cowboy boots, a tank top with something about .357s on it, and a big, heavy, black leather jacket from *Kung Fu, The Legend Continues,* climb into Annie's huge black GMC SUV with the Harley sticker on it, with Thunder, my Bernese mountain dog, in the back (he goes everywhere with me), and haul over to Quentin's pad in the Hollywood Hills. I'd been there before, to watch movies in his vintage movie theater, but had never been inside the house. He buzzes the gate open and I growl up the long driveway. I leave Thunder in the truck, and ring the doorbell. It takes a while before Quentin opens the door. He's in short pants and a Hawaiian shirt. "Yeah, yeah. Come on in," he says. "I'll be right with you." And he disappears. I go in through a big foyer and work my way through a maze of movie posters and memorabilia, in four or five languages, all over the walls, chairs, and floors. I find a space on a couch and sit down. He reappears, and says what do I want to drink. I say coffee, if he has it. He's got an espresso maker, but he's never used it. Doesn't know how it works. We fuck around with it for a while with no success, and finally I settle for a Coke. He has a beer, and we go outside to the terrace. We start talking about everything under the sun, except the film.

But it's all about movies. Orson Welles: We both agree that *Citizen Kane* is not the best movie ever made, as the American Film Institute claims. It's too black and white, in every sense of the term, and he overacts. Anyway, it's not even Welles' best. That would probably be *Touch of Evil*. He lets himself hang out almost embarrassingly in that flick. Incredibly self-knowing performance. And I try to imagine him, grumbling and stumbling through that performance, and then saying "Cut!" and " Now put the camera over here." Boggles the mind. But it's not the best movie ever made.

Steven Spielberg: Quentin and I sort of disagree about him. I feel that his massive and remarkably popular body of work doesn't hold a candle to the few pictures that David Lean made: *Lawrence of Arabia*, which gets my vote as the best movie of all time, and *The Bridge on the River Kwai*, a close second. Lean's philosophy is always intact and consistent. Steven's is all over the place. I feel he's forgotten the kid who used to climb the fence to try to get to talk to the bosses at Universal. Now, he's such an institution that some of the humanity is hidden away behind the mogul. Quentin says no, and he probably knows better: He actually hangs out with Spielberg.

Marlon Brando: so huge, tragic, like one of the Olympian gods. Ernst Lubitsch, who Quentin is very big on. I'm really not very familiar with his stuff, but then I saw those pictures so long ago, before Quentin was born!! Marty Scorsese: We both wish the Academy would loosen up and give him the award. Francis Coppola: *The Godfather* and *Apocalypse Now* will be watched a hundred years from now. And, of course, Roger Corman. Quentin loves the B picture guys. Roger is the king of that, though he hates the term, and I've done nine films with him and his wife, Julie. Roger made the action flicks and the sexy exposés, all of that, while Julie made brooding character studies. Sometimes they worked together, as on *Boxcar Bertha,* the film I made with Marty Scorsese. Roger told Marty, "When you talk to the press, don't say anything about labor unions or social injustice," though that's what the movie was about. "Just keep talking about robbing trains, shooting guns, and visiting whorehouses."

We also reveled in our esoteric knowledge of little-known films: *The Three Penny Opera,* a musical version starring Laurence Olivier; a version of *Don Quixote,* with Feodor Chaliapin, the great operatic basso, and he sings in it. This is probably one of the earliest screen musicals ever made; sound had just come in. There's a film made in Germany in about 1956 called *The Devil's General,* about a *Luftwaffe* general who changes his mind about the

Nazis and does a kamikaze raid on his own factory, blowing up it and himself. Curt Jurgens gives the performance of his life. I saw that picture about six times in Berkeley, while I was auditing at the University of California. He's a much better actor in his own language. I've based my else.

It's pretty hot by Quentin's pool. And blinding (the conversation, *and* the weather). Quentin has his shades on. I put on my own dark glasses, for a while, anyway, and take off my jacket, and eventually, my boots, and try to look cool and easy. Actually, I feel like a college kid taking his oral exam, and awed in the presence of one of the lesser gods to boot. He tells me that, for the whole three years or so that he's been writing this movie, he hasn't found anyone who really *gets* it. And he's lonely. And do I *get* it? Yeah, I *get* it. Kung fu, samurai, spaghetti Western, gangster love story, Japanese anime, I get it all. We talk for two hours. I say I have to go. He walks me to the truck. He meets Thunder. He's still rapping away about the movie, all excited. He says, "Now, do you have any other obligations we have to worry about?" "Well, yeah," I say, "concerts, autograph conventions, personal appearances, but almost all of them on weekends." He says he can live with that. I send Thunder off to take a pee, and say, "So what about Tuesday?" He had said that's when training starts, with the wire crew from *Matrix* and *Crouching Tiger, Hidden Dragon*. I say, "I don't want to miss the first day." He says, "Well, if you come Tuesday, you have to come Wednesday." Thunder peeks out at us from behind a tree while he pees. "Okay, yeah. I'm in." We shake on it. I mention Rob Moses, my long time trainer and guitar buddy, who's been by my side since *Lone Wolf McQuade*—that's twenty years. I'm thinking he could finally get his SAG card. Can he be along in the training? Quentin says sure, if it's cool with Yuen Wu Ping, the wire guy—"The Master." He's the last word on the training. I wrangle Thunder into the truck and drive away, leaving my prescription sunglasses, my cigarette case, my Dunhill lighter, and my brain behind.

I should add here that I started working on Quentin way back in 1996, when I tracked him down at the Toronto Film Festival. I figured he could be my salvation. He did it for Travolta, and I'm much more his style. And I really dig the guy. I managed to keep in touch with him from time to time over those years, culminating in the visit to Austin. I'm pretty sure that's where the campaign gelled.

There was also the niggling realization that he was lumping me with all the losers, the faded almost-stars, the totally faded TV guys, and, of course, *the bad boys*. True enough, all of it. For the last couple of years I'd been supporting myself with autograph conventions. I was always the biggest thing there, but that's not saying too much. Guys from old TV shows, the girl from *The Little Rascals* movies (now in her seventies), Linda Blair of *The Exorcist*, and the guy who was inside the "Black Lagoon" creature suit are typical examples. Scotty from *Star Trek*—anybody, actually, who'd ever had any kind of a part on any of the incarnations of *Star Trek*. Very near the end of the line, by my standards anyway. Scary. I could hear the coffin nails being driven in.

But those are the people he loves the most, more than the big, successful stars. A guy like Quentin has got to be rooting for the underdog. He reaches out a hand to those he thinks aren't too far gone, and whom he thinks are worth saving. The cool part of it all is that he picked me to work on this time. I'll sure as hell do my best to come up to his expectations.

One interesting result, though, of the autograph thing: A guy who writes for *High Times* came by my table, somewhere in Ohio. He said it was funny they'd never done me. I agreed. Yeah. Funny. So, they sent a very cool unregenerated beatnik/hippy to my house and we rapped for an hour or so. They offered me the cover, but I declined. They knew I would. Celebrities always do, it appears. He asked me if drugs were legalized today, what would I have in my pocket. I told him, "An apple. Been there. Done that." Then I said, quoting my big brother, Keith: "You know, there's a reason they call it 'dope.'" The issue should have been on the street in a couple of months, but I never heard any more about it. Guess I was too straight for them. He also, though it was clear to him I'm not really into it anymore, gave me a little present, de rigueur for the magazine, I guess: a huge bud, so powerful that from inside a plastic ziplock bag in a tin box in a drawer, it stunk up the whole house. I gave it away to a friend. Well, actually, I used it as bait, to get this particular friend, whose muscles and appetite for hard work are legendary, to help me move some heavy items of furniture up and down the stairs. He appreciated the bud, and Annie appreciated getting rid of the skunk odor.

At "The Night of a Hundred Stars," in front of all the TV cameras, I didn't know if I was supposed to talk about the movie. I figured Quentin might want to make his own announcement, and the Warren Beatty thing was probably a little delicate. So, I tell them I'm about to do this big, wonderful movie, but I can't say anything about it yet. Annie says, "You're allowed to be coy." That I dig. I act coy. I wish I could tell *someone,* though. Inside, Michael Madsen whispers to me, "Do you know if Warren drops out, you've got the part in *Kill Bill*?" I whisper back, "It's a done deal." Feels great.

Monday, March 25

I'm to take a meeting with Harvey Weinstein of Miramax and Quentin's partner, Lawrence Bender, who will produce the film, at the Peninsula Hotel. I have a hard time finding the place, as it's so exclusive it doesn't have a sign, and I really don't want to be late. Then, in the lobby, where I'm supposed to meet them, I can find no one. I almost collide with Steven Seagal in the doorway. He says, "Are you okay, David?" Staring down at me from his Brodingnagian height. I say, "I'm great! [Are you kidding?] Good as I get!" That appears to make him happy. It's hard to tell with Steven. I wonder if he had seen the lampoon we did of him on *MADtv*. Then, I say, "I've gotta go." He seems disappointed. Well, I'm on a mission from God.

After wading through several extremely stuffy and unctuous officials, waiters, etc., I finally have the meeting with Miramax on the terrace behind the dining room. Harvey is very sweet, as he's always been, every time I've met him. Lawrence turns out to be extremely hip and sharp, with a definite elegance. I can't tell if he's a good guy or a bad guy. A perfect match for Quentin, though. We talk about wardrobe. Harvey wants to see me in Giorgio Armani suits. I know that isn't going to happen. But, I know what that is about. He thinks something has to be done to make me more like Warren. I know, though, that what Quentin wants is to capitalize on exactly who I really am. After all, he'd built the whole script around that idea. I knew Quentin would have his way, with Harvey and Miramax, and with me. We'd all bend over for him. None of this really matters, though. It's clear to me this meeting is chiefly a matter of protocol. Harvey wants to be part of the mix.

I know I said some stupid, naïve things. When I'm talking to Masters of the Universe like Harvey Weinstein, I always feel like a little boy. And I try to say something smart. When I feel at ease I am smart. I should learn to listen more when I'm insecure. The strong silent type is a better bet than the kid who's trying to be a wise guy. It's like the thing I have about names. I can't remember them. So, my solution to that has become . . . simply never calling anyone by their name. It works okay, though my old buddy Jeff once pointed out to me that a person's name, when they hear it, is like a caress. Better safe, however, than sorry. I remember once at the Sundance Festival calling Glenn Close, whose work I absolutely love, "Meryl." I tried to fix it by pretending I couldn't see without my glasses. But I don't think I fooled her.

This whole ambience was part of some other league that was completely out of my ken. It didn't matter. I couldn't blow it unless I farted in his face; I found out later from Harvey himself that that was pretty much the case. He and Lawrence were checking me out to make sure Quentin was right when he said I wasn't crazy. If I passed the psycho test, I was in.

Tuesday, March 26

Then we go into the negotiation thing. Gayle Max, my sainted new manager, is ecstatic and supercharged with this opportunity. It's just what we've been looking for, and a lot more. And we're going to make a lot of money here. They have me training for two months and then shooting for four, at least. That should be worth a lot of dough.

Not exactly. It turns out that actors' salaries are not what Quentin intends to spend his forty million on. Lawrence Bender tells Gayle no one is taking any money for the film. They're all working for scale or double-scale. Warren was. Daryl Hannah, Lucy Liu, Vivica Fox—they're all willing to work for nothing, just for the chance to be in a Tarantino film. He reminds us what a great opportunity this is, how much *Pulp Fiction* did for Travolta, all that. Gayle, bless her, tells him, "Yeah, well, those people are all rich. David does this for a living! He's going to have to turn down work at his regular price." They cough up a few more bucks. But, they stick on all the little extras. Nobody gets those, they say. The biggest thing being all the training, eight hours a day, five days a week, for two, three months—for nothing. Also, it starts to look bad for all my little appearance and concert dates, as the shooting is going to take place in China, Japan, Mexico, and the Canary Islands, as well as Southern California. I'm going to have to cancel a lot of gigs. And nobody remembers my conversation with Quentin about Rob Moses, my trainer. Gayle attacks that one with definite gusto. She's touched by my loyalty. Well, shit! Rob has been by my side "through everything I done," like Bobby McGee, for twenty years, and never got much out of it except my company.

Wednesday, March 27

Quentin brought me and a few others in for a rehearsal at his Culver City Citadel, a supermodern spread-out facility totally out of character for him—but, hey, he's the boss. The place was humming with the Apart Band, a bunch of thoroughly Quentin-like people—though no one is, of course, like Quentin. Kindred, though. Everybody smiling and happy in their "apartness." On hand were Uma and some of the others. Quentin was putting us all through our paces, utilizing for each of us one of our best scenes. I got to work with Uma a little, and then they sent me to the front, where I gave the costumer my sizes, talked with props about watches, cigarette lighters, and gun rigs, and met with the set designer, where I got a look at the fabulous locations they had found and the equally spectacular sets they were planning to build there. We talked about what would be a good car for Bill to drive. In the script, it lists a Porsche. I was fervently hoping that wouldn't happen. The designer was talking about a Cadillac. He thought Bill should drive American. I agreed, and told him about the Cien, the new V12 sports prototype I'd seen at the auto show. I suggested maybe they'd loan it to us. Quentin said, "If they won't, we'll build it."

Today was Tarantino's birthday (thirty-ninth). There was a thing with a birthday cake at the office before we all split, and Uma, Ethan Hawke, and some of the others had arranged a party for the evening. Quentin's idea of a party always includes watching a movie, so they had set one up to happen in his sacred screening room, "The Church." Quentin knew all about this, but the name of the movie was a secret. The picture was to be his surprise present. I showed up, with Annie, knowing she'd get a big kick out of the event (everything is an event at Quentin's). We ate some pop-corn and sushi, and I drank a Coke, while Annie sampled the Merlot. Then we all sat down as Ethan Hawke introduced the evening's entertain-ment. He tried to be coy about what the movie was, but Quentin guessed it. He jumped up and yelled, "*Bound For Glory*! I love it!" For Christ's sake, this old movie of mine was everybody's idea of what Quentin wanted most for his birthday! They had tracked the print down at some art house and borrowed it for the night. It had to be back in the theater tomorrow. Also included was the salacious trailer for *Summer Love*, I think it was called, a movie Daryl Hannah made right at the beginning of her career. Every-body had a hoot over it, and Daryl was appropriately blushing, but I saw that movie when it came out. It's actually a pretty good movie, and Daryl is fabulous in it. I had said to myself at the time, Who is this girl? I told everybody who would listen that she was going to be a star, for sure.

I should have spoken up while Quentin and his minions were making their fun, but I was still too shy with these people to butt in. Maybe I'll get Daryl aside someday and set it straight. They also screened the trailer for *Boxcar Bertha*. That brought back some memories, mostly good. None bad, actually, just some sort of bittersweet. Barbara Hershey and I were so in love then. It was maybe the high point of our romance. It's almost painful to watch us together on the screen.

March 27, 2002

"Kill Bill"
Supércool Manchu, Inc.
10950 W. Washington Boulevard, Suite 150
Culver City, CA 90232
Ph: 310/555-6480 Fax: 310/555-9033
Att. Lawrence Bender

To all concerned:

As you may know, on Academy Sunday when Quentin and I struck our deal, I made it clear that I had some previous commitments, which were all weekend gigs, mostly concerts. Quentin assured me that we could work around those days. Here is my schedule. As you will see, having seen the tentative shooting schedule, I've stripped away a couple of dates as impossible, too close, or too risky for the production.

The other issue is that of Rob Moses, my "trainer." In the same conversation, I asked if he could be included in the practice. Quentin said: yes, as long as, of course, it was simpatico with the master-at-arms, so to speak. Rob has worked with me for twenty years. I have never been without him. He is the disciple of *my* master, Sifu Kam Yuen, a 35th-generation master of Tai Mantis, making Rob the 36th and me the 37th, if you care to look at it that way. We descend in a direct line from the creator of the 37th chamber. Quentin knows what that means. Rob's inclusion in the process would be as organic as things get. He's prepared to quit his school for the duration to participate. Unfortunately, he can't give his time, forty hours a week, for free. He has to live, as do I. If something can be worked out here, that would be great: for Rob, for me, for the movie.

As for the 3rd issue of the car and driver, I will bite that bullet without further discussion, paying for that myself. The only boon I would ask is to let me use someone from the company rather than an outsider. Ben is a perfect candidate, and he lives in the valley, making it an easy ride for him.

David
cc: Quentin Tarantino

Thursday, March 28

The negotiations have finally been set in stone. The driver issue got extremely sticky. I have had a driver assigned to me on every job I've had, from the fattest bloated studio behemoths to the tiniest semipro indies, ever since the last year of *Kung Fu,* when I fell asleep on the way to work one morning and woke up in the middle of an accident. Lawrence was adamant. No one else has a driver. On location, yes, but not in L.A. Well, no one else had a driver in L.A. on all those other pictures either, but *I* did. And, hey, Uma has a driver. "That's different," Lawrence says. Well, yes, it is. She has a new baby. She's getting paid, too. Well, that's different, too. The show is written around her, and she has been a collaborator with Quentin on the script. Well, it seems to me the show was written around me, too, and I have apparently been an absent collaborator of sorts. The debate goes on, back and forth, between the negotiators. No, Ben can't do it, even if I pay for him. He could pick me up, maybe, but he doesn't get off at five, so he couldn't take me home. Never mind. This issue, we stress, Gayle and I, is not a deal-breaker. Hey, nothing is, actually. There is nothing I can think of that would be, unless they decided to

ANDREW COOPER/MIRAMAX FILMS

actually kill me. So, no driver. That's done. The deal is struck. Rob is in, though: I accomplished that much. He volunteers, eagerly, to pick me up and drop me off, so that's solved as well.

Meanwhile, Tuesday had come and gone, and training hadn't begun. Yuen Wu Ping, the wushu-and-wire master, and his band of circus acrobats were engaged in finishing up their work on *Matrix II*. The new date to start was April 1, but April 1 went by without the training beginning (ha ha, April fools). I should have known something right then about the schedule of this movie. It was destined to change radically many times before it was over.

Friday, March 29

This, now, was the main event: a reading of the script with as many of the principals as could be assembled—Uma; Daryl; Vivica; Julie Dreyfus, who sat beside me, a lovely English lady with a command of French and Japanese, which skills are part of her role; Michael Madsen; Michael Jai White; Michael Parks, who was there to reprise his lawman role from *From Dusk Till Dawn*; and Parks' son, who was to play his deputy. Ricardo Montalban was slated to play the Mexican pimp who was Bill's surrogate father, but he was a no-show, so Quentin asked Michael Parks to read that part. We read the whole script, with Quentin doing the descriptions (I should say "literature," for that's what it is) between the lines. This took a good solid while to do, with two hundred pages to get through. Not that anybody minded. We all knew we were embarking on maybe the best journey of our collective careers, with a seasoned captain who knew the waters. Halfway through, we broke for a catered-in lunch. I got a lot of compliments. Michael Jai White went on about how great my voice is. Funny. I've always thought I just had a voice, like a human, you know. But I keep getting this comment, so I suppose they all know something I don't. Anyway, it all felt great. This is going to be one kick-ass movie.

Something I noticed that strengthened my belief in Quentin's abilities was the realization that his huge brain is capable of multitasking far beyond what the experts say is possible. He was standing by the table giving instructions to an assistant, talking on his cell phone, explaining to all of us how the day was going to go, and ordering lunch all at the same time, without skipping a beat. The human brain is not supposed to be capable of that. But Quentin is not your run-of-the-mill earthling.

Michael Parks as himself. He is deep. *DAVID CARRADINE*

When we sat down to read the second half, Michael Parks surprised everyone by giving what I swear was a better version of the character than Ricardo could have done. Quentin hired Michael on the spot. Ricardo was out. I'd say we all decided at that point that one thing none of us were ever going to do was miss one of Quentin's meetings.

Part of the deal is that Uma, Daryl Hannah, Lucy Liu, Vivica A. Fox, and I must report to a gym in Culver City, and study samurai with Sonny Chiba, the king of samurai movies these days, as well as kung fu: actually wushu. Rob Moses calls it "kung fu circus." It wouldn't work on the street, he says. (He oughta know.) And wirework with Yuen Wu Ping's troupe of *Crouching Tiger* and *Matrix* fame, plus free weights and that hamster shit on treadmills and bicycles that don't go anywhere, all this 9 to 5, Monday thru Friday, for two solid months.

Monday, April 8

We report to the gym they've put together in Culver City. They said 9 to 5; Rob and I show up at 8:30. We're the first ones there. I like that. The facility couldn't be better. A huge room, with about a forty-foot ceiling, to accommodate the wires. Big mats, pads, free weights, all kinds of machines, a big bag and a rubber dummy to beat up, mirrors, ballet barres, lots of towels, and a kitchen with tons of nonfattening food and drink available nonstop. A nice surprise is a private room for me to hang out in with my name on it; well, "Bill's" name.

We start out stretching, which we will do for an hour every day. Little by little the group shows up. Quentin is the first. He goes straight to the treadmill, and as the ladies arrive, they join him and talk animatedly while they jog and then walk, for a good half hour or so. Then the cadre arrives: A trainer for each of the actors. Wu Ping and his assistant—"Fish" is his name. He is sort of the ship's doctor, dispensing Chinese liniments and Ace bandages. Sonny Chiba, the samurai master (and virtually worshipped star of *Street Fighter* and *Shadow Warriors*), and his assistant, Tetsuro Shimaguchi, who will become my fast friend, in spite of a huge language barrier. Wu Ping doesn't work out with us. He commands lots of respect, looks darkly at everyone, and goes outside for a lot of smoke breaks. He is a master of not looking at you. Through you, or right past you, but not at you. It will take me a month to get a "Good morning" from him. When I finally achieve that, I know I've been recognized by him as a member of the human race—an honor which doesn't come easily with Wu Ping.

Once we're stretched out, we start kicking. Hundreds of front kicks, side kicks, roundhouse kicks. Then punches, punch-and-kick combinations, and moving on to bits of choreography, some of which will make it into the film. I had figured my thirty years playing around with kung fu would put me ahead, but these girls are hot, and relentless. And this stuff is very different. Wushu. More balletic than martial, though I certainly would not care to go a few rounds with any of these trainers. They are all superb athletes, in the greatest condition. At one point, I wonder if I'm going to make it here. My head is spinning and I can hardly lift my leg, but I slog on. Got to. Everybody drinks a lot of bottled water. I stick with green tea and Matte. Lunch mercifully arrives: catered-in Chinese and Japanese grub. I confine myself to a big fresh fruit salad with a pile of cottage cheese on top. After lunch Quentin gives us a lively introduction and history lesson, then shows a videotape of some classic kung fu or samurai movie. Then we practice the wires. I love that. There is a formal samurai lesson from Sonny, assisted ably and delightfully by Tetsuro. This is where I start to really get off. You'd think I wouldn't like it. Everything is very formal: the bowing; the precise way you move your feet; how you draw the sword; how you put it back. But I really dig it. Later on, we'll be learning some fancier stuff, but for now, we're just dealing with the basics. In between all this, we find time for cardiovascular activities on treadmills and bikes, and weight lifting, and tummy crunches. I need thousands of those, no doubt about it. At five, we quit. Whew!

Rob and I ride back to Tarzana together, an hour and a half at least in the rush-hour traffic, talking up a storm. When I get home, I can hardly get out of the car, I'm so crippled up.

Then I've got to make it up the stairs. I sleep like a rock.

Friday, April 26

So that's my life now, for the next two or three months. There's no time and no energy for anything else, just the workout. I've never worked this hard at anything before. Back in 1965, I lifted weights three times a week at Sigmund Klein's Gym on Seventh Avenue; Klein's the legendary trainer who brought up a few Mr. Universes, and who worked with actors, too, such as Laurence Olivier. For a couple of years, I ran seven miles every day on the beach in Malibu. And, of course, I've practiced kung fu off and on for over thirty years; but doing weight training, wushu, the wirework, samurai, and jogging on a treadmill, all in one day, five days a week, 9 to 5: That's more dedication than I ever thought I could muster up.

Of course, it gets easier every day. Rob has to go out of town and I start braving the trip in the Maserati. One morning I've just had it in the shop, giving it a thorough mechanical once-over, when something goes wrong with the transmission. No way I'm going to be late, so I press on, with terrible grinding noises and the belts slipping like crazy. Then I start to smell burning Bakelite, one of my favorite aromas. Especially in the morning. Smells like . . . expensive repairs. Well, I made it to the gym, and on time. Barely; I mean the Maser's transmission barely made it. My perfect attendance record was intact, though. I called Franco and he sent a tow truck for the car. It turned out (surprise surprise) the tranny was fried. One of the cooling hoses had broken. Fortunately, the car has a Chrysler transmission, a common item, so it cost only fifteen hundred bucks to replace it, instead of five thousand or so.

Rob returns, and we're back to our old routine while the Maser is in the hospital. The cadre doesn't know quite what to do with Rob. Maybe they're intimidated by him. In some ways he's far ahead of all of them. He wanders around, sometimes just looking for something to do. He's usually off doing his own thing while we're all working hard at the wushu exercises. Suddenly, we hear a resounding whack! We all turn to look, and there is the rubber man, lying on his side, the water which is supposed to weigh him down so he can't fall over leaking out all over the floor. Rob has decked him, with one punch. I've never seen anyone do that before. Didn't know you could. Rob sheepishly sets the dude back up, gets some towels, and mops up the water. He's really embarrassed, but we're all amazed. Well, that's Rob. "Humble" doesn't begin to describe him.

Every Friday, at the end of the day, Quentin gives a "State of the Union" address (his name for it). He gets the cast into his cubicle, and we all sit on the couch and prepare to cringe while he tells us how we've done this week and what we can do to improve the process. Rob Moses is there, too, sitting on the floor off to one side, his back against the wall. This Friday, Quentin's particularly tough on us. He harps on slow starters in the morning. "No one is to be still suiting up, or having coffee, after nine," he says. "Come at eight-thirty, and get all that done." When the clock strikes nine, he wants us all on the floor, starting to sweat. The other issue is flagging energies after lunch and late in the day. He says he can see people starting to look at the clock and treading water by around three-thirty. There are still two hours to go, he says, and he wants us to keep crunching right to the end.

Vivica raises her hand, and asks, "Wait a minute. Are you saying now the workout is eight-thirty to five? You want us here at fucking eight-thirty?" And before Quentin can get in a good answer, she's off! On a tirade! We're giving our fucking all here. We are getting up at seven, braving the traffic, sweating all fucking day, same shit traffic on the way home, no time for family, shopping, or any other thing, and all for free, and now he wants *more*? As far as slowing down later in the day, she's beat, she says. After 500 front-kicks and 240 tummy crunches, yeah, she's starting to watch the clock! And it so happens, she adds, that every single one of the girls is at a certain time of the month right now as well (part of the reason for her tirade, no doubt), and "Back off, motherfucker."

While Quentin is unusually, or should I say "uniquely," stuck for an answer, suddenly, all the girls get going. He's hit with back talk from all sides. Vivica is still leading the pack, but they all get on the rag now. Rob Moses sits on the floor just keeping his mouth shut, and trying to look small, while Quentin is busy trying to deal with what could shortly be called a mutiny. He says, "Hey, I'm working right alongside with the rest of you." Vivica is not impressed. He comes around, yes, she says, and does the treadmill while he gaily raps with Uma and Daryl, and he does some workout stuff, but he's treated "a little special" by the cadre, and in the afternoon, he closes the door of his cubicle and does administrative stuff, or he takes field trips, scouting locations. She's on fire. This is Labor versus Management, and she's not budging.

Heartened by Vivica's courage, or you could I suppose call it "sass," I pipe up. My gripe is I feel unused. He had told me in his State of the Union two weeks back that Wu Ping's guys were afraid to tell me stuff because they had so much respect for me as fans. I had said, "What? Go for it! I'm here to learn!" Then, last week, he said that on the wires, I was "the one to emulate." Since then I've not been on the wires once. Meanwhile, I don't feel like an actor here. I'm just a rusty athlete training for the Olympics (or maybe the Special Olympics or the Over-Forty Olympics). It says in the script I'm supposed to be so good with the sword that I fight with one hand in my pocket, and I'm not getting any of that. Sonny tells me that is absolutely forbidden. Some kind of samurai protocol. I know this doesn't hold water, as the most famous samurai of them all, Matsumoto, was famous for doing just that.

Matsumoto was a total renegade. He violated every rule, every tradition, and never lost a fight. (Well, of course he didn't. You lose a samurai fight, you're dead.) He often didn't even bother with a sword—he'd take on his opponents with a stick. One famous story concerns the tradition of washing one's self before a contest. The idea is you must purify yourself before a battle, to show respect for The Art and for your opponent. They brought him a big basin of water, and he tilted it up to his mouth and drank it all down, and went on to do the fight dirty from his travels. He won it, of course. I think our Bill is more that kind of guy.

I'm not getting any style going here. I'm just taking a big class in basic samurai. I get no feeling at all of this guy Bill's take on all this, which is what I'm here for. And as for this late-afternoon-slump thing, I'm wandering around looking for something to do and no one is using me. What he's asking me to do is *look busy*. That's not what I'm here for, and, anyway, it's too late in life for me to resort to that kind of water-treading. Give me something real to do, and I'll do it!

The session ends with Quentin getting himself back in the captain's chair and masterfully putting down the rebellion, with expert diplomacy; though, Vivica later remarks that he managed to arbitrate us into silence and out the door without really agreeing to change anything. He's great at that, she notes. Still, I know I, at least, have made my point.

Wednesday, May 1

Yes, there are changes. I'm starting to get special time with Tetsuro. I've talked him into teaching me stuff that's not in the basic program. I now know several flashy ways to draw the sword, for instance, and several equally fancy ways to get it back in the scabbard. And we're working on choreographed numbers, routines that are mini-sequences in some samurai movie of Tetsuro's imagination, full of very cool moves. I'm having a blast, acting out the implacable samurai warrior. Tetsuro loves to die. He insists that after I take him out in these battles, I give him an extra coup de grace. He writhes on the floor and begs for mercy, then expires with great agony when I plunge the sword in and give it a sadistic twist. This is all huge fun. And, yeah, a lot of one-handed stuff. "Bill" is coming alive for me.

Today, Quentin pulled me aside and asked me to assemble some tapes of the fights I've done over the years. David Carradine's Greatest Hits. Well, there are about 180 of those, but most of my tape is in storage. I start to scramble together what I can, and make an appointment at ProStar in the valley to edit the stuff together.

May 3, 2002

Q,

Okay, given that most of my past lives are in storage, here's as close as I can come at this time to a representative sampling of my fighting career. Unfortunately, I don't have anything from *Shane* or much of the original *Kung Fu*. In those days, I never looked back. I probably should have included the fight with Sylvester Stallone in *Death Race 2000*. I left it out because I'm wearing a mask.

I've found you a cross section, though, that spans a couple of decades: hands, feet, knives, swords, and guns. I couldn't resist including some of the scenes that go with the fights. Sometimes they're too rich to leave out. I also felt that the tape should add up to a charming piece of film, let us say, in itself. I think it does, with a roughness born of speed, and a very likeable *heroic naiveté* that goes well with my mystique.

Then, Annie, my Goddess, my Geisha, told me I have to lay something special on you: a promo reel for *Mata Hari* which I made to show at Cannes in 1980, made up of scenes from the first three years, '77, '78, and '79, starring my daughter, from fourteen years old in India to her execution at the age of seventeen in a forest in Holland (doubling for France: trees are trees).

Some of the fights are not the greatest copies, but, hey, some of the movies don't deserve better. Some of it's great, even when the movies weren't. Some of it's pretty funny, not always on purpose.

Hope you enjoy it all. It took me many hours digging through tapes in dusty places, and a long afternoon on the computer, to put the bits and pieces together. I think the order is:

Kung Fu. The rice paper. October 1971. This was the first kung fu move I ever performed on film. I hiked up my robe so I could show my great legs and improvised it on the spot, using something like ballet moves, with a little Inca emperor thrown in.

Kung Fu, The Legend Continues. Mostly from the premier two-hour episode, made in '92. I've cut it up a little, to put together a mini-movie about epic kung fu fights. Rob Moses figures big in it. I do a couple of awesome kicks in every one of the fight scenes.

The Silent Flute (Circle of Iron), made around Thanksgiving '77, in Israel. One of my absolute favorite fights. Performed in a ruined fort, which had guarded the pass to Jerusalem for a couple of thousand years or more. We set up with the sun going down, surrounded by silhouettes of Israeli soldiers standing all around the parapets, Uzis over their shoulders, watching us pretend to kill each other on ground soaked with thousands of years of the blood of marauding Saracens, Jews, Crusaders, etc.

P.O.W. the Escape, a Vietnam piece for Cannon, shot in the Philippines, just before Marcos' fall in '85. That's the late Steve James, All-American, as the sergeant, and Charles Grant, now an investment counselor, as the punk. The Japanese captain who gives the order at the beginning is Mako. I should have left in more footage of him.

Lone Wolf McQuade, a great, dirty fight, which Steve Carver and Chuck graciously allowed me to choreograph. Very Sergio Leone, even more so on film, in scope and surround. Proves over and over that I can take a punch with the best of them. You'll see me get knocked down a lot in this tape.

Future Zone, a barely futuristic bounty hunter movie, which I moonlighted in in the summer of '90 in Mobile, during a three-week lull for me on *Bird on a Wire* in Vancouver. A lot of fast draws, and two great fistfights.

Mr. Horn, August of '78. Some truly remarkable gunplay, while playing a drunk scene, a performance very reminiscent of Cole Younger. Includes the acting debut of Pat McCormick, who got shot between the eyes in an outtake. Take particular note of the utterly foolhardy spin at full cock right in front of my right eye.

The Long Riders knife fight, of course. You can't see on tape that the knife I put in my belt at the end is rubber, but that's why I have trouble getting it in the sheath.

The Warrior and the Sorceress, a Corman movie shot in Argentina in the early '80s, *Yojimbo* on another planet. I come off more like Clint than Toshiro. This picture has a Sergio Leone quality too (if produced by Joe Levine), though the *Hollywood Reporter* thought the fights must have been edited by a blind man.

Deathsport, in the fall of 1977, right after *The Serpent's Egg,* another Corman flick, which taught me that you really *can't* make a silk purse out of a sow's ear. The review in the *Reporter* said: "Don't let the fact that David Carradine is terrific in this film talk you into going to see it, as it's the worst movie ever made." But the sword fight is very special. Richard Lynch is godlike in his ruined beauty. I left in a snippet of Claudia Jennings as a gorgeous madonna. This was her last picture.

Gary Graver was responsible for the photography, some of it breathtaking. For the last six years or so of life, he was Orson Welles' cameraman, including Orson's unfinished masterpiece, *The Other Side of the Wind,* starring John Huston as the great director—as Orson, actually. (I've seen some of it. It's awesome: epic fantasy and utterly natural documentary realism, if you can ever call John Huston or Orson natural.) A movie within a movie within a movie. Gary brings some of all that to this picture. Jonathan Yarborough, now the male half of The Pendragons, the Vegas magic act, staged the swordfights. The swords were supposed to be carbon crystal from organic material in the ruined city (people), fused into sheets of diamond by a neutron blast. The props, though beautiful, in a *John Carter of Mars* sort of way, were made out of Lucite, and extremely breakable. We couldn't let them touch each other at all, leading to some unique choreography.

And to cap the whole thing, for a cooldown lap, the end credits of my *Kung Fu Workout* video, made in about '87. Kung fu as tai chi, in a cute sleeveless outfit, against a red background, with credits rolling by. Very sweet.

Enjoy,

David

Monday, May 6

Today, a camera crew showed up with a video camcorder to shoot a documentary teaser for the Cannes Film Festival. Quentin started out the day telling us that at a certain point the camera would follow him out of his cubicle and pan around the facility to show everyone breaking their butts. It was to look extemporaneous, so just go on with what you're doing, he said. Of course, this being his first chance to direct something in about five years, it wasn't going to be that off-the-cuff. He had Uma laid out on the floor in an impossible stretching posture, and Vivica trying to take off her trainer's head with spinning back kicks. I was set up to be working with the sword, and I did some directing of my own. I timed it so that, when the camera pans around to us, I've got Tetsuro on the floor and am cruelly delivering the final blow. Quentin loved it.

Wednesday, May 8

Wrote a letter today to my old friend Jeff Cooper. Jeff probably knows me better than any other living person. We met on a plane going to Hollywood for our screen tests back in 1964 and worked the movie scene in Hollywood together for almost thirty years before he retired to his birth city of Hamilton, in Ontario, Canada. He is a legend in his own special way, to those who know. Jeff and I were sort of mentors to each other throughout those years, and pretty much still are, though the monkish existence he has dedicated himself to in later life makes him the master, I think.

May 8, 2002

Old Buddy,

Well, Jeff, this Tarantino thing changes everything. A couple of days after the announcement, I got calls from Richard Donner and Tom Cruise—well, not from them personally: from their companies. When you're warm, you're warm. Maybe I'll make a name for myself yet. And, then, the pensions are kicking in, so if I stay away from Ferraris and don't start financing my own movies again, I can always say fuck 'em all, not that that's much of a change for me, it just feels better without the attendant lack of bread. I could even take a page from our old friend and kung fu teacher, Mike Vendrell, who has moved to the Big Island in Hawaii. I get e-mails from him. A happy man. My health is great these days. Even some of my chronic problems have faded back or disappeared. I am pretty fucking buff, man.

This Tarantino film requires me to train, train, train. Unlike workout kings like you jocks who love the act itself, I've been lamely and vainly promising myself to get it together for years. Now, I've *got* to, as happened on Broadway with *The Royal Hunt of the Sun*, with the series *Kung Fu, The Silent Flute* aka *Circle of Iron*, and *Lone Wolf McQuade* (wasn't going to show up half-flabby to face three-time world champion Chuck Norris). I'd be in a rocking chair if it hadn't been for the need to get my tough up for those projects. My congenital laziness is equaled only by my fierce ambition.

Quentin is training right along with us, in preparation for his role as Pai Mei, the evil kung fu master. He is subjecting himself to at least as much torture as the rest of us. And grinning through it all, every minute. Or maybe that's a painful grimace. I'd have to get to know him better.

The training will go on till the picture ends, in Beijing, Tokyo, L.A., Baja California, and planned to finish in the Canary Islands, appropriately on Halloween. This stuff is hard. My piddling studies of kung fu over the years help a little, but the ladies are close behind me. I have to hustle. I have some question whether it's a good idea to teach already ball-busting women these moves. Watching Vivica A. vent her black-ass street spleen on her little Chinese trainer is positively scary, particularly at certain times of the month. The hours spent are sweet for me, though.

The thing I've really taken to is the samurai sword. You'd think I'd hate it. You have to do everything just so, but I love it. It's real warrior shit, much more than the kung fu. And I love the style—totally arrogant, and superpolite at the same time. As Kung Fu Caine, they never let me near the weapons.

Then there's the wirework. It's painful, but who cares. I'm flying through the air and swinging a samurai sword at the same time.

Tarantino is an interesting guy—not one of us, but not one of them, either. Educated, though not learned, and definitely with the spark of insight and outsight without which he'd be an ape. He's a very lucky guy, but he deserves at least some of it. He's not Hal Ashby, but he's a lot more fun to talk to.

So, that's about it for now. The dawn is imminent, so it's my bedtime. Let me know that you receive this.

Your friend, as always,

Davey

June 25, or so; I can't keep track

I fly to London for a convention, and then catch a Lufthansa flight to Beijing, with a few thousand British pounds in my pocket. Right away, I start working out. The whole cadre is already there, and they've taken over half the studio, including a gym that hovers around 110 degrees and 90 percent humidity.

Uma has dropped her "baby fat," and is looking strong and confident, also incredibly beautiful. Quentin amazes me with his kung fu. He has the Pai Mei routines down pat, and lightning fast, working them nevertheless, over and over. It's funny as hell, and charming as well. He does it all in character, making it look so easy. Well, Pai Mei has been doing these moves for over three hundred years. They'd have to be as familiar to him as combing his beard.

Rob Moses is on hand. It's a godsend that I got him onto the picture. He shows me easy ways to look busy, really necessary to keep from passing out, and we do our own thing whenever we can, the hard-core Shaolin moves, which seem to amaze the cadre. Chinese gung fu is, after all, the mother of them all. All this, while feasting our eyes on these pretty females, whose bodies get tighter and righter as it goes along. Then, in my suite at our five-star hotel, just down the road from the Forbidden City, we play the blues.

A big plus has been getting to know Ethan Hawke, who is traveling with Uma. He plays decent guitar, writes Tom Waits–ish songs, and recites Gregory Corso. He's written two novels, one of which I like a lot. He's somewhat responsible for my good fortune, as he was reading my autobiography, *Endless Highway,* while occupying a guest room in QT's house, and he kept interrupting Tarantino's writing by emerging from his room and saying, "This guy is fantastic!" and reading passages to him. Ethan's a real punk and a savant at the same time. It's valuable to talk to someone who's still growing up. Gives me a take on the future of mankind, and makes me laugh: the most important thing of all, or so my mentor taught me. Actually, he put it forth: "Love, Art, Music, and Laughs," he said. But according to Tony Quinn in *The Savage Innocents* ("Quinn, the Eskimo"), in Inuit the word for "love" and "laugh" are the same.

One evening, after the workout, I get a call from Quentin. "Do you smoke cigars?" he asks. "Yeah," I say. "Well, there's a cigar lounge in this hotel. Do you want to meet me there?"

Well, sure. Any opportunity to meet with Quentin one-on-one is always a gas. It's a completely different experience from when he's surrounded by people. He lets his hair down.

We light up a couple of giant Cubans and talk about all kinds of shit, some of it very deep; Quentin has something he wants my opinion about: something about his life's ambitions. I'm not going to say here what it was about, as I consider it a privileged communication. I'm flattered that Quentin respects me enough to care what I think, and I do my best to help him out. One of the subjects we get into is comic book superheroes. It starts out with a comment I'd read in a magazine denigrating Christopher Reeve's performance as Superman. There's never been a great film Superman. How could there be? He's Superman! Actors are mortals. But he was an absolutely perfect Clark Kent: right out of the pages of *Action Comics*. We go from there to a whole diatribe about alter egos. Quentin decides he wants another cigar. He picks out a Davidoff, which he says is a great "second cigar." He has me try a drag. I tell him it tastes like a milk shake. Quentin laughs, and says, "God, all I'd have to do is write down things you say and people would think I'm a genius." I say, "Well, you are, Quentin, but feel free." Six days later a new rewrite of the script comes out, and he's taken our whole conversation about Superman's alter ego and dropped it into my mouth as one of those typically delightful non-sequitur monologues that are at the heart of all of Q's movies.

I had to fly back to New York to play a concert with the band; something I just couldn't cancel. Annie arranged to meet me at the airport with my guitar. She showed up looking like a Russian spy, in a trench coat, with nothing on underneath it except lingerie, and guided me to a limousine with one of those partitions, which we left closed for the whole trip. Well, it had been a long fast.

Friday, July 5

Q,

Well, okay. Annie and I spent half a day at the Chinese Embassy, trying to get a reentry visa. A very weird experience. The embassy is across the street from the *Enterprise,* the vintage aircraft carrier that they've made a museum out of. I knew the guy pretty well who started it. Retired field grade officer of some kind. He's dead now. There were a half dozen or so Chinese people squatting on the sidewalk in front of the embassy, with a ghetto blaster playing Oriental music, rocking back and forth. We stood in line with a whole bunch more Chinese expatriates for an hour, and when we were two people away, the guy closed the window and just left us all standing there. We had to stay while this accursed petty official had his lunch or lose our place in line, only to hear when he came back that the letter we had was, according to him, stamped by someone who had no authority to "invite us to China." No appeal. To get rid of the bad taste, I took Annie to lunch at Café des Artistes, for the nude paintings, and coffee in the fancy bar at the Pierre, always good for a laugh.

Now, we're on Fifth Avenue, walking down the steps out of Saint Patrick's Cathedral, when her cell phone rings. It's Damiana, saying, "Take him home." Annie says, "This is a joke, right?" No, no joke, and no, he's not fired.

I can't say I'm unhappy to be back in L.A. for a couple of weeks, and Annie's ecstatic about it, as are the kids, but I missed the action immediately, such as it was. Yeah, I was sort of hanging around, but it felt a lot like being an astronaut waiting for the countdown to begin, and I would have liked to have been on the sidelines when you made the first shot. Plus, I was really looking forward to some more evenings in the cigar lounge, and Tetsuro must feel like a jilted bride.

Yes, I've read (and reread) *Kill Bill Revisited*. Well, let's see. You've pared it down to 197 pages. The movie is becoming positively minimalist. All the new stuff is great. The shit with the gun works. The Superman rap is priceless. Everything that's gone hurts like a tooth extraction, but that's Show Biz, ain't it? I was sort of hoping you'd shoot it all and then skinny it up in the editing room, rolling up the extra pieces of gold carefully, and stashing them in a safe room until the world cried for the long version, which I would suspect would be before the release. Certainly, Cannes would love to see it all, and the DVD would be the richer for it. I suppose finance enters here somewhere, but you're probably sticking to your artistic guns. I just can't see the forest for the tree stumps.

The one lost piece of the puzzle that really hurts is The Long Long Long Long Road. I'll tell you why (as though you, in your infinite wisdom, don't know). First, The Road, so much more impressive in the angles of the location photos than in the cheap movie where you found it. And, of course, everyone of us wants to go to the Canary Islands. Then, the shot itself: the metaphor of Bill and The Bride rushing to each other's sides across the desert at CanAm speeds (even without the Caddy prototype).

And then, the total surprise! *BLAM!* as they would say in a *Batman* comic. Smashed window, blown-out eardrums, and proof positive that Bill does not screw around.

Pictures need surprises. They're totally fucked without them. Audiences want them, love them, and crave them. This was a great one. To replace all that with a guy on a patio and a girl on a grassy knoll holding cell phones to their ears is, well, okay, I guess. We want to study Bill's face, and it would be nice to watch him move around. We haven't seen much of him. And Uma will look great out there in the day, with the sky behind her, maybe her hair blowing in the wind a little. But, I love to be shocked. And then, what about, a little later, the Carmen Ghia viewed through Bill's front door behind The Bride, with the windows shattered? A small goodie in itself.

The other thing I miss is Bill arranging flowers and sharing his eagerness, like a bridegroom, with the housekeeper. Shows how much he cares for the broad, making sure the place smells good when she comes to kill

him. I loved that scene. It was so fucking upside down, mixing the warrior
mystique in with the romance thing. And a killer so pure he can be dainty
about it.

Ah, well. I'm not questioning your genius, just waving a fond farewell
to my favorite ounces of fat. It'll all be there in the novel, I'm sure.

Speaking of Caddy prototypes, art director David showed me pictures
of the De Thomaso Mangusta. Yes, it's a pretty car. The only thing is, Bill
gets a million dollars a hit, right? The Mangusta is a $30,000 buy, about
the price of an old Vette. And it doesn't really qualify as a Vintage auto. It's
a Ford, with an Italian body. Sort of a kit-car. What the Auto Trader would
call "miscellaneous," listed along with the replicars. To give it its due, *Hem-
mings Motor News* would treat it with more respect, giving it its own heading. But, how about the Mercedes C300, I think it was called, looking like
a landlocked F15, with a three-rotor Wankel. They made only a handful, all
promised to Arab sheiks before they were out the door. Probably impossible to get one. But, there's the BMW Z1, a great-looking thoroughbred,
which makes the Z3 look like a Miata. A few of them slipped past the feds
and made it over here to the States. You could also look at the BMW Z8.
Maybe the most beautiful car ever made. You never see the coupe version.
Very new, and very rare. Very pricey, too, but I've heard Jay Leno has three
of them!? Maybe he'd loan us one. All this is kind of unimportant if the car
is just going to sit in front of Bill's hacienda, I guess, but I'm a car nut, and
for guys like us, the car is The Man. Probably, there should be *a few* exotic
pieces of machinery parked outside his pad, and maybe a Harley, and a big
truck of some kind would be good, too.

One last idea, though. Annie (she's a car nut too, as well as a Harley
freak) pointed out that Bill is, or at least was, a *"Bad"* James Bond. A shiny,
brand-new Aston Martin Vantage V12 coupe would certainly be his speed.
It shrieks of Wealth, Power, and Arrogance, and it's gorgeous. If I had a
spare hundred and seventy grand, I'd be driving one right now. In silver,
maybe, though they're awesome in basic black. Bottom line, however: I'm
plenty happy with the Mangusta if you are.

Well, I'll try to stay in shape while I'm impatiently luxuriating here in
La La Land. Give my love to them all.

New subject: I'm afraid I did you a disservice, when you asked me "point blank" to give you my opinion of your Broadway stint in the revival of *Wait Until Dark*. I wasn't very point blank. I probably won't be now, but I'm going to try. (This is risky, so know in advance I love you like a brother.) I think your experiment came too soon, and you used too much of your clout to get the part. All that put you at a disadvantage. That's part of it. Then, there's this. If you want to parade around on a stage, you have to have total confidence, to the point of arrogance, or you have to be utterly humble, and make that charming. I don't know if you can fake the latter—I doubt it—but you surely have the chutzpah for the former. You just have to say, "Fuck 'em all!" and go for your own vision. If they don't like it, shove it down their throats.

My first time on Broadway, in *The Deputy*, the producer-director, Herman Shumlin, bless him, tried to fire me after a few weeks. It was weird. People were crying in the audience, and he'd started out loving my performance, but now he was saying I was ruining his play. I said, well, okay. But you have to pay me every week till my run-of-the-play contract runs out. He wasn't willing to do that. I did the show for another four months or so, knowing he hated every night of it. The next season, after I opened in *The Royal Hunt of the Sun*, a buddy of mine who was in the show with me had a conversation at a party with some actor who'd seen both plays. The guy wouldn't believe the same actor had given both performances. His opinion of the first one paralleled Herman's, and it fucked with his head that any actor could go from awful to magnificent in one season. The point of all this being, don't let anything stop you. How you can know so much about other actors, and what makes them good, and not know yourself is beyond me. Maybe it's like that psychic's thing where you can't help yourself. I also don't understand why directing pictures that blow the minds of superradical people doesn't get you off more than watching a lot of blue-haired ladies stare mindlessly at you from the crummy seats of a Broadway house. No accounting, I guess.

We went to see *Minority Report* today. Spielberg is becoming increasingly like Stanley Kubrick. But someone should point out to him that Stanley, dark and scary though he could be, always hit us with fucking rainbows. Think how scary *Clockwork Orange* is, with all the horror looking like hard candy. Why does everyone think the future is going to be sort of black and white? All the greatest pictures are full of supersaturated color, from *The Wizard of Oz* and *Gone With the Wind* to *Lawrence of Arabia* and *The Bridge Over the River Kwai*.

I love you for your color. *Pulp Fiction* blazes. *Jackie Brown* looks just like a mall. Pam Grier glows! Something else about Steven: He understands violence, or at least how to show it. You, on the other hand, understand violent *people*. What's inside them. I think, while you were suffering on Broadway, you might have forgotten that that guy you were playing, at least one of him anyway, was such a person. You seemed to be apologizing for him. But what the fuck do I know?

Love you, miss you,

D

July 15, or thereabouts

Quentin, wanting, as ever, as much input from me as he could get, sent his wardrobe staff to my house to rummage through my closet, looking for good stuff for me to wear in the movie. The two girls he sent loved everything, and pretty much emptied out the closet, taking it all down to show to Quentin. I was left with nothing to wear. Quentin looked at it all and picked out a bunch of things to be copied. This gave me an idea. So, while I was unsupervised in Los Angeles, I took a page from Brother Mike's experience on *Jackie Brown*. He had furnished his character's apartment with crap from his own pad, so the cop he was playing had a real life that was Mike's. I lured Sandy, the set decorator, down to my storage facility. They forklifted out the four modules, and we spent half a day pawing through it. We selected out a pile of sacred artifacts: my mother's couch, a bunch of Chinese lacquer furniture, a dozen paintings, pre-Columbian sculpture, a bronze Buddha, a sculpture from some Hindu temple of Krishna and Govinda in a Kama Sutra pose. A museum replica of a Rodin sculpture, swords, knives, Indian blankets: all kinds of shit. They took it away in a truck to store it until it was time to send it down to Puerto Vallarta for the shoot.

I took the opportunity to gather some things for myself: a stereo, my scanner, some silk Hawaiian shirts I'd bought on the Big Island. A really good teapot from Ireland.

Meanwhile, I'd been hearing stuff about the movie, through channels and on the grapevine as well. It was all over the Internet: wild rumors and speculation. They had started shooting. Then, they're behind schedule and they give me another week in California. We've started going to a lot of movies, knowing we won't be able to see this stuff on the big screen in Beijing. There *are* no big screens in Beijing.

Sandy sent me a big book with Polaroids of all my stuff. Ninety-six of them. I had to attach values to it all for the insurance.

"Kill Bill"

Supércool Manchu, Inc.
10950 W. Washington Boulevard, Suite 150
Culver City, CA 90232
ART DEPARTMENT
ATT. Sandy Wasco
July 30, 2002

Sandy,

Yeah, when it's all down in that book, it looks quite impressive. Well, I guess it *is*!

Here is the list for insurance. Some of this stuff it's very hard to assign values to, the "forgeries" for example, so the figures are pretty arbitrary in those cases.

The Picasso would have to be appraised. I have no idea of its value. Hope this works for you.

As Always,

David

hey david!

how's it been going in china?? peter told me all about it, and that sounds fantastic! and i love that story, too. how perfect is that?

i was asking peter about you because i wanted to find out if you're going to be in l.a. from july 27–31. i'm producing this animated feature by my cousin, the brilliant and insane animator bill plimpton, and we would so love to have you do a voice in it if you're around. we'll even pay you!

let me know what your schedule looks like for that week. we'd need to record you for a couple of hours only, and then sometime in the future we would do some retakes once animation is complete. we also would love to have everyone sit around a dinner table to go over the script and punch up the gags.

so far, here's the cast: peter, my dad, hayley, matthew perry, craig bierko, tom noonan, zak orth, beverly d'angelo, sarah silverman, ed begley jr. and myself. it should be a total blast so i hope you're around!

sending you much love and warmest salutations!

xoxo martha

Martha, My Dear,

Well, shit! I'm in Beijing at that time for that little picture with Quantum Tarantooni, Uma Thermal, Daryl Woo Woo Hannah, Vivica Hey Hey Foxy, and a bunch of little Chinamen. Oh, and Mad Michael Madsen. Leave on the 22nd, if they don't fall even further behind schedule, which I would not wish on the poor dude. I'm going a little crazy. I haven't shot a foot yet, though I've been in training since April for the job. (Am I buff? I am buff!) I spent three weeks in Beijing in a minimum security prison, no, a witness protection program (an antiseptic apartment with three bedrooms and two and a half bathrooms. I never knew where to sleep or shit). It was okay. I'm on salary, and it turns out the Forbidden City isn't really forbidden, but I felt like an astronaut when they stop the countdown because of bad weather or faulty preparation. Sitting there in the safe house in my space suit, becoming gradually scared to go up. Remember that one guy that pissed in his suit? Too early in history to take advantage of the space technology that distills the junk out of his piss so he can drink it later. Then they sent me home to save themselves some per diem. Would love to sit around a table with you anytime. Have to pass, though, unless there's a monsoon in China, which could happen.

I will, however, talk to production and see if I can delay my blast-off.

Cross your pretty little fingers

Unca Dave

JULY 23, 2002

To: All my friends
Subject: TEMPORARILY INSANE

Anyhow, that's my plea, though the condition may actually be a permanent, or at least chronic one.

This here is an attempt to gather up the unraveling strands of my various sadly neglected epistolary relationships (romances?) before they dissolve for lack of attention. I apologize for the generic mass-communication, but I only have time for one of these. Forgive me if this gets redundant for some of you.

I'm languishing in La La Land here for just a few days, supposedly in the middle of the movie I'm making in Beijing (Quentin Tarantino's *Kill Bill,* in case you are totally out of the news-loop—I'm Bill). I say "supposedly in the middle" because I haven't actually shot anything yet. I, along with a half dozen beautiful and largely famous multiethnic ladies, have been training since April for this epic (and "epic" it is). Eight hours a day, five days a week: To say grueling is too kind—stretching, kung fu, or rather wushu, samurai, wirework, weight training, and those hamster machines where you run and cycle without going anywhere. Plus, of course, the choreography. These fights are now so ingrained in my brain that I will be able to try them on New York muggers when I'm ninety. What I've really cottoned to is the samurai. You'd think I wouldn't. It's so disciplined, so specific. You have to do everything just so. Not usually my kind of thing, but I love it. And I'm great at it. Well, as Caine, I was never allowed to play with weapons. Always empty-handed. Swords are a gas. And the style gets me too. Superpolite and Arrogant at the same time. Then the wirework—painful, yes—I have scars from the harness—but who cares! I'm flying through the air swinging a samurai sword!

Anyway, back to the "supposedly": We all went to Beijing to continue the training while they did prep there. Then I flew back to New York for a concert, and while trying unsuccessfully to get my visa renewed so I could go back, I was told, "Go home." I had the shit down, you see, I mean DOWN, and everybody knew it, and I wasn't going to work for weeks. I was just hanging around, going through the motions, at their expense. They've been shooting now for a few weeks, and they are way behind schedule. Well, a director who's never shot outside L.A., in Beijing, with a Chinese crew who don't speak English, with special effects, stunts, and Maoist bureaucracy to deal with: Duh, aren't we surprised. I'm due to go back imminently, to start work. Best role I've had in years, of course, and Quentin is a dear boy.

Meanwhile, I'm a very happy man. Finances are improving (I am on salary). I'm living in a big house with a doting family: Annie, a jewel, with four kids with whom the love is fabulously mutual. This idyll could last a while, but of course, one never knows. Still my record is fourteen years, and that one wasn't even that much fun for most of it. This time "fun" is the operative word, so, be happy for me, and for the doting family too. They're getting my best sides. Someone's parent wanted to know if I was I-don't-know—the superficial glamour Hollywood thing, you know—and was told by Annie, "Well, he cleans up the dog shit."

Today, I had to go down to the preschool and convince a very nice lady not to expel Max (from preschool!!). He had thrown a chair at someone (because he tried to take his lunch) and thrown a shoe at the teacher. Max is three. Well, he watches me work out.

Back to "supposedly": The only thing is, I feel like an astronaut—they train, train, train, and then they're told they're going to go. They get all suited up, and on the tarmac, and then Houston starts delaying the countdown. No training now, just sitting in some safe room, in their space suits, waiting, getting scared. Like gladiators, cooling their heels while they get the lions together. Remember that one guy who pissed in his suit, and they had to peel him out of it, and put him in someone else's ill-fitting rig? I just want to get on that firecracker and GO before I lose my nerve.

It's hot here, well of course, but just beautiful. I love L.A. I totally disagree with Woody Allen and all the other L.A. bashers about the town. I'm glad though that they don't want to live here. It's too crowded already. That's the only downer. The greatest thing of course about this place is the lack of humidity and BUGS. No mosquitoes, no cockroaches, unless you're in Beantown or Watts, I guess. Smog? How about Beijing for that? The King! Beijing was (is) a trip! Very different from my visit three or four years ago. The trappings of the Cultural Revolution are fading fast. I didn't see one of those Mao jackets, and the loudspeakers that played martial music and "big-brother"-style announcements at lunchtime have been silenced. They're tearing down a lot of the old stuff and putting up twenty-story buildings a block wide—a BIG block wide—that look like jukeboxes or Cuisinarts and toasters, sometimes with a pagoda roof on top of it all. Streets are unbelievably wide; I guess they have a lot of space over there.

There's still Tiananmen Square to remind us that it can get ugly, but it's a happy place in general. People are friendly, and there's jazz and blues and crack houses, or so I hear. The experiment didn't take. The power of Western decadence to seduce is supreme, it seems.

There's this place called the Peace Hotel, really just a bar, where the Peace Orchestra plays. These musicians were playing counterrevolutionary music during Mao's tenure, which is to say, rock & roll, blues, etc., maybe some John Denver, in secret. If they got caught doing it, they were executed. Finally, they buried their instruments and played dumb to stay alive. When the regime fell or softened or whatever it did, they dug them up. They're all in their seventies and eighties, and they can only cut about a twenty-minute set, and then they have to take a break, but there they are. It's cool.

My new band, incidentally, and sometimes incandescently, the Cosmic Rescue Team, is alive and well, though pretty much on hold until I get back from China (after I go there). The gig in New York was awesome. Our shit is really coming together.

I'm telling everyone to go see *Road to Perdition*. I know; it's obvious. Newman, Hanks, and all. But check out the scene near the beginning

The Cosmic Rescue Team in concert

when Paul and Tom do a piano duet together. Rates as one of the greatest movie love scenes of all time. I just wish they'd let the hero live once in a while. In *Insomnia*, it would have been so cool if Pacino woke up in the hospital and it turned out he hadn't died of bullet wounds, he'd just finally taken a little nap. Well, it would be cool if Hamlet didn't die either—too? Guess that's why my favorite movies are things like *Groundhog Day* and *The Wizard of Oz*.

Recently saw several renderings for what is going to go up in Ground Zero, to replace the Twin Towers. All very beautiful, with towers, spires really, the tallest a mere seventy-five stories, and parks and memorials, of course. It's sort of a contest. I hope they build one of them quick. It would help *me* to heal, and it might do something for Wall Street as well. I'd like to see all that, not put behind us, but moved to a better frame, something positive, unrelated to getting those bastards, and beyond the tears. I'm so tired of the political crap, and the War Against Terrorism. I no longer talk at all to my old friends who have opinions about this, some of whom will be on the list to get this letter. I am equally impatient with the bleeding heart liberals and the militant hawks. The activist redskins, brownskins, and black-and-blue skins. There is no attitude that can be had which is not flawed in almost every way. Every agenda has, after all, its own agenda. All we can do that is not suspect is to be as kind as we can to those within our reach. Not to say that I don't care. I do, passionately, about oceans, coral reefs, whales, wolves, water, land mines, child abuse, abortions, and bad movies. And I really would like to see Osama, Sadaam, and Yasir thrown into a gravel pit, but none of that has anything to do with what I'm supposed to be concentrating on.

My introduction to Gabriel García Márquez was during a Western shoot in Santa Fe, New Mexico. At a bookstore near my Adobe-Disneyland-Hotel I picked up a thin volume entitled *Of Love and Other Demons*, which totally hynotized me. I underlined wonderful sentences that I had wanted to remember, until I realized I was underlining the whole book. Then I found out about his political moves—hanging out with guys like Castro and Kadafi, imparting a certain delicay, if not gentility to those Raging Bulls' machinations—and his Nobel Prize, and all. And, of course, I read some of his other stuff: *Love in the Time of Cholera* is pretty good.

Márquez, like people such as Pablo Casals, Jacques Cousteau, Muhammad Ali, Bob Marley, Mother Theresa, Jimi Hendrix, and George Carlin, to name a few—the list is huge—used his art to make more difference than he could possibly have accomplished by carrying a sign or by voting for his favorite compromised candidate or mucked-up new restrictive law. Fuck all that.

We will all miss little Gabriel if his fears of imminent mortality come to pass, whether we know we're missing him or not. Fortunately, he has been a prolific writer. There's enough of him to last me for quite awhile. If we could all live our days the way this dude wishes he had, and, truth be told, did, it would be a better world for all of us. Take heed: Márquez has it down.

Don't be strangers, all of you. I'm very busy regenerating a career. Still trying to make a name for myself. I'll be back.

I love you all.

Your David

July 31

Quentin,

Well, L.A. is still here; and so am I. Waiting and waiting. Doing errands, taking the kids to ding-dong movies.

Did a voice-over for a feature cartoon, *Hair High,* Bill Plimpton's creation. I don't know if you're aware of his "award winning" very weird stuff. Paints directly on the film. I'm playing a chain-smoking biology teacher, Mr. Snerz, who, while demonstrating electrically stimulated reanimation on a dead frog, coughs his guts out (literally), and his students, using their excellent knowledge of anatomy, get it all stuffed back in successfully. Pretty weird shit. My niece, Martha Plimpton, and cousin of Bill, is producing the thing. More like Zap Comix than *South Park*.

I'm going to the foundry Monday to work on the wax of a bust I made of one of my ex-wives, preparatory to pouring a bronze. I finally have enough distance from the bitch so I can see the sculpture as a sculpture and not a voodoo doll. Some TV show is going to shoot me (with a camera) working on it.

Aside from that, waiting, waiting. Itching to be back in harness, though I understand my harness is cut. They tell me, in the new rewrites, I don't get to fly. The girls get all the fun. I hope Pai Mei's sword-balancing act is still in.

Quentin's dress-up day ANNIE BIERMAN

Everything I do these days, I think of how Bill would fit in. Surprisingly, he always does. I can see him taking The Bride and my daughter BB to *Lilo & Stitch*, shopping for miniature bathing suits, even shoveling dog shit. Then, of course, there's the sword practice. Rob Moses, as you know, is back in town, and I'm teaching him the routines, so I won't return to you completely unprepared.

Rereading the El Paso Massacre, I've come to agree with you about the 9mm automatic. Much as I hate to lose the fast draw and that beautiful two-gun rig your people whipped up for me, the auto is definitely the right tool for the event. Maybe they can adapt the rig, or give me two Army .45s in snap-down holsters, like The Phantom.

Saw *Men in Black II*, speaking of FX, just exactly as good as the first one. Lara Flynn Boyle makes a delicious villain. Tommy Lee Jones arrived late, and just took over. On Forty-second Street, there would have been cheers when he showed. It's amazing how much mileage those suits from *Reservoir Dogs* are good for.

Also seen, due to a complete dearth of Hollywood flicks worth my time, two foreign films: *Sex and Lucia,* from Spain, sexy, or at least erotic, in a weird Spanish way, almost a good film (Annie loved it, as she gets all the jokes, having been brought up in Chile), and *My Wife Is an Actress,* from France, very French, with a pretty funny sequence where an entire film crew works nude to make the actress in the love scene more comfortable: the boom man, the script girl, the ADs. The director's bum, as he assumes that stooped-forward, hands-on-knees, watching-the-take posture, is the capper. Terence Stamp is wasted, but right on, as usual (he doesn't undress). And then, a happy ending. Apparently, the existential angst thing has run its course there in France. Too much black & white, though. Well, you know how I feel about that.

Sending along these two comics I found, which smack faintly of "The Bride." Elektra, in her original incarnation, by Frank Miller, was a killer. These are amusing, at least.

Hope everything is going smoothly. Should be, the slowness aside. Hey, foreign location, Chinese crew, post-Mao bureaucracy, sweltering heat, stunts, special effects, *duh,* what else to expect. Anyway, it's an epic. It's supposed to go slow.

I tried to keep this down to one page, as I know you're busy, dancing in discos all night long. It got away from me.

Yours forever,

D

August 16

Back in Beijing. We've been here two days now, Annie and I. After a flurry of semimadness, getting it together to fly to China for three weeks. Having delivered the Maserati to Franco's for its long-overdue restoration, I spent the last two days running around in my little Toyota rent-a-car getting shit together. Picking up dry cleaning, batteries for my camera, vitamins and herbal remedies to protect us from the dreaded third-world water, stuff like that.

The twins, Max and Olivia, had to find a new preschool before we left. Max was close to being kicked out of Pinecrest. He threw a chair and one of his shoes, supposedly at a teacher, though he says he just threw them and they happened to fly in the direction of the teacher. God knows I've been there a couple of times. Then a few days later, he bit someone. I don't remember ever doing that.

So, today they picked me up at nine-thirty to take me to the set. I was scheduled to shoot an over-shoulder, an easy way to start, but that didn't happen. We ran into Bennett Walsh, the line producer, who's lost fifteen pounds, and looks sort of fragile; but his energy is high and he's in a bubbly mood. He walked us through all the sets, including the House of Blue Leaves, where Uma had just finished killing about a hundred of Lucy Liu's bodyguards. The set was just awesome. Every detail was perfect, down to the Japanese "exit" signs. They'd made everything here—the artwork on the walls, even the furniture. It was cheaper than buying it. Then, of course, they'd ripped it all to shreds in the eight weeks of samurai sword battles. Scarlet, my faithful Chinese interpreter and watchdog, appeared to take us to the training studio. "He" (that's his name) was working out with the boys. "He" is the master now. "He" grinned to see me again, and he let me stretch out and do some kicks on my own for a half hour or so, and then assembled the guys and we went through the street fight I'm going to do on film in a week or two. "He" and I were both amazed that I hadn't forgotten the routines. I had them down perfectly after one run-through. So I killed five guys, "He" playing Michael Jai White's part. All of us sweating profusely. It was really hot and humid, and the smog is fearsome. You can look straight at the sun. It looks like the moon. We did the routine about twelve times, and then I worked alone with him ("He") for a few more reps of the part of the fight with Michael.

I went to wardrobe to try on some new shirts that had just arrived from L.A.; they had made them up for me, copied from one of my silk combo Chinese/cowboy things, only in blue. It's deliciously cool, cold actually, in the wardrobe room. I was dripping wet and for the moment totally beat. Still catching my breath, I took off my T-shirt and took a wrestler's bath (a sponge bath with a towel) from the waist up, so I wouldn't trash the shirt with kung fu sweat. The first shirt was about two inches too short. That was a bummer, but the second one was just fine. Annie remarked that it was a great color for me. She thinks I look good in blue. Helen, the wardrobe mistress, gave me a new Calvin Klein tank top from wardrobe and said she'd wash my T-shirt and get it back to me tomorrow.

After that, they put the wigs on me. First, we tried the double wig, which made me look like "Pearl" in *Sonny Boy*. Then they put on the other one, which had been made from scratch, just for me. It was as though I suddenly had grown four more inches of hair. It looked just like me, only a touch thicker, especially on top, which was the whole point of the exercise in the first place. We walked over to the set, down alleyways strewn with trash, and past the basketball court, where the stunt guys were playing soccer (this after a whole morning of grueling martial arts training) to show it to Quentin. We passed a slew of familiar faces hanging out at tables in the heat, past a sign that said "Please Don't Spit" and into the dark foyer, where I found an ice-cold Chinese Coke. Quentin was sitting in the dark on the soundstage, behind the set, with Top 40s music blasting. He loved the wig; I've never seen him so happy. He took us into the

My first day on the job ANDREW COOPER/MIRAMAX FILMS

light and examined it minutely. Manny, the hairdresser, was intensely relieved. Apparently, it doesn't always go that way with Quentin.

Outside, we ran into Uma, who looked fabulous. She'd lost all of her "baby fat" and was rippling with muscle. Totally back to Poison Ivy (her role in *Batman and Robin*) and more. We talked for five minutes or so, without her realizing I was wearing a wig. I guess she must have thought my hair grew really fast. We went back to Manny's digs (the guys were still playing their extremely animated soccer game) and the wig was carefully removed. While Annie took a nap in my dressing room, Manny trimmed my real hair for me. Now that I was sure the wig worked, I could do that. We talked a lot while he snipped with his $500 gold-plated scissors. Manny's a very interesting guy. He worked with Bill Murray on several movies, before he moved on to do for Jean-Claude Van Damme. No one, it seems, works with their own hair.

We talked a lot about *Groundhog Day*, and he agrees with me that it's a really deep movie, even a metaphysical statement. The whole idea of being made to do it over and over until you get it right is a truly delicious one, and sounds very much like Hindu and Buddhist ideas of reincarnation. A guy who finds it impossible to successfully commit suicide, and so, decides to do some good instead. Totally inspiring. I've watched the movie several times and will undoubtedly do so again. The mystery was finally solved for me of how many days Bill Murray had to wake up to "I Got You Babe" before he finally got it right. A year. That's the story. Well, that's neat and tidy, but I disbelieve that anyone could become a concert-grade pianist in that time. I'm still working on it after sixty years. Have to accept it, though, the source being the director of the film. Manny said they also shot a scene where Bill becomes a pool shark. That, too, takes a little time. They cut that one out. Guess pool is a really tough one to get down, though two years in the Army, I can attest, will do the trick. I've heard that in the original concept, Bill had to repeat that awful day for ten thousand years. That's more like Greek, or maybe Hindu, mythology. Americans are too much in a hurry for that story.

August 17

Yesterday was my first day in front of the camera. They picked us up at 11 A.M., and I waited until after 5 before I was called to the set. Nothing unusual about that. Anyway, they were busy chopping a dummy in half (supposedly a Japanese warlord), and it took many takes and many buckets of movie blood and suits of clothes to get it to work. As I walked on the set, I heard the Chinese crew murmuring, *"Beer, Beer, thas Beer? Thas Beer?"* What's the big deal about beer? And why are they whispering? No. Not beer; translated: "Bill." This was the fiftieth day of shooting on this movie called *Kill Bill*, and no one had seen "Bill" till this moment.

My first scene was only on my hands: an easy start. Julie Dreyfus, as Sofie Fatale, who has had her left arm chopped off by Uma to get information from her, sits in a wheelchair crying, while my hands caress her shoulders and hair and my off-screen voice comforts her. Julie was wonderful. I told her they were worried that she wouldn't be able to pull off the scene, but I had told them she could handle it with one arm tied behind her back. It got a little smile from her, and a huge laugh from Quentin.

After the first rehearsal, Quentin sort of caught me on the move and whispered, "Don't do that breathing, that exhale thing." Quentin whispers his directions to you, which is cool; makes one feel like an accomplice. I said, "I got it." I walked a couple of steps, then said, loud enough to reach him, "And you're right." And then, more to myself, "It's a crutch!" It had hit me that that mannerism was a stupid trick I'd got into the habit of. Like my dad with his eyebrows. Not real acting. I'll never do it again. I decided I was going to like this guy.

There was a big thing about a watch. Props had given me one that was a close match to my gold-and-titanium Jaeger-leCoultre, which they loved, but Quentin thought it would be cool if I wore the same rare Rolex that he had on Uma. I said, "Well, this is a pretty cool watch." He said, "Yeah, it's pretty cool. What do you think?" I said, "Well, a Rolex is the cliché of the absolute most desirable watch." He said, "Okay, let's look at the Rolex and see which one we like better." While we waited for them to find it, he said, "Look, if you love this watch, wear it." I said, "You know, Quentin, if it looks just like the one Uma is wearing, there's no contest. It's the right watch, no matter what it looks like." We hung around for a few minutes, waiting. I took a drink of bottled water, and drank in a little of Annie, sitting primly in the chair they'd brought for her. There was an empty one next to her. She said, "They brought this chair for you to sit in." I shook my head. No way I wanted to sit down right then. Then, suddenly, Quentin said, "We're going with the watch you have on; forget the Rolex," and we started to shoot. We did four or so takes of that scene, with little adjustments, Quentin loving every one of them, but just wanting more, and then broke to move to another stage for my big scene of the day, one of the longest speeches I have in the movie, one of the longest I've had in any movie, I think. A trial by fire. Well, not really. Just an opportunity to excel, actually. Piece of cake for me. I had the words cold after four months of studying them. The only thing I didn't know was how I was going to play it, but I never do.

Quentin took me aside to the Japanese bar set where they had been bifurcating the dummy to tell me about a new scene he was writing for me, which would allow me to have a kung fu fight with the actor who was now playing Pai Mei, the evil master: Gordon Liu, who'd actually been in the Pai Mei movies, and was famous in China for playing Shaolin monks, as I was in America. Cool!

We put the shoulder-length (Bill is hip) wig on me, darkened slightly and pulled down on my forehead a couple of millimeters to account for a ten years' flashback, and I went back to work. The scene was with Uma and me around a campfire, me telling her a bedtime story about the massacre of a Shaolin temple by the immortal who was about to become her teacher (yes, the very same evil master, Pai Mei). The soundstage was already hot, and they had a blazing fire going. This was going to be a very sweaty night. We did a rehearsal with me roasting marshmallows while I talked. I got a good laugh from the crew while trying to get Quentin's words out with a mouthful of hot marshmallow.

Quentin said, "Why don't you try it playing the Silent Flute."

I said, "While I'm talking?"

"Yeah."

Okay, so I tried it: telling the story and playing the flute between sentences. Uma looked about fifteen years old in her sleeping bag, her hair pulled back in a ponytail, so I talked to her as I would to a child, and what with the flute passages, it took on a *Peter and the Wolf* character. We did a lot of takes. The flute and I almost burned up, but I nailed it good. At the end, the crew applauded, always a good sign. Everyone was very impressed, from Erica, the rep from Miramax, and Lawrence, the producer, down to the grips and gofers. I had to stop to be complimented over and over, all the way down the hall and up to my dressing room. "Your voice is so powerful," "Your flute playing is so beautiful," and so on. I was lucky: Sometimes the Silent Flute won't play at all, it has so many cracks in it.

Quentin was ecstatic. Well, so was I. He's just great to work with. Makes you feel great, so you *are* great. And Uma was hot. All I had to do to make it work was look at her. Annie told me later that Quentin was jumping up and down with glee while I was performing. Well, he's been directing huge fight scenes for eight weeks, and he finally got to hear some of his dialogue, a lot of it: the wild, peculiarly Tarantino writing that is the real heart of his movies.

They wrapped me about ten-thirty, and went on to do another scene without me. Annie and I were both beat, but wired at the same time. We decided to go up to our suite and clean up, and then hit the lobby lounge for a snack and a little wind-down time, but in the middle of my shower to wash off the layer of sweat, we got a call from Deedee, the associate producer, inviting us to join her, Uma, Erica, and a few others in the bar. We dressed up a little and went down. The place was pretty empty, except for the movie people. I noticed there was a grand piano. I devoured some tempura, and Annie sipped Merlot while we hung out with the girls, talking about children, preschools, nannies, and such. Uma did a whole routine about how she could avoid having a fight to the death with me—with Bill, actually. She's fallen in love with him. She's a sucker for a good story-teller. Like some girls are for musicians, or men in uniform, or mimes, she has it for raconteurs. Annie asked me if I didn't want to play the piano. I shook my head. Not in front of all these people; I'd have to perform. When the party broke up, Erica mentioned that she'd like to arrange a dinner with us the next night. I said, "Sure." I climbed on stage, now that the place was empty, and played a little piano while Annie beamed at me from across the room.

Monday, August 19

I know, I've skipped a few days. It's really hard to keep up with this. Okay, the dinner with Erica turned out totally different. Erica couldn't go; she had to stay in and watch the dailies. Uma wasn't interested in another bout of what she called "summer camp madness," dealing with multiple conversations and sophomoric games. However, Deedee was putting together something at the Meditteraneo restaurant, a kind of Italian/Spanish/Greek place, where we could sit outside. The excuse for it was a farewell party for Howard, the makeup/special effects artist (which is to say blood-spouting gashes on faces, arms, legs, necks, etc.), whose work here was finished (though my impression of Deedee is that she needs no excuse to throw a party).

When Annie and I arrived, there were already about two dozen people sitting at a long, long table, reveling up a storm. They added another table to the stretch, making it a long, long, long table. This would go on for the rest of the evening. Lawrence showed up and immediately began producing—making sure the wine flowed, and later, making sure it didn't flow too fast. The menu looked pretty good. It included a beef carpaccio, one of my favorite things, so I went for it. When it came, there was no shaved Parmesan, which sort of takes some of the fun out of it. I asked for some, and they brought, of course, a bowl of grated stuff. I was ready to accept that, but Lawrence jumped in and explained to the waiter, after only about three tries, what I wanted. I said, "Okay. We're training them, huh?" That made Lawrence smile. I liked that. He doesn't smile that much. Producing a movie is a tough job.

People kept showing up, getting a cheer and applause every time. The game of Chinese Whispers (the Beijing version of Telephone) started up, and never really ended, passing around the huge gathering statements that were so salacious, so demeaning to the parties in question, and so weird and funny, that they could scarcely be made weirder or funnier in imperfect translation. In the middle of this, Quentin arrived, and proceeded to have fun, I've got to say, *diligently*. Quentin is very determined about having fun. He pursues it with a resoluteness, a rigor that is irresistible and cannot fail. My Parmesan still had not arrived, and finally I just had to dig in to the carpaccio. It was really great, Parmesan or no. The whispers thing went on, now going around the table in both directions, which kept becoming longer and more closely packed. Then, they started passing shoulder punches, and knee bites. I remarked to Lawrence that this could get serious. At this point, long after the carpaccio had disappeared, somewhere in the middle of the main course, a huge plate of shaved Parmesan arrived, with a bunch of slabs in the middle arranged to form a little house. We had a good laugh about that, but between Lawrence, Annie, and myself, we ate it all. Quentin found a moment to ecstaticize again about my first day's work. He went on about a certain smile that was *so* Carradine that I'd let slip out, and then about a long, pregnant pause that had been sheer genius. I decided not to tell him that the "spontaneous" smile was totally premeditated and choreographed, or that the "pregnant pause" was because I couldn't hear Uma's dulcet voice over the roaring campfire and didn't know if I should say my line. Why spoil his fun?

We left the party early, probably the first casualties. The rest of them went on till two o'clock, and then Quentin took the stragglers to his room and showed them an exploitation movie, starting at 3 A.M. That's Quentin. Wherever he gets his energy, it's not from this plane.

Wednesday, August 21

The Summer Palace. Very beautiful. Huge place, with its own artificial lake and a half dozen or so different buildings and shrines spread around the shore and on a little island, all accessible by long boats with dragon heads and tails. Thousands of people. We took a few rolls of 35 mm film, and Annie captured a lot of it with her camcorder. Afterward, we looked all around outside the gates for the shop that Rob had told me to check out for sure for great martial arts stuff at superlow prices. I think we finally found the place, a little stand buried around the side, but they didn't really have much to sell at the moment, and communication was too difficult to go on with after such a long day, so we didn't buy anything.

Back at the hotel, we found out I needed to go out to the location the next day, the White Lotus Temple, an hour out of town. I was definitely eager to work so this was exciting, until we found out it was for a wardrobe fitting. Didn't make much sense, to go an hour away and back for that, when I had to be wearing the same clothes up there I had worn at the campfire for continuity.

We went up to the eighteenth floor, where there was a private happy hour for hotel guests. It was okay, with pretty good tidbits of grub, but you couldn't smoke there, so we split after a few bites to the lobby for cappuccinos. For dinner, we dressed up and went to the Astor Grill, where we ate on the terrace. Very nice. The weather this evening was just right, and the service was, like everywhere else around here, utterly sweet. Julie was there with Chris, one of the special effects guys, who looked pretty much like a special effect himself. She was quick to let us know that this was not a beau. She has one of those in New York, though she lives in Tokyo and works in L.A. They brought Annie a porterhouse steak big enough for three. She took some of it to the room to save for breakfast.

Thursday, August 22

We decided to visit the Great Wall. We called up Scarlet, our faithful assistant and translator, on the international cell phone that we all carry. It's the only way we can stay in communication without going through operators, who are not likely to speak English. Scarlet jumped at the chance to buddy around with us. After we'd had a good breakfast at lunchtime, she showed up at the hotel with our driver, whom we knew only as "G." He'd given us his name, but I couldn't get it with my firearm-damaged ears. He said, "G," and then gave up, so that's what we called him. The first time we ever saw him, walking with little baby steps to the

A couple of happy wall climbers *SCARLET*

下肢残疾人免费乘缆车
LEG DISABLED FREE FOR CABLECAR

China has a heart *DAVID CARRADINE*

car, Annie said to me, "Laurel or Hardy?" I checked him out and said, "Both." It was true. He had the physique and face of Ollie and the personality of Stan. We called him "Laurel and Hardy" to each other.

We took off for The Wall, about an hour-and-a-quarter drive. There are a lot of jokes about Beijing drivers. "Laurel and Hardy" was okay; he didn't quite drive all over the road, and he got us where we wanted to go. The section of The Wall we were headed for was the main tourist destination, which gave us some trepidation, but it was also the easiest. None of us had the desire to climb the mountain to get there, and this place had a cable lift. There was a sign over the ticket window which in English meant "Free to people with handicapped lower limbs and children." The view was outstanding, even from the cable car. We could see a lot of China, with The Wall winding through the mountains. The view of the long drop to where we'd parked the car gave a little extra excitement. If the cable broke, we were definitely toast. The Wall was great, just as I'd thought it would be. It entailed a lot of walking: uphill and downhill, and through narrow passages where the guard towers were. I noticed relatively modern gun emplacements here and there, implying the place had still been used for defense fairly recently. We took a lot of pictures, and then Annie gave her camera to Scarlet and she got seriously into becoming the official photographer of the two of us. I stopped a German couple and coerced the man into taking a picture of the three of us.

I played the bamboo flute I had made for *Kung Fu: The Movie*, the two-hour movie for TV with Brandon Lee as my son. Played it all over the place.

I noticed some very startled Chinese tourists, though nothing can beat the snapshots I've seen of my brother Keith playing his bagpipes on The Wall on a trip for the State Department back when that was the only way you could get into the country. Before we went down again, we bought a bunch of T-shirts that said, "I climbed the Great Wall."

Friday, August 23

So: 8 A.M. pickup at the hotel, except there was a flood in both of our palatial bathrooms. The drains were spewing up shower water, the toilets were spewing up sewer water, and the sinks were stopped up. We called our "Butler," and he showed up with a couple of dish towels to solve the problems. No way! So, the whole plumber SWAT team was sent in. We couldn't wait. The set was calling, so we left them in mid-plunge, hoping we'd have a home to return to. An hour and a half on the road took us to the four-hundred-year-old Buddhist temple we were going to shoot at. The place is superbeautiful—though the bathrooms lacked elegance, even for *two* hundred years ago. This last observation is a vast understatement, as anyone from the shoot will verify. Only the hardiest (or the most desperate) were willing to brave a visit. I began to miss my merely flooded facilities back in Beijing.

We found Quentin and Uma, and watched them shooting her climbing the stairs to meet Pai Mei. She did it just like Annie's twelve-year-old Amanda. Uma is really good. Then we all had a little interview with the boy from *Entertainment Weekly,* intruding on Uma's space in the woods. She runs away from these people. I just give them what they want, and they go away. I think his favorite quote from me was something to do with my opinion of Quentin, or Uma; I can't remember which, maybe both. I told him that intelligence was not the most important thing, but it was certainly helpful for a genius to be smart. Annie and I hiked the nine hundred steps and took some photos of the cemetery, which seems to be the main focus of the place. The last empress' grandfather is buried there in a big cairn, alongside some lesser late monks or whatever. The trees are the

This was worth the whole trip *ANNIE BIERMAN*

objects that seem most sacred, and the Chinese authorities know that, too. They're all numbered with little plaques nailed into the trunks, and there's a 6000 RMB fine (about $750, but of course that changes every day) for fucking with them.

Bennett showed up and told us there was a fifty-fifty chance that I would work today. We didn't care. It was groovy to be here with the company in this extremely cool location. (In every sense: The thunderstorm had greatly improved the air.) We had lunch and read old magazines and napped, and still, nothing was happening.

Then, just about the time I figured I wasn't going to work today, I was told to go to makeup and hair and prepare for my scene with Uma. We did that, and then, after a brief pause, the word came through channels that I was wrapped. Manny said, "Well, how did you like our practice session?" "Great," I said. "Let's do it again tomorrow."

I walked over to where Daryl and a crew member and some of the others were gathered around an Epiphone guitar. They flipped over my Argentine Armadillo "Charanga" guitar. I left it with them for the night rather than break up the fun. We really wanted to get "home." Annie went off to exchange the Versace sunglasses she'd bought yesterday for 1440

RMB ($182); she had decided for sure they were fakes. They couldn't credit her American Express, so they gave her cash. She bought another pair of fakes for 108 RMB ($13). When she got home, she was delighted with the family of panda bears I'd bought her in the gift shop (*toy stuffed* Panda Bears, not members of an endangered species), the bottle of 1993 reserve Chilean cabernet, and the Taitinger's champagne, which was chilling in the minibar, the various beers, etc. having been moved to the hall to accommodate it. I gave her a kiss, and told her she tasted like a big box of wishes come true.

Saturday, August 24

Today I had a reasonably late call. Uma was now shooting the scene where she meets Pai Mei, at the top of the endless stairway. After suiting up and going to makeup, I tried to find the set, and ran into Gordon Liu, who is playing Pai Mei. He had just finished his scene with Uma, and they were, as we spoke, moving on to the next location. He was wearing the shoulder-length white wig and white beard, and looked totally cool. The hair in the wig and beard is so white it's almost transparent, and it's set off by thick eyebrows which scoot off to the sides like Nike streaks. We hit it off right away. He's a musician, and wanted to know where I got the Armadillo guitar, then was very disappointed to find out he'd have to go to Argentina to find one like it. As a consolation, he had the still photographer take pictures of it.

I went on down the long steps to the road where we'd be filming my scene. This would be my first time working with Uma. I had no idea what to expect. A few crew members were clustered around a rugged-looking jeep. I wondered what the history was of an old Army jeep in China. Quentin was there with the cinematographer, Bob Richardson, a very hip guy. He had cut off his chest-length white hair just before he first met with Quentin, in March. I guess Band Apart had saved him from knuckling under to the establishment. He had been contritely and gratefully growing his locks back ever since. Quentin was very excited. Well, he always is. He apologized for having a plan for how the scene would be blocked. His sensitivity to actors is touching. It's not as though he can't just tell us what he wants.

What he had in mind was great. Bill would come down the stairway, which was eternally long and hellishly steep, like the steps of a Mayan pyramid. Then, the whole scene would be on the move, with Bill telling the fifteen-year-old Uma how to stay alive around Pai Mei, while busily loading her down with her two backpacks and bedroll, ending with me burning rubber and driving off in the jeep and her left alone to contemplate the long, long stairway.

Heba and a "scar specialist" made my face up to look as though I'd suffered some injuries in the fight with Pai Mei, which we would shoot later. I thought it would be a nice touch if it looked as though he'd dug his nails into the flesh around my eye, implying he could have plucked it out if he'd wanted to. Came out looking as though I'd been attacked by an eagle's talons, which was perfect. Quentin loved it.

We rehearsed the scene a few times, and then there was talk of breaking for lunch, but Quentin, after conferring with Bob, decided to push on. Uma and I rehearsed together on our own a couple of times, while the camera was set up on Bob's shoulder.

On the second time through, at the moment when I was supposed to say "Adios," I paused and stared into her eyes. So beautiful, I thought. I, as Bill, wouldn't see her again for years. Suddenly, it became real, and the air

Me and Bob ANDREW COOPER/MIRAMAX

around and between us practically crackled. Then it was time to put it on film. Quentin told me to start halfway up the stairs. I said tell me when to stop, and ran up, about sixty steps, taking them two at a time. The camera rolled, and I ran down—yeah, two at a time. He hadn't told me to do that, but I figured if I didn't the shot would take forever. I was a little out of breath at the start of the scene, which seemed right, so I played it up a little. We did that three times, and then Quentin said to try it without being out of breath. He suggested that I start near the bottom, since he had that part in the can. I said I'd rather do the whole thing, as it set me up for the scene.

Now, by this time, I had been up and down those steps about a dozen times, what with the rehearsals and the takes, running every time. I could have taken it easy going up. No one was in a hurry, but I was damned if I was going to let them see me show my age. I managed to do the scene without gasping in the least, and maybe it was better. After two more takes, we went into the coverage. Uma was wonderful, looking straight into my eyes, and giving me everything I needed. Quentin said to her at one point, "You know, you probably don't even know you're doing it, but it looks great when you lean on the rearview mirror like that." Uma laughed and said, "Yeah, right: Of course I have no idea." It's a great actress who can fool not just the audience, but the director into thinking what she's doing is not thought out.

After we got it all, they put the camera on the ground and I tried to throw dirt at the lens while tearing away in the jeep. The jeep's engine was barely capable of about 3,000 RPM, so this wasn't easy. It took several tries, the Chinese grips shoveling a lot of loose stuff around the rear wheels, Quentin right down there beside the camera taking it in the face.

Then he wanted a separate shot of me going down from the very top of the stairs. Back to the run up, run down routine again, this time about a hundred steps. I fairly flew. Well, I was inspired. This had been a great day. I relaxed for a few minutes and watched them get ready for Uma to carry buckets of water up those steps on a pole across her shoulders. Annie was amazed that she could do it. I saw that the buckets had false bottoms, so they weren't quite so heavy. Even so, it had to be a bitch.

Quentin, under "pressure from upstairs"—I supposed that meant

Lawrence—had decided to shoot the fight with Pai Mei on the back lot. There was just no time to do it here, and there were plenty of good temple nooks and corners in the studio. Think of *Crouching Tiger, Hidden Dragon.*

Then it turned out the Silent Flute was missing. I put out the alarm, and several people ran around, trying to discover what had happened to it. It turned out it was in the jeep, on the way back to the studio. As we trudged up the steps to the car, Annie said, "You know, you should take some of this bamboo home." I stopped dead. "My God!! Of course!" Flutes made out of bamboo from the White Lotus Temple in China! I had to have it! I took my American Eagle Buck knife to the roots. I wanted to get the whole tree, the base of the trunk where the roots spread out looks so cool. Quentin walked by, and thought it was a great idea, but wondered if I was allowed to do that. I said, "Well, bamboo is a pest, after all." But I knew he was probably right.

Scarlet showed up with a shovel. I started hacking away with that. It broke just about when a crew member brought another, better shovel. I was working feverishly, because any minute some official would probably arrest me for doing this. Then, Scarlet brought in an axe from somewhere. I got two whole trees out, the perfect thickness. Someone called down, "You better get out of there! Somebody's on the way to stop you!" I whacked the stuff into lengths of about eight or nine feet and lopped most of the branches off. Then I hurriedly propped up the useless little top sections, too skinny for flutes, to look as if they were still growing, hid the cuttings in the underbrush, and ran. There was no evidence, for the moment, that we'd been there, except the huge bundle of bamboo in my arms. With

The thief at work *ANNIE BIERMAN*

The happy surfer with his stolen bamboo *ANNIE BIERMAN*

any luck, if it rained soon, the tops would take root.

Getting the pieces in the car was tough. And the authorities were getting close. I had visions of a Chinese jail cell. G and I managed to fit them more or less into the car, and we made it out clean, probably just in time.

I was in a total sweat. As I laid my head back, I thought, You know, in March, before I started this workout program, I could never have done this day. Then I thought, Hell, *twenty years* ago I could never have done it. I don't know what's going on here, but I seem to be living backward in time.

I must have been a strange sight, parading through the marble lobby of the St. Regis with a bundle of twelve-foot bamboo stalks on my shoulder, trailing temple dirt from the roots all over the plush carpet. Fortunately, six-star hotels have tall elevators. That night, before I went to bed, I cut the stuff down a little, mostly to get rid of the split sections which I had butchered with the axe. A great day.

he happy couple in better days. (Doesn't she look fantastic?) *ANDREW COOPER/MIRAMAX FILMS*

功夫

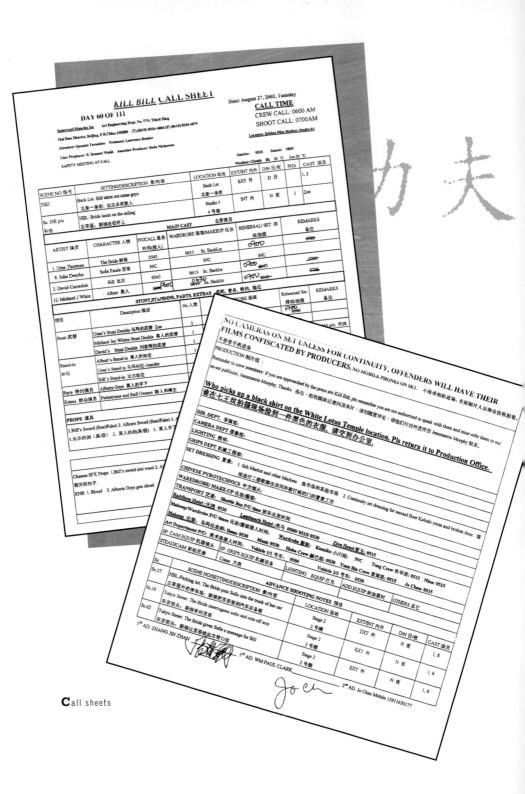

Call sheets

So, I'm taking a break. You got a problem with that? *ANNIE BIERMAN*

功夫

功夫

goddess walking? *ANDREW COOPER/MIRAMAX FILMS*

ma's gonna watch Bill kill a few guys. . . *ANDREW COOPER/MIRAMAX FILMS*

. . . **W**hich he does without even working up a sweat, one hand in his pocket.
ANDREW COOPER/MIRAMAX FILMS

Jai is amazed *ANDREW COOPER/MIRAMAX FILMS*

DC suggests, Q digs it, Uma's not so sure *ANDREW COOPER/MIRAMAX FILMS*

Takin' out Jai requires a little practice *ANDREW COOPER/MIRAMAX FILMS*

The bigger they are . . . *ANDREW COOPER/MIRAMAX FILMS*

功 夫

. . . The harder they fall. *ANDREW COOPER/MIRAMAX FILMS*

This is hard work! *ANDREW COOPER/MIRAMAX FILMS*

He likes it! *ANDREW COOPER/MIRAMAX FILMS*

Wednesday, August 28

A 5:45 call to start my big samurai fight with Michael Jai White and his four henchmen. I'm up and ready long before that; eager to get it on. I love this samurai shit, and I've been practicing the routines now since early April. I am extremely hot to trot. Traffic has picked this day to be especially brutal, and I start to get nervous when, halfway there, Scarlet gets a call from Lawrence wondering how long we're going to be. Quentin had scheduled a rehearsal before everyone went to makeup, and we were going to miss the target time. When we get there, though, Bill, the first AD, is totally cool. Quentin is still at the hotel. Uma is nowhere to be seen either. I get a cup of coffee, and Annie wonders if she'll be able to take pictures on the set. There are signs everywhere and a notation on the call sheet that cameras are strictly forbidden and film will be confiscated from any transgressors. I discuss that with Andrew Cooper, the still photographer. He says that I should check it out with Lawrence and Quentin and they will undoubtedly give us permission.

The set is a Chinese street on the studio back lot. I love back lots. You can feel all the other movies that have been shot on them. At Warner Brothers, I have rolled in the same dust as Gary Cooper, John Wayne, and for sure, my own father. Today, I'm going to eat the dust of scores of Chinese kung fu flicks, going back to long before the Bruce Lee days.

The Chinese back street has been dressed with street vendors, baskets of fruits, and wrong ends of weird vegetables. Smudge pots spew out atmosphere. It looks more typically Chinese than anything I've seen in Beijing, though not any more so than the sets I worked on in Hollywood or Toronto. Still, it feels more real somehow, and it certainly smells authentic.

Tips from The Master *ANDREW COOPER/MIRAMAX FILMS*

All in good time, Quentin arrives, and Wu Ping, Fish, "He," and the rest of the fight crew assemble. Michael Jai White shows up in a blue sweatsuit and Quentin orders the trainers to show him the routine. This is a slow starter, as Wu Ping is having "He" do my part and one of the other boys who actually doesn't know the routine do Michael's moves. "He" has really never done my part; he always played the other side, with me doing me, of course. So, essentially, we're watching the two guys learn the routine. Michael, who has worked the fight only once, back in L.A. last May, is not getting much from this, and neither is anyone else. Meanwhile I, who have been living this fight in my waking and sleeping hours for five months, am just standing there watching.

Okay, I step up and say, "Let me and 'He' show it to you." This creates a huge rumble from everyone in Wu Ping's camp. Some bullshit about protocol. I ignore all that and "He" and I dance through it at lightning speed, every move perfect. It kicks ass. Still, though, Wu Ping's delegation is scandalized. Michael, on the other hand, suddenly brightens. He finally sees what he's supposed to do. Quentin, no doubt encouraged by my little revolt, suggests a big change which will make the fight even more exciting. He now has decided that the first samurai exchange between Michael and me will be done with bare blades, instead of sheathed swords, as has been planned and rehearsed for three months. The main reason being, he wants to see me do the flashy draw he's seen me perfecting in my spare time, wherein I hold the scabbard in my left hand and jerk it upward, causing the sword to fly out and arc through the air to land in my right hand, ready for action. It's a very cool move, and I had always regretted that it wasn't going to make it into the film. Wu Ping objects strenuously. Then he suggests some other kind of draw, one more his style, but not anywhere near as flashy. I say, "No way. That's the draw I want to do." I give the set back to them and wander off. Quentin becomes engaged in a long, incredibly patient debate with Wu Ping and Fish. They don't want to budge from what's been established.

After a while, not from argument or butting heads of any kind, but simply from not giving up, Quentin, of course, gets his way. He comes down the street to talk to me. I've just started to compliment him on his patience and diplomacy when he cuts in and chastises me for violating the protocol. I say well, maybe so, but it just wasn't working, and add that Michael had thanked me for the display, saying that each run-through he had seen of the routine up to then had been different; my demonstration was the first time he'd had a clear idea of his own moves. After all, "He" had been living Michael's part alongside me for five months, too. Quentin

Quentin makes it fun for all *ANDREW COOPER/MIRAMAX FILMS*

Lawrence and I get it on. That's Wu Ping behind us. I don't think he likes me.
ANDREW COOPER/MIRAMAX FILMS

got it. I said, "Hey, I don't want to fuck with Wu Ping. On the other hand, I really do want to fuck with Wu Ping." Quentin smiled that great grin of his, and his eyes crackled with conspiratorial glee. "Yeah!" And off he went to set up the cameras.

At this point, Andrew, the still man, asked me to pose for him with the sword. He set up a very artistic shot in front of a very tall stone disk with a hole in it, sort of like the wheels in the *BC* cartoons, and shot three rolls of film with his Hasselblad. He told me I should be sure to get some of these shots, as I was looking awesome in them.

Bob, the cinematographer, was directing his crew to put up huge silks over the street. This would keep the light looking constant throughout the day, and we'd be able to keep shooting even after the sun had set, as we surely would, with the light matching perfectly. I was sent off to makeup and wardrobe. Annie and I stopped at the little cantina run by Helen, which had been set up for the company, for some espresso. It occurred to me that there was still no scene written. It wasn't even clear where this fight was going to fit into the picture. It gradually unfolded, while I sat in Manny's chair. That's where most information comes together. (I think it's always that way. After all, we'd never have known about Marilyn Monroe's affair with Bobby Kennedy if it weren't for her hairdresser.) This sequence would take place while Uma and I were on the way to Pai Mei's temple, and would be introduced in a narration by Uma. As Manny was gluing the wig to my head, a "script" for the scene arrived, handwritten by Quentin with a Magic Marker on the back of a call sheet. It's short and very sweet, just enough to justify the fight being in the picture, and it's, of course, great writing, and right up my alley, as it would have been for Clint Eastwood, Mel Gibson, or Humphrey Bogart. Quentin's writing is, like the stuff in *Dirty Harry, Raiders of the Lost Ark, The Maltese Falcon,* or *Gone With the Wind,* just so good that anyone who gets to say these words, who's not a complete pussy, is going to shine.

I commit the words to memory, getting it exactly right, letter perfect, as I'm doing with all of Quentin's dialogue, as homage to the auteur nature of his talent. I don't always do that. Normally I fit the words to my sense of my own mystique, but I trust Quentin to do that for me here.

They call me to the set, and we start working on the scene. Michael has changed into his costume, a chocolate brown silk kung fu outfit with long flowing sleeves. It looks great on his massive frame. The action is:

Bill shows them all how it's done *ANDREW COOPER/MIRAMAX FILMS*

Uma and I are walking down the street, minding our own business, when we spot Michael and his four henchmen blocking the way. Michael issues a challenge to me, ready to slice me in two as revenge for my having killed his master. I suggest that, since I'm with a lady friend, maybe we could do this another time. Michael demurs, and the mayhem begins. To my amazement, Quentin has asked Michael to do the whole thing in a New Zealand Kiwi accent; that's the voice you always hear dubbed onto Chinese kung fu movies. Michael is really good at it. Not only that, he can do it so it looks as though he's slightly out of synch. It's truly hilarious. I can hardly keep a straight face. Uma takes it all in stride, as she does everything.

I notice that the same redheaded weirdo I've been seeing on the set for days now (he was at the long, long stairway) is sitting in a canvas chair just outside the action, with a laptop computer, a Mac, on his lap. I want to know who he is. This dude is very weird: three hundred pounds or more, wild, long, curly red locks, and an equally long curly red beard. He looks like a clown, or a redheaded Santa Claus. He walks with crutches; I don't ask what that's about. It turns out that this is Harry Knowles, the proprietor of a Web site called aintitcool.com. He has paid his own way to Beijing to be on the set, and is sending his comments to the Web site daily.

This guy is utterly mad. I have to include some of his stuff here, if I can get his permission. He has his own totally unique take on the material. So, here it is, with all the typos, weird syntax, and madness intact.

BIG HARRY IN GIGANTIC CHINA: KILL BILL SET REPORT #1!!!

China . . . I'm really here, this isn't some delusion, some bit of gravy or undigested pork curdled around a strawberry margarita spiked with hashish . . . This is the real thing. China.

I am in the Temple of the White Lotus Clan to see a very old man that some worship as a god and others fear as a devil, Pai Mei. I quickly gather

Harry gets the scoop *ANDREW COOPER/MIRAMAX FILMS*

my bearings. I see Quentin talking with Daryl Hannah in her Elle Driver training under Pai Mei garb. Raggedy loose clothing drenched in blood for her eye has recently been plucked clean out, and bloody rags cover the socket. Still, through the blood and the loose clothing you can see quite clearly the exquisite beauty that is Daryl Christine Hannah. I'll never forget discovering her at the Fox Theater in Austin, Texas when I was 10 years old as I watched BLADE RUNNER alone. I fell madly in love with her and hated Harrison Ford for killing her. She was exquisite innocence combined with the skills of a killer. Talk about your Beauty and The Beast. She's both. Quentin is set to do another take inside the home of Pai Mei, sees me, waves and heads in to direct the scene with Daryl and Pai Mei.

Lawrence Bender comes over and we sit down. This Chinese man stocky strong and determined looking lets out a scream in Chinese that I assume means "Quiet on Set" but sounded like a war cry to me. This war cry is picked up, up and down the mountain by other assistants. It is quite something to hear. All human noise is gone. Suddenly you are struck by the sounds of this forest covered mountain. The cicadas and birds. A second guttural cry lets out, which I have to assume means, "ROLLING" and then through the door to this multi-thousand year old temple home, I see Pai Mei.

My heart skips multiple beats. HOLY GOD Pai Mei! I can't believe it. There he is. Gordon Liu! I begin to have the most intense smile you can imagine. He's belting out Mandarin at Hannah's Elle in a scene not in the script. Because the script is out, I will not ruin this new scene, but I will tell you this. Elle is a treacherous little bitch, I'll tell ya that much.

Quentin comes up and says, "Welcome to China."

I learn that in Japan, the same people that build models of Tokyo for Godzilla to crush are building a miniature of Tokyo for Uma to fly over. Quentin wants it to have that look that Toho Tokyo look. He is after all making the greatest cult exploitation film of all time" and he knows the devil is in the details. He wants Uma's arrival to Japan to be like Godzilla landing. I CAN't WAIT. There will be 3 days of shooting in Japan very soon. Then a couple of weeks off, while they prep for shooting in Los Angeles. Then they move to Barstow and El Paso ending shooting in Mexico.

As this latest take of Pai Mei and Elle Driver ends, Quentin brings over Daryl Hannah. She's barefoot, bloody and beautiful. Her lone blue eye staring back at me. Quentin reminds her that I'm the guy that said, "PRIS TO STAR IN KILL BILL," which thankfully kicked off good memories. Daryl and I begin to chat. This is her first day of shooting on KILL BILL. Up to this point she's been training with Master Yuen Wo Ping (but everyone here just calls him "THE MASTER") and Sonny Chiba. Instantly "What is training with Sonny Chiba like?" escapes my mouth with a smile attached. I could feel my ears perking forward awaiting to hear what that experience was like.

Once again they return to shooting the scene I will not spoil. This time instead of focusing on the action, I take in where I am.

Pai Mei's home is ancient and decrepit, the sides cracked, as is the cobblestone courtyard. That iridescent moss is everywhere. Plants are growing in-between the tiles of the roof, weeds, flowers and what not. And further still directly in front of me is an archway that has stairs that lead to a higher level still of temples.

This looks exactly like what it is supposed to look like, which is what it is. A multi-thousand year old temple of disrepair. I love it here. The sounds, the history, the culture. This is grand.

The Chinese crew begins breaking the equipment down and heading down the treacherous Pai Mei steps at impossible velocities. I'm told they are breaking for lunch, but will return. I elect to stay where I am, rather than endure the certain doom of trying the steps too often. As I sat in Pai Mei's courtyard, I am a bit bemused to see poor Hiromi (Miramax Lady) being eaten alive by Chinese Mosquitoes and Fleas which don't dine on redheaded Buddha Leprechauns. Muhahahaha

Soon I learn that the crew won't be coming back up to where I am, so I have to descend the torturous stairs of Pai Mei. I am in awe of my powers of concentration. I focused out all of the surrounding vertigo effects focusing only upon the next stair. When I got through the 72 million slippery steps, I found my arms cramped, my palms soaked in a sweat I've never before experienced. Even now as I type this my hands are sore from my Kung-fu Death Grip.

I continue my journey via car to the very most bottom of the stairs that

I had first seen from the road. Here I watch Bill's return to the Bride after getting Pai Mei's permission for her to train along with his leaving her there. Here's the scene:

THE BRIDE: **When will I see you again?**

BILL: **That's the title of my favorite soul song of the Seventies.**

THE BRIDE: **What?**

BILL: **Nothing. When he tells me you re done.**

THE BRIDE: **When do you think that might be?**

BILL : **That my dearest, all depends on You. Now remember, no backtalk, no Sarcasm Least not for the first year. You re going to have to let him Warm up for you. He hates Caucasians, despises Americans, and Has nothing but contempt for women, So in your case, that may take a Little while.**
     Adios.

Now, this is my first chance to see Uma and David act in the film. David Carradine is magnificent looking as Bill. He has a full head of peppered gray and black hair. A very lean face, the training he's been doing with THE MASTER is apparent. He has some recent bloody torn flesh aside his face that he got from Pai Mei in his "talks" with him. He's wearing a royal blue silk shirt with red piping styled across the shoulders. Upon closer inspection, you can notice a series of Asian patterns in the fabric. VERY COOL SHIRT. He's driving the dirtiest meanest looking jeep ever.

Uma here looks a bit like a little lost girl. Her blonde hair dirty and in a ponytail. She has a white loose Vera Cruz style top, a sweats top with a hood down, and knee high pants leaving those well-formed calves available for flexing in her ascent of Pai Mei's steps.

Listening to David go through that last paragraph of dialogue Killer. Absolutely killer. If you've ever seen Carradine's COLE YOUNGER in Walter Hill's brilliant THE LONG RIDERS, reference the tone, timbre and look in the way he spoke to Pamela Reed's BELLE STARR. He's amused by the Bride, but it is a tough love, not a gushing type. There is a certain delight to the pain he knows he's going to cause her, and a sadness for making her live it.

Uma on the other hand is playing the young pre-THE BRIDE character as having a certain amount of innocence and you can clearly see the doe-y eyed love for Bill here, which we'll obviously see a change in by the end of the film.

David is going to kick people's ass when they see this film, I knew it before and now that I've seen a bit of how he's playing the character, I know it again. YOU'LL SEE albeit either at Cannes or October of 2003. Yeah, I know that sucks.

As for Quentin's directing style I'll go more into that after I have a full day watching him on a soundstage. In brief he is very excited, extremely focused on the impact of the moments he's attempting to capture. He is directing every single foot of film shot on this movie. No second unit. 100% Quentin. When you see tire wheels spitting out dirt as David Carradine drives off abandoning the Bride Quentin is 3 inches to the side of the lens getting dirt thrown in his face and demanding a second take. He shoots very very quick, getting what he wants and moving on. There is no play-back monitor, he checks the framing of each shot before it begins, but stays focused on the reality of what he is shooting. He is there for extreme support for his actors, plays with his crew and engages everyone on the set.

Basically what you see on the behind the scenes of the PULP FICTION dvd, that's how he is on set.

In one break in shooting, Quentin is talking to David Carradine about how he wants him to peel out like he did in CANNONBALL, he then says, "Which I showed in Austin at my festival." David grimaces a bit, seeming to not have the fondest memories of that films dramatic merit. I say, "Yup and it played like gangbusters." David looks at me, then Quentin says, "Oh yeah, it hit em like gangbusters, it was great." Then David is in the jeep ready to peel out.

After this shot was wrapped, Gordon Liu makes his way to set in full

Pai Mei make up. I'm in awe. This is Gordon Liu, I'm in China and this is Gordon Liu! Quentin brings Gordon over to meet me, repeating to Gordon via an interpreter what I had written about him verbatim, which is extremely creepy and humbling to hear coming from Quentin. But Gordon is delighted. I literally am beside myself. It is very rare where I am literally a star

Well, you see what I mean. Harry's a little special.

So, back to the day in question. The camera is set up to get Uma's and my side of the exchange with Michael. Later, they'll get Michael's angle. This is all happening, you understand, in a narrow Chinese alley. You have to point the camera either up the street or down the street. There's not any real space to shoot a good side view. We do several takes of the verbal exchange. Then, we get down to the first part of the action. A little Chinese guy is going to come running at me, leaping and dancing, swinging his sword around his head. I will take him out with the little throwing knife that nestles on the side of the scabbard, getting him in mid-charge, *thock,* in the forehead. We will shoot that part later, as right now, the actor is walking around with the knife already sticking out of his head, courtesy of Chris, the special effects makeup guy. We can shoot my side of it, though, and go on to the next bit, where I plunge my sheathed sword into the ground in front of me and, just before Michael's minions get to me, whip it out and wipe out the three of them with a single swing of my "Hanzo blade," while the little guy lies in the street between us with the knife sticking out of his head. Then I manage to plunge the bloody blade back inside the scabbard before it falls over. Impossible, yes, but a classic Hong Kong kung fu movie bit. This would normally require a little special FX, but what we do is shoot it backward, which is just how it would be done in a Chinese movie.

Then we do some close-ups of the little knife coming out of its hiding place. For these, I suggest we use the real throwing knife. Nobody else has thought of that. Well, the reason I do this is because I'm really tired of seeing me put away a rubber knife at the end of the knife fight on the video, and now on the DVD, of *The Long Riders*. It's the only flaw in the whole sequence.

Probably no one else can see it, but I can. This stuff we're working with here is not rubber, but it's not bright steel, either. Aluminum doesn't quite have that sheen. Annie immediately gets up and moves her chair back about fifteen or twenty feet. Someone next to her says, "Why are you doing that?" She says, "I know how he throws." Everybody clears out of the way after that. Someone tells Harry Knowles, who's sitting very close to the camera, that he'd better move too. He says, "If I get killed by a knife thrown by David Carradine, I'll be a happy man." He stayed where he was. Good thing. Right by the camera was the safest place he could be. That sucker flew.

Somewhere around here we break for lunch. Everybody walks out of the closely guarded arched portico and down the studio street to the lunchroom. Annie asks if we're going there. I say, no. I've been there before, on my last visit to Beijing, during the workouts. Hot, loud—full of scintillating conversation, yes, but that's not what I need right now. Cool, quiet rest is more to the point. I always try, on every shoot, to get a little nap at lunch. Well, I don't sleep at night a lot. And I couldn't care less about the food. So we repair to my dressing room. Scarlet shows up with two plates of assorted East-West cooking, though, and I find a couple of icy Chinese Cokes. I manage to squeeze in a ten-minute nap.

After lunch, Michael and I rap a little while the crew is turning the camera around to get his dialogue and re-dressing the set, which entails clearing away the piles of equipment and all the people in canvasback chairs that would now be in the shot. This is going to take a little while. I remark to Michael that it's going to be some time before we get to do our thing together, maybe not even today. On the schedule we're supposed to do this whole scene in one, maybe two days. I can see we can scratch the "maybe." Two days, at least, it's going to take.

Before they turn the camera around, they decide to get a shot of Uma watching the action from the doorway they've put her in. Quentin moved her out of the way so she wouldn't have to stand around all day, but we need her reactions. I get together with "He" and we go through the whole fight off-camera to give her something to look at. Then we turn it all around. Michael does his bit. In the first rehearsal, he does his out-of-synch routine, just like in a dubbed Chinese movie. He gets a big laugh out of everyone. Then he gets serious. Somehow he's able to make the crazy

欢 迎
您 再 来
PLEASE COME AGAIN

That's Scarlet *DAVID CARRADINE*

Kiwi accent his own. The way he plays it, it's not even funny. He's awesome in his flowing silks, as big as a genie. At Michael's signal, the four minions run at me. Then, finally, the one guy who's been walking around all day with a knife sticking out of his head gets to do his running jumping dancing bit, but it has to be without the knife. That takes a while, removing the device and smoothing out his forehead. He's quite wonderful in his moment of glory, pushing himself to the limit, leaping, spinning, almost flying. In one take, he gets carried away by his momentum, his head getting way in front of his feet, and he actually sails through the air and does a nosedive. He turns it into a forward roll and lands on his feet again. He's sheepish, but everybody loves every bit of his stuff.

Now, it's time for Michael and me to do our thing. But we're running out of daylight. We get into it just a little, to get it started. Then, it's a wrap. It's a long ride home.

Thursday, August 29

Six o'clock call. I'm told to go straight to the set for a rehearsal. I do that, but the place is empty. A few of the Chinese construction guys are milling around, but that's it. I take a tour through the area, just to make sure, and go for coffee. There I get the word that Manny is ready for me; well, Manny is always ready. I take my coffee up to his room and submit to the wig. We have a great time, talking about all kinds of things. Dave, the third assistant director, sticks his head in the door and says, "How long?" I answer, "Couple of weeks." Everybody laughs, and Dave goes away. It takes as long as it takes.

When I get to the set, Quentin hasn't arrived. He's so cool. He knows how to get everybody ready, and he never shows up until he's needed. Then all day long, he works like a dog, and expects everyone else to do the same, while being extremely caring toward us all. Walks a razor's edge between the obsessed visionary and the doting mama hen.

So, Michael and I now start to fight in earnest. Take after take, angle after angle. Every few shots, someone comes up and changes us out of our sweaty shirts. They seem to have an endless supply of these. Good thing. We go through the first sword routine, get it down pretty great. I get the coolest compliment from Quentin. He says that I seem to move in a sweet, easy slow motion, while Michael is all speed and power, and yet, I'm up to speed with him, and totally in control. It's as though we're in different universes, kind of a quantum thing, is how he puts it. I say, "Is that all right? Do you like it?" He then lights up and says, "It looks great! I *love* it!"

We do inserts of my sword (the real one; I keep making sure that anytime we're not in imminent danger because of doing it, we use the real shit) going slowly into the scabbard, ending with a satisfying *snick*. And then there's a special setup for Michael to twirl his big sword, in the gold-encrusted scabbard, decorated with dragons and such (and it is a really big sword, and a really big scabbard), and plunge it into a heavy wooden table through a basket of dried chili peppers. Then he'll pull out the sword, leaving the scabbard embedded in the table. Very cool bit.

While they're shooting that, I take off my shirt and hang out with Harry Knowles for a while. Sweat runs down my back, even with the shirt off. We start out talking about Mac computers. He's very curious about *The Long Riders,* so I tell him some stories. Then there are the usual questions about the *Kung Fu* series. Turns out he's a fan, of course. He goes on about the myth of Bruce Lee being the creator the first choice the etc. for the series. I try to set him straight.

Harry, like everyone else, is not too clear on my role in the movie. He wants to know if I'm the bad guy. I laugh. "Well, there aren't any good guys in a Tarantino movie." Think about it: *Reservoir Dogs, Pulp Fiction, Jackie Brown*—everybody has an agenda. You root for them but they're all bad. Michael joins us, having finished his shot. "Actually," I point out to him, "you're the only good guy in this whole picture. You're avenging your master that I've killed. Fucking noble is what you are." Well, there are a few actually nice people in the picture: The innocent wedding party that I'm going to blow away later on is what I'm thinking of. But, in true Tarantino fashion, they will evince no sympathy from the audience.

Before I leave to go back to work, Harry's assistant gives me the next installment of his aintitcool.com report on the shoot. I hand it to Annie for safekeeping. Can't read it now.

Now, the past two days, I've been doing a lot of time with Michael Jai White, who is a very cool guy. Andrew Cooper (the still photographer) asks if Michael has his eleven-year-old son studying martial arts yet. Michael answers no—mainly, he says, because he feels that martial arts in the United States has become more of a business than a character-building ethos to carry through life, as it was for him. Today, it is more about the fighting abilities, the marketing of the skills into film and shit like that. Just about anyone, he says, can achieve a black belt today, and that devalues the meaning that the belt once had. Hey, I'm with him on that. Hell, I've been personally responsible for a lot of that commercial explosion. Not what I had in mind at all.

Harry Knowles draws a parallel with what happened to the Boy Scouts of America during the nineties, when the qualifications were softened so that folks who were handicapped or lived in urban areas where they never had an opportunity to camp could become an Eagle Scout through substitution badges such as computers, electrical engineering, and various other "bullshit badges" (Harry's words) that have nothing to do with the philosophy behind what Scouting is about.

Michael agrees. But then he demonstrates almost the opposite view with a kind of parable, trying to get to the heart of what martial arts is for him. He says, "Okay. Say I can kick a thousand times before wearing out, and you [Andrew] can kick three hundred times before getting to the same place."

Hiromi (the Miramax Lady) interrupts with, "And I can kick two times."

Michael continues, "Okay, and you can kick two times before tiring. Well, in martial arts, my training wouldn't really begin till kick number a thousand and one; yours [Andrew] would be at three-oh-one and Hiromi's would be at three. Now lets say I kick in my training to one thousand and five, but you [Andrew] kick to three-twenty. In the discipline it took to go farther past your limitations, who is the better martial artist? You are. It's about being able to know your limits and going past them, realizing that though you have your limits, you will push beyond them."

Harry interrupts, "So, basically, due to my conquering of those damn Pai Mei steps the other day, that means I'm ten times the martial artist of all of you!"

Michael very seriously agrees that Harry's defeating that internal fear and conquering that physical limitation was built on a personal inner strength that is at the exact core of what martial arts is about.

I just keep my mouth shut.

Michael has his thing, and it's well thought out and right on for him and his kind. I like the guy a lot and didn't feel in the least like getting into a philosophical debate right then, on the back lot of a Chinese movie studio.

My take on kung fu has evolved from an entirely different perspective. I have no interest in competition, certainly none in fighting. I also don't care about "testing" my endurance or stamina; and the need for a system of self-defense has never entered my mind.

These things I've mentioned are the very reasons why most people take up the martial arts. Well, I've always been able to take care of myself, and my strength, speed, endurance, and agility puts me in good stead. Also, I hate to work out. It's boring. Around the time I was doing the series *Kung Fu,* the way I kept myself in shape was by living at the top of seventy-five rickety wooden steps. I had to carry groceries and shit up and down those stairs, and usually did it at a dead run. And I had a beam ceiling in my little shack which I used as a jungle gym. That was enough, and it wasn't boring.

At lunch in my dressing room, Annie reads the aintitcool report, while I try to nap. She tells me, "You've got to read this. It's all about you. This guy really digs you." I think, Huh, and that's before I talked to him. Cool.

Now it's time to go on to the second section of the fight, the one-handed kung fu match. But, right then, a huge wind comes through and the silks that are covering the set start to rip. People run to the rescue, but, no, the wind whips up, and the whole cover, thirty or forty feet of it, comes apart and billows down all over everybody. There will be a pause of about two hours while this is repaired. This absolutely ensures that we'll finish the scene tomorrow, not today.

So, we hang out. No one worries, while the American and Chinese crews collaborate beautifully to put it all back up.

Finally, we get started. Same shit as before. Take after take, angle after angle. I am having more fun than I've ever had in my life. So is Quentin. He's just dancing with glee, every minute.

"One more," he yells, "because we *love* making movies!"

Finally, we run out of light. Before they send me home, Lawrence buttonholes me with the information that first thing in the morning, they are going to shoot an overhead shot of the fight. They want to do it with my stunt double. It will be used only for a quick cutaway, he says. It also means that I can sleep for an extra hour. I'm very doubtful about this. "No one moves like me," I say. We finally decide that I can do it if I want to.

As I'm walking away, it suddenly occurs to me that I've been looking at this poor guy for two days now, dressed up like me, with an identical wig, whom they hired in L.A. because of his brilliant martial arts skills, and who's traveled halfway around the world to be just standing there, ready to work, day after day, and who will probably never get a chance to show his stuff in the whole movie if I don't give it to him. And, hey, I'd get an extra hour's sleep for my magnanimity. So, I tell Scarlet, "Okay, let him do his thing. I'll sleep in."

Michael, it turns out, has been nursing a very bad ankle, an injury he picked up a few weeks ago. Annie suggests I put him in touch with Rob's Donna, now Uma's therapist, since Michael seems to be sort of sweet on her anyway.

Michael always heads straight for the buffet when he gets to the hotel (his massive frame needs a lot of feeding), so he's easy to find. I catch him at his table and we rap for a while. I give him Donna's room number.

Then, to bed.

Okay. Here's Harry Knowles' version of the day, in all its mad splendor.

BIG HARRY IN GIGANTIC CHINA: DAY 2 ON THE SET OF KILL BILL!!

I m on the set of a Beijing Backlot used for RAISE THE RED LANTERN, THE TAI CHI MASTER and many more the sets are frankly extraordinary. The sets look like those from IRON MONKEY and all the classic cool old Chinese sets of old Carvings, filigree, and style everywhere you turn to look There are bundles of dried sticks and bamboo fruits, vegetables and at every turn you expect the 3 storms to just start kicking ass.

As I round one corner in particular I see Quentin and his crew setting up a shot with David Carradine, Uma Thurman and some Chinese Extras. Now, I know that Michael Jai White is supposed to be around here somewhere, but I don't see him yet.

This is a scene that I can't remember being in the script. Uma is wearing the same blouse that she was wearing when Bill dropped her off at Pai

Mei's Very cute, very soft, not the hardened killer look yet. She's got 80's era levis, where the stitching is all readily apparent ya know, yellow flip flops, a Oaxacan wove belt, a soft suede purse with yellow, red and green beads hanging from the fringe. The blouse is white with blue embroidery, if you remember I had described it before as looking very Vera Cruz in style Today I especially want to stress that, because that is what it looked like.

Bill Is wearing an off white, almost tan loose woven Asian style shirt, black pants and some sort of I think Adidas style shoes, black and grey. Oh wait, he's changing shirts ahhhh much better, same color, definitely cooler. This shirt has the traditional black ties where the buttons are supposed to go. He has his Hanzo sword it is awesome looking David just came over to talk about the miracles of APPLE technology. Then let me handle his Hanzo blade. On the black sheath is the image of a DEVIL head. Built into the sheath is a removable throwing knife. The sword he currently has is a real one. I must see if I can make off with it. I must own a Hanzo blade.

Ah, here comes Michael Jai White and he is wearing a loose cotton almost hospital gurney's outfit. His blue outfit is universal tops and bottoms he has a CD player on a tune black belt with yellow and gray. His head is shaved, and has an evil goatee. Michael's sword is one of those wavy blades a bigger more imposing Chinese blade doomed before Hanzo steel. Now, Michael is huge I mean the man has that perfect superhero physique. I mean, all those muscles where there are not supposed to be any. And I know they aren't supposed to be there because I don't have them. After a bit, they begin to put Michael in his actual costume for Michael's character it is a silk kung fu Burgundy outfit with the white fold back cuffs, the black Nikes.

Behind Michael are four of his back ups. They are traditional Chinese red shirts only wearing that traditional all black Chinese kung fu garb. Right now there is one of them with a blade stuck in the center of his forehead, for some odd reason, I don't think he's about to survive his attack on Bill.

This whole sequence was created by Quentin yesterday He wrote it in his spiral notebook in Orange Felt Tip. I managed to make off with a Xerox copy of the page, because well I found it in the dirt and possession is 9 tenths of the law . . . wait that is ok back home oh man, I'm gonna end up painting Uncle George's action figures all assembly line fashion for sure now.

As the scene begins, a man on a bicycle rides by. There's a man behind Bill pushing an enormous cart with grain bags piled on it. Bill and THE BRIDE are laughing when suddenly they see Michael and his goons

    BILL: **Gentlemen, Can I Help you**

    Do Moe laughs, then spits out

    DO MOE: **Bastard all you can do for me is DIE.**
              You killed my master Da Moe and now I'm going to kill you too.

    BILL: **You see, I'm with a lady friend . . .**
          Can't we do this another time

    DO MOE: **Nice Try, but today is the day**
             you die.

    BILL: **Kiddo, if you don't mind. This**
          will only take a minute.

Bill hits this pose like, he couldn't care less it is the antithesis of an action pose—blade relaxed upon his shoulder Bill then gestures for the future dead people to attack.

    DO MOE: **You Arrogant Bastard, Get HIM!**

Michael sends the first poor soul into battle He's going to be leaping and swirling his sword around like he's some sort of talented badass, but due to the KNB appliance of an embedded blade in his forehead all BATTLE ROYALE style, he's been rehearsing his blade movements and his death move. He's very happy with himself, but serious at the same time. He's got this great, "I'm fucked" face. Very expressive fellow.

As they rehearse the shoot for the knife throw, behind the camera, Quentin is running at David with the blade acting like a madman to get David to crack a smile of bemusement at the ineptitude of the foes he faces. This is absolutely classic. I notice there is nobody DV-ing this moment. This is sad. Somebody should be archiving this. These are the moments we geeks die for.

Right now they are shooting THE BRIDE'S close up of her watching Bill beginning to kick ass. Meanwhile off camera, David and Victim number one just practice killing and being killed. David says he and his doomed opponent are purely responsible for anything that is being elicited from Uma Thurman's BRIDE here. In fact David says, "Of course it was great, it's the brilliance of our off camera efforts paying off!" Fun guy.

Ok, back to master shots The First guy is down. After that, David stabs the hilt of his sword into the earth. Then three bastards attack him with swords drawn. With one hand still in his side pocket, he suddenly unleashes his Hanzo sword, and in the first motion slashes the nearest victim/would be challenger from hip to shoulder then on the return motion disposes of the other two. Leaving the street awash with blood bodies and his final opponent Michael Jai White standing before him.

This shot is a huge two camera shot, so I was cleared pretty far away from the coverage in a blind spot Quentin is now directing the deaths of the various victims acting out each of their particular deaths their howls, their grimaces, their pained collapses. Meanwhile, as Quentin does this, David is practicing classic Samurai motions. Elegantly swiveling and making all the moves that Warren Beatty would have looked plum stupid as hell doing. This is literally the part that David Carradine was reborn to play. For him, this is his UNTOUCHABLES Connery part. Where everything he had been before culminates into this performance, albeit a supporting performance, but a performance that haunts every moment of the film, because ultimately he is what the film is about

The Silk that is balancing the light over this long streetway of this back-lot has begun to tear in the ferocious Chinese afternoon wind reminding me of the disasters experienced by mariners in those unfortunate movies where the sail cloth tears dooming them to back in the unmoving water as the sun drifts across the sky. Here however, it is a matter of removing the existing silk, and getting Steel Reinforced silk in place this being China there is always extra silk around somewhere. Ya know what I mean.

David has gotten out of costume and into a muscle shirt to cool off. When the shirt came off the first thing you notice is the very NON-sixty year old physique 2nd the plethora of cool old school tattoos. Very cool.

After this shot, it's finally time to turn around for Michael Jai White's reaction shots to all this stuff, his lines, the various attacks and dispatches Right now Michael is singing Dewey Bunnell's THE HORSE WITH NO NAME as originally sung behind me as he gets into his Do Moe outfit the Burgundy silk kung fu outfit covered in intricate design work through-out . . . He is also getting the right pair of Nikes on.

The shot is going to be a hard crash SHAW BROTHERS style zoom onto Michael Jai's cackled threat. This is a Shaw Brothers ZOOM as shot by multi-Academy Award winning Cinematographer shot with a PRIMO ZOOM 11:1 lens from Panavision. I guarantee you, there will never have been a higher class SHAW BROTHER zoom in history. The wonderfully youthful silver haired Robert Richardson looks like he's having the most fun ever on this shoot he told me a story yesterday about screwing Quentin's shoe to the ground during a HOUSE OF BLUE LEAVES sequence, because Quentin was so focused on the rehearsal, that he never knew Robert was doing it. So beware of Robert Richardson on your sets.

The knife head guy is getting his great performance moment. He's wielding his blade like a badass. Very thrilling!

"One more because we love making movies." Quentin Tarantino exclaims after a particularly good take!!!

There is a break in the action here as it is time to remove all the silk, so they can capture the last few moments of the Magic Hour light, for the end of the day's shoot. You ever wonder why Chinese films always look so beautiful? I can tell you. The secret is the ability to cover vast areas with silk for that perfect magic hour lighting. Not only that, but due to labor being as cheap as it is here, the rigging on these lighting set ups Well, just looking at this breakdown, there are easily 40 or so folks yanking on ropes, gathering in the silk, moving bamboo ladders and catching falling objects. The magic of the beautiful Chinese film is solved. SILK and MANPOWER. That's all there is to it. Oh and a great DP probably doesn't hurt!

"We're whistling and skipping our way into darkness." Quentin Tarantino exclaims as the ticks of the sun dial he is living is coming to a close on this very hot day!!!

Now one of the things I haven't mentioned about this day is Michael Jai White's accent. He is performing his entire role in an exaggerated KIWI accent. The result is absolutely startling on set. It is like the most perfect dubbing ever for a Shaw Brothers film, because it isn't a dub it's real, it is live and it is the actor himself doing it. Michael is having trouble though because he keeps wanting to deliver the lines with his lips not-synced to the sound he is delivering. When he demonstrates this to me, I nearly cry laughing, because it is better than even the work in POLICE ACADEMY if you re a geek, you know the scene, but it's a bit much here.

However, Quentin comes over and does a candy bar commercial with Michael, with both of them doing their KIWI voices. I'm not going to repeat it here, but if you ever see me ask me about it, I'll perform it live. It's killer.

Soon the sun is down, and it is time to wrap. There's a couple of loose bits that I'll leave you with. First David from Austin really wants Mexican Food. If you know David from Austin, please send him Mexican food. Just address the food to David in Beijing.

Lastly, there was a profound bit of wisdom that Kwai Chang Caine imparted upon me at a very significant moment of sharing. He called these . . .

THE RULES OF SLURPS
1st one is an accident.
2nd one is just to be sure
3rd slurp is pure greeeeed.

There you have it, my 2nd Day on the set of KILL BILL

Friday, August 30

I arrive on the set at a leisurely seven-thirty. The overhead shot is over with. I guess it went okay. Michael and I square off again, and we fight all day. At one point, the set dressings, tables with baskets full of vegetables, smudge pots—everything is pushed out of the way, so we can get a side angle. They set up a dolly track and follow us through the kung fu portion of the fight. These are lightning-fast moves, and we really travel, so the dolly has to really whip along to keep up with us. Then we do the same for the steadycam, which has a more fluid movement, and more intimate feeling.

The operator has to back-pedal like crazy to keep from getting run over. The sequence ends with Michael attacking me in a flying double front kick (which is like watching a freight train coming at me). I slip around him and, as he spins and charges me again, I trip him up and flip him. He sails through the air, hits the ground hard, rolls, and comes back to his feet. That pisses this Kiwi off and we go back to swords. We do all that several times from several angles. It's hot as hell. We're both sweating like crazy. Michael is changing his silks every few takes. I don't think they could possibly have that many of them. They must be drying and pressing them in an assembly line.

I take a blow on the arm from Michael's huge sword at one point. I go on to finish the take, and when Quentin says, "Cut," I take a look and there's a big red stain all down my sleeve. Well, I always get hurt some way or another on every picture. People gather around clucking, with Band-Aids and stuff. I get the shirt off, and take a look at the wound. It's not bad, just a lot of blood. And, *hey*, a wound from a samurai sword, gotten in

China, on a Quentin Tarantino movie . . . Badge of fucking Honor! I think briefly about rubbing salt in it, so it won't go away. But we clean it off, and bandage it up. People around are amazed that Annie isn't freaked. Well, she has four kids; cuts and scrapes are no big thing for her. They hand me a fresh shirt, and we go at it again.

Now, we do the sequence where I do my flashy sword draw. Quentin sets up a special isolated angle to show it off. About twenty takes of it. Sometimes it works. Sometimes it doesn't. Sometimes it's pure magic. And there's a hilarious one where the sword gets completely away from me and flies across the set into the vegetable table, scattering chili peppers everywhere. Then, Quentin says, "Give me some of those high-flying ones." These are where the sword gains ten feet or so of altitude before it spins back down to land in my hand. Hard to get right. After quite a few of those, he says, "Give me one of those and catch it without looking at it, and I'll suck your dick." It takes a few tries, but I pull that off at least once, though I'll pass on collecting the reward.

Okay. Now it's time to cut Michael's throat. While I've been throwing samurai swords around, Michael has been outfitted with a rubber neck, complete with a sliced carotid artery and a plastic tube connected to a pump. When I lay the sword into the slice, someone off-camera will work the pump, and blood will spurt out. Michael will go "Ow!" or something and fall down.

Harry Knowles has set himself up in a chair right next to the action. Someone tells him the blood will spurt quite a distance, and he should move back to avoid getting movie blood all over him. Harry laughs, and says, "Are you kidding? You think I'm going to miss getting blood sprayed on me by David Carradine? That's what I came to China for!"

We're having trouble getting the thing to work just right, so Quentin steps in. "Let me try it, so I can see what the problem is." When he gets his hand on the sword, his eyes light up. He loves this shit. Between the bunch of us, we get the trick to work, while Michael is standing there in the middle of it, waiting to bleed. I ruin the first take by being visibly grossed when the blood spurts out. I can't help it; it's a really shocking effect. We reset the effects, and do it three more times, each one a jewel. Michael screams and falls down, writhing on the ground. As I snap the sword back into the scabbard, blood spatters on my face, which is cool. I look down at Michael and watch him die. No expression at all. Quentin wouldn't go for me making any faces. I know that.

Great day. Quentin announces Michael's completion of filming and my finish in Beijing, and the crew applauds us. It's traditional.

BIG HARRY IN GIGANTIC CHINA:
DAY 3 OF THE KILL BILL REPORTS!

I find the crew picking up where they had left off yesterday Now they are shooting Michael and David's fight to the death in the TAI CHI MASTER alley way. This is just the bomb, the first exchange of sword attacks Very cool. This shot was a series of three sword clashes and a missed death blow by Michael, looking to decapitate Bill. David Carradine has a ferocity in his face, that I don't know if I've seen before. Very cool. Absolutely no nonsense.

As that shot ends, Quentin is shooting a trick sword removal by Carradine where he throws the blade up out of the sheath into the air and then landing in his hand in a high position for a downward slice. Very cool move. I really can't believe how cool that looks. It is funny when it goes too far out, but David always seems to catch it and bring it back into frame, though the time it hit the table with all the peppers caused David to crack up pretty hard.

Right now, David is shooting a close up of his side of the attack of Michael Jai White. The putting away of his blade, followed by a viscous [vicious] physical hand attack at Michael's face. Behind the camera is The Master Yuen Woo Ping He tends to pace around, but here he was rapt attention on what Carradine was doing, and after the thrust, he begins excitedly nodding, pivoting and smiling. He very much approved of what he saw. Very cool.

The second that Quentin closes up a shot, the Chinese crew leaps into action Pointing at everyone on the reverse side of the camera and shouting out "In da movie . . . in da movie!" and pointing at everything. Suddenly it is all moved. And I mean WAY FAST. 5 minute turn around max. I mean this track is laid out, cleaned, and smoothed out quicker than a runny nose in January.

Robert Richardson is up in the on high seat on the dolly, does the push on the Michael Jai White Chinese Stand in. Then without notice Quentin is back, replacing Robert in the seat, watching the push from the place, and then he's ready to go. Now, there could've been all sorts of notice, but all I know is everything that gets screamed on this set is either a war cry or some Chinese phrase that probably means, "Quiet On Set!" "Turn Off Your Cell phones and Radios!" "Cut" "Rolling" or the typical phrases of film production. Although there is a lot of screaming of "STEEEELLLLLLLLL-LAAAAAA!!!!" on set too, but I think this refers to someone named Stella that handles costumes for the principles or something. All I know is at least twice a day the crew gets a big kick out of yelling her name in all their anguished glory.

Now, about 5 feet in front of me, off camera way off camera is David Carradine literally going through the off camera motions every single take for Michael to reference. What a giving performer. He doesn't have to do this, but he's there every take being the reference his fellow actor needs. After a bit he retires to a seat next to me and we begin talking at length as Michael is jamming his sword hilt into and through a table it looks like. There's a lot of technical stuff to this shot, getting the sword to land in the exact right spot off of a grand sweeping motion all without looking at the spot.

David comes over and really was overly kind about the stories that have appeared on the page thus far. I am of course humble acting, but inside I know it is all true ahem riiiiiight. I just have great material to reflect upon this trip. If I was on the set of CHARLIE'S ANGELS 2 right now, well my neck would be tired of my head following the swirling motion and I m sure I would constantly just be drooling.

However, giving that I was having hardly any drool issues today, though Michael Jai White's implants (well, that's what he calls em) well Ok, I won't go there. Anyways, I had a long Conversation with David Carradine about THE LONG RIDERS One of my all time fave westerns For me, it is my all time favorite Walter Hill movie, and frankly I've always been curious how the project came together. Turns out that it was James

Keach and Bob Carradine's brain child / pipe dream. They came to David to try to get him to do it, and after they d told him what they were thinking, David just hemmed and hawed and let them know that he felt it would never happen. That it was a pipedream of youth. At the time James Keach and Bob Carradine were just a pair of saplings Young kids that hadn't really done much of anything at that point, but James said that Stacy Keach had signed on. David told him that if Stacy was aboard, he d do it, but that it would never happen. Immediately after David committed, James and Bob went to ask Stacy if he d come aboard. They decided to bring in the Quaids and the Bridges brothers. Walter Hill came on, and then it was trying to get United Artists aboard. Well, United Artists was intrigued, but felt that they d never get all the brothers and family all together at any given time to pull the project off. They said to name a date, and when they did, they through a big ol' party all the brothers showed up, got drunk, sang and did their bit to convince UA that they were serious. After that it all moved forward. On the set it was great fun. Keith Carradine had recently had a personal relationship fall apart and was pretty down, and David was kind of wondering why he was on this film, because his part was just so small. Since he had so much idle time, he figured that he d occupy himself with making Keith laugh. Walter would overhear him saying something smartassy to Keith, then tell David to use that in the movie. From there, the character was expanded. And when Pamela Reed came aboard. He knew the film was working. Because they just had such a great connection on the set. He feels that even though she's barely in the film, though she was literally coming from out of nowhere, she nearly steals the whole film. Speaking of Belle Starr, on the set there was a ton of moonshine, singing, firing guns, riding horses and. Atlanta whores. At the time David had his wife on set. However, anyone that was lonely wasn't lonely for long. He also felt that those women were some of the nicest, most friendly, good spirited women he d met. We then talked about the brilliance of the action, but right when we were about to get to the nitty gritty

On set, there was a sudden transition to the reverse of the initial fight with David Carradine and Michael Jai White. That first volley of attacks Watching from the opposite side this time, being able to see Michael's expression during the shoot is very intense he had a "don't fuck with me feeble white man" look. Very cool.

Now as they continue to shoot, Quentin starts off one particular take with, "Can we pick up the speed a bit here, I m going for Lightning Swords of Death style action here."

After nailing that take with a bit of Ogami Itto action going on, they again decide to focus on more of Michael's shots. So again, David comes and takes a seat next to me. Having this sort of talk time with David is quite cool, specially for someone that grew up on DEATHRACE 2000 which I still haven't brought up! CIRCLE OF IRON, LONG RIDERS, LONE WOLF McQUADE, Q and of course KUNG FU. For a child of the seventies and eighties David Carradine means quite a friggin' lot and having him just plop down to shoot the shit is great. There is zero pretension, and he's got a wicked sense of humor. When he takes a seat, he begins telling me about the Campfire Story sequence in KILL BILL!

Campfire story? What fucking Campfire story? Well according to David, the Campfire Story is essentially The Story of Pai Mei in the script it takes place in the jeep as Bill takes the oh so youthful one day BRIDE to the sadistic hands of Pai Mei. Now, instead of a conversation in that dusty jeep, it takes place at night on the Chinese Countryside, the night before he arrives at Pai Mei's Originally Quentin wanted them roasting marshmallows as he told the story, but the monologue didn't flow quite right with a steaming hot molten marshmallow in David's mouth, so Quentin asked David to try it with the Flute.

What FLUTE? Well it turns out that David brought along the CIRCLE OF IRON Silent Flute That's right, Bill will have the Silent Flute in the film. And he uses his flute to help tell the story "Peter and the Wolf" fashion. How cool is that? Now, as the story goes, back before CIRCLE OF IRON started filming, David planted the bamboo plants, let them grow, harvested the bamboo, dried it out, treated it and turned them into the silent flutes. There were three Silent Flutes, and they all got banged up to hell, given the amount of head banging and ass bruising they caused, and on most days they will rarely give out a note, but on the night of the Campfire The flute treated David and the crew to a rare sonata of a performance. The scene starts off with David improvising out some flute work, then going into the story of well . . . you know, it goes:

BILL (V.O.):   **Once upon a time in China, some believe around the year, one-double naught-three**

As each part of the story unfolds, David plays PETER AND THE WOLF fashion musical interludes for the characters and storyline that comes. Now will this still be over old Pai Mei footage from the Shaw Brothers era? I'll need to ask Quentin that. However, the other people I asked on set about the Campfire scene all declare it a classic. And Quentin came over at the tail end of David's telling of how it went, and said that it was actually the first monologue of his he heard for this film being delivered. David interrupted that it was pretty much the only on-camera monologue Then Quentin stressed that he felt that David's SUPERMAN monologue was most definitely a monologue, which David quickly conceded. Quentin then mawkishly looks at me and says, "Oh yeah, that's another new thing that isn't in your version of the script!" THE BASTARD!

Knowing that Quentin is in a coy, fuck with Harry mode, I don't ask him about the "Superman" Monologue, but instead sit on it, wait for Quentin to get busy else where.

Quickly, Quentin is called back into action, leaving me alone again with David. I look at David with angelic innocence and say, "Superman monologue?" This is apparently a new scene that takes place between Uma, David and that other character that I don't want to mention because of the spoiler nature of the final chapter of KILL BILL, but as David says it, this is a doozy. He looked me dead in the eye and says that the SUPERMAN monologue is one of those just ingenious trademark brilliant Quentin monologues that he's famous for. Dealing with the whole Clark Kent/Superman and his place in things sort of stories. How this ties in to such a powerful sequence as when The Bride and Bill finally meet. Well, that's a story he wouldn't get into, but from the fire agate flame of giddiness in David's eye it really must be great stuff.

David is again called into action and as I look around for my ever watchful eyes to pick up on something, I notice the Master Yuen Woo-Ping is playing with the paper label from his water bottle. Folding the paper, smiling at the paper, looking at the water bottle, but ultimately bored with the water bottle. Apparently the label didn't hold the secrets of the universe, or maybe it did, but him being The Master, he knew the secrets of the universe long ago, and is bored with such revelations. Suddenly he is paying attention again to the "sliced button" take.

The SLICED BUTTON TAKE?

Well Michael Jai White's character does a sweeping Slice one of Bill's buttons in half moments. There's a whole special effects complexity to this shot that I could never really fathom. But then I'm a simple man from Texas.

Next they begin rehearsing the one armed fight, as Bill has his sword behind his back, and Michael has lost his sword when it is thrust all the way through a solid wooden post, not easily retrieved.

I watch David tossing that poor fool named Michael Jai White who dared to step up to the plate with the Grasshopper. Ewwww, these are brutal throws. Man, Spawn getting ass whupping lessons from Kwai Chang Caine. Somehow I really feel that's appropriate as all hell. It'd be like watching Kirk kick shit out of Picard. Just something that needs to happen from time to time.

Frankly I am really unable to conceive of having to wait till Cannes. That's just not fair. I mean, this shit is all tickling the privates and getting me ready, with a 10 month wait for release Fuck that. I'm mortal man. I need to see this fight scene pronto. But that will be a story for another day, because as all things must this story has reached its end!

Well, okay. That's all you get. I can only take so much of Harry.

On the way to the hotel, we discover that they have booked us on a plane for L.A. tonight. No way that was going to work. Annie gets on my cell phone and sets it up for tomorrow. Tonight, we will sleep.

Saturday, August 31

Well, we didn't sleep much, because, of course, we had to pack. That took most of the night. We piled our mountain of luggage into a company van, and G drove us to the airport. On the way, however, we had to stop at the Friendship store to pick up as many sets of silk sheets as there were colors. Had to. We may never get the chance again, and lying in silk sheets has got to be the ultimate. Scarlet accompanied us all the way to the barrier, where she gave us a tearful good-bye. So many times I've said farewell at the end of a shoot to someone who has become like family. There were no skycaps anywhere, so we loaded our bags on two carts and made our way slowly and confusedly through the endless red tape of getting out of China. The X-ray machine spit out two of my bags. There was an interesting moment when they found my rubber practice single-action Colts. It took a while for them to decide they weren't dangerous weapons. The heat was enormous, the humidity even worse.

Soon I got my bags back together and was on my way. Now I was really sweating. Finally we were through the line, and, shortly, on the plane—747, which is my favorite way to fly. China Air's version of first class was nothing special. But we were on our way home, and, luxury, or even comfort, are not the most important things on earth, or in the air. With the war on terrorism, people starving everywhere, and, for that matter, a good chunk of a solid performance in a great movie at my back, I could scarcely take myself seriously complaining about my first-class seat back to the Home of the Brave.

"Our arrival at LAX brought that feeling home for sure. They waved us through the "Nothing to Declare" line. The customs guy said, "Hi, Dave. Where you been this time?"

"China," I said.

"A movie?"

"Yeah. Quentin Tarantino's new film. *Kill Bill* . . . I'm Bill."

"Way to go, David."

Limo driver waiting. All things beautiful. Even the weather was per-fect. Home looked like heaven. Well, it is.

Thursday, September 5, 2:54 A.M.

I just woke up from a terrible nightmare. Well, terrible for me. I'm still actually trembling, after two glasses of water and, being a good boy, Thunder's doggie antibiotics, which I am taking to try to get rid of the bronchial invader that had got into me in China, and having lit a cigarette to try to calm down. Suddenly, I thought, I gotta write this down. My fingers hardly work. But this is too bad not to talk out.

I showed up for work on some distant location, not China or Barstow, someplace with grass, trees, and a big, serene lake. The set was I guess a castle, though of course it's a dream and everything is changing all the time. It's funny how I always just accept completely such paradoxes. As though I have no brains in my sleep. You'd think I would still have *some* of my higher judgment center working. Maybe that part of the brain is what needs the sleep. The hippocampus, fried by the work it's done all day, goes into a coma. It shuts off like someone threw the switch. And out comes the emotional, illogical, frightened child that lives in the frontal lobe.

Quentin was shooting some other scene on the grounds of the castle. There were a thousand extras and he'd changed the whole movie. It was now a period piece. I didn't know my lines, but I wasn't worried. He'd be a while, I knew, and I'm a very fast study. All I had to do was find a script. Well, there was no one who could find me one. There wasn't an AD, or a PA, or even a gofer anywhere. Nobody in wardrobe either. But there were actors everywhere. I asked everybody to loan me their script: I would only need it for a few minutes. I haven't once in forty years as an actor gone on without my lines. Hell, in the old *Kung Fu* series I never even read the scripts. Yeah! I would be in my dressing room playing the guitar or talking to lawyers or, in the final season in particular, working out with Kam Yuen and Janet, learning forms, kicking and stretching. Jim Weatherill would appear at the door (it was always open) and say, "They need you, *Kwai*." I'd go out to the set, which I wouldn't have seen before, and Jim would say "Piece of cake" usually (which it usually was) and walk me through the moves. Then while they were doing the final touches I'd go over to the script girl—"Plain Jane," everybody called her, because she was so beautiful. I'd say, "Can I look at the pages for a second?" I'd look at them for less than a minute (quotes from the *Tao Te Ching* maybe, really hard stuff), flipping the pages back and forth, and say, "Thanks." It looked as though I was just taking a last look, but it was actually my first and only one. I had no idea what the story was about. It all really worked. It was like I was from another planet. A stranger-in-a-strange-land, just like Caine. I never told anyone, particularly the directors. They'd freak, I figured.

(I'm just calming down enough to breathe again, but my fingers still won't work!)

So I found my costume. It was gorgeous, kind of Shakespearean, with tights yet. (I've got great legs.) I'm still trying to find a script, and things are going wrong when I try to put on the duds. The little short diaper thing like padded Jockey shorts that go with that kind of outfit was made in two pieces. It had a zipper that went right around to my ass. It was hard to get on, and the zipper kept unzipping, leaving me exposed to all the people. There were beautiful women, though not Uma or Daryl or anyone I knew. And there were older ladies, clowns, vaudeville acts, magicians. Like a Fellini movie. Still no script. I was starting to panic. Then a swarthy gent with an Eastern European accent who's changing out of a gypsy costume says, "You can haff a loook at my script. I dunt need it anymore." He hands me what looks like a circus poster, but it turns out it has only his scene in it.

Then a PA or something showed up and said they were ready. I couldn't go out there like that, with my ass showing, so I changed back into my Hugo Boss trousers. Then I couldn't find any shoes. I went out there barefoot; nobody would care. I told the PA I needed a script. He said he'd get me one. The scene was, I think, a funeral, and I had to give the eulogy. I found my mark among the crowd, and the PA, who had now become a young girl, slipped me a scrap of paper with the words I had to say written all over it in tiny longhand.

I couldn't read it without my glasses. Now I've got to find the glasses. Of course, I can't. Suddenly I've got the costume on, only it's transformed itself into a black suit. Then I find out the movie has become a musical, with a big chorus of singers and dancers and the whole bit, and my lines are lyrics. I've got to learn a song in five minutes, and I don't know the tune and can't see. Quentin calls "Action" and I blow the scene. Quentin is pissed, monumentally angry, and he's even taller than the six-four or so he is in real life. Like an angry god. I say, "I'll get it together, don't worry. I just have to find my glasses." Lawrence Bender steps in and says, "That's it. You're out!" I cry, "No no no." Quentin says, "You've betrayed me! Why do you hate me?" I say, hysterical now, "No, man. I love you!" Then I find the glasses in my pocket. "Hey, I found them!" But they won't change their minds. I'm pleading. Quentin now is laughing, which he really is most of the time—I mean in real life, when I'm awake. He says, "You know, you'd make a good Parson." That's the very much smaller part that Bo Svenson is playing in the real *Kill Bill*. The way he says it, though, I know I won't even get that. It's just a mean joke, totally out of character for Quentin.

I'm crazed and desperate. I say, "I'm going to do it. Just give me one chance. I'll nail it." Lawrence says, with a tolerant smile, "I'm sorry, David. You're fired. That's it!" I run and climb up to the set, and I still can't read the damn words. They come and try to drag me away. I'm hanging on to the railing and pleading. More crew members show up and they're all pulling at me and trying to pry my fingers loose. I scream, my voice about an octave higher than usual, "I don't want to hit anybody!" I think I'm starting to cry. They all give a mighty heave and my fingers almost break trying to hold on, but the bunch of big tough grips and electricians, along with the ADs and the PAs, are too much for me. They drag me off and throw me down the mountain. I land in the lake and start to drown. I'm still yelling, "I CAN DO IT," while I'm drowning. They all turn away and just get back to work.

I wake up then, in my big bed, Annie beside me, under our champagne Chinese silk sheets. I just *slam* up, my head full of that groggy paralysis, still really in the dream, shaking all over. I guess I cry out, because Annie wakes up with a start and says, "What's wrong?" She never knows with me. I gasp—climbing, almost falling out of bed and reeling to the bathroom—*"I just had a terrible dream!"* Still in the hysterical-chipmunk voice.

Well, the great thing about nightmares is you wake up and it's not real. I've calmed down now. I realize it's all going to be all right. Suddenly I'm energized. I know I'm going to be great in this part, and I'll do everything I can to make the movie the best it can be. For Quentin. I really do love him, like we all do—adore him, actually. We'll do anything for him. Follow him down any rabbit hole he dreams up. Yikes! There's that word again.

I'm reminded of a dream I had once where I was desperately sad about being rejected by my father when I tried to hug him. I was attacked by a monster in the turgid dark of a house that always appears in my dreams. I fought the monster off and killed it, only to discover that it was my best friend trying to comfort me. When I woke up I knew that I had to be extra careful because at the core, I'm insane; every once in a while I'm wrong about everything.

Ouspensky's *In Search of the Miraculous,* which I always say to people is my favorite book, tells us that we're all dreaming. We wake up in the morning from one dream into another one. With a lot of mental work, we can wake up from this dream into yet another. Somewhere up that ladder is reality, which only a few of us ever get to, and it's always possible to slip back if we're not paying attention. Ouspensky once asked Gurdjieff what he thought about psychiatry. Gurdjieff replied that psychiatry was all very well for human beings, but we're machines; what we need are mechanics. Ouspensky said, "But surely there are some people who are human beings." Gurdjieff said, "Of course there are. But *YOU* don't know any."

Once, when I had taken dozens of buttons of peyote, Mescalito came to me. (He's the god of Peyote: they say you haven't really experienced a real peyote trip unless you've seen Mescalito. Well, I have.) Looking like the Jolly Green Giant, he stepped over the mountains, and bent down to talk to me. "Time to go, Dave," he said. I said, "No no no. I've got all this stuff to do—songs to write, women to make love with." He said, "That's already all happened. Time is a circle. It's all been done already. You don't have to go through all the pain." I said, "I don't mind the pain. I want to do it all in these baby steps." He just shook his head and said, "All right, whatever you say." Then he straightened up and walked away, stepping over the Santa Monica Mountains. Was that real? Was that UNreal? Seemed real. What's real?

Einstein said it's all pretty much an illusion. The Hindus say none of what we do makes any difference. The Pope says repent and it's like it never happened. Sometimes it's clear to me that nothing *does* matter, but at the same time it's important to go through it all, for some higher reason. And we *are* allowed to have fun. I find it comforting that eating and shitting, waking and sleeping are not what it's all about. Can't give up on making love. Sometimes that seems to me to be all there is that's worth anything. All the rest is just to make a place and a time for that. And Art and Music; gotta have them. Other times it seems as though the whole thing is happening underwater—none of it real, except the embrace. That always feels like it has real substance. Certainly, the pain isn't real. Thank God for laughter.

Okay. It's five-fifteen. I've been writing this crazy digression for two and a half hours. But I got it out. I'm cool.

Only, there's no way I can get back to sleep. No, wait! There is. I could try to read *Acting: The First Six Lessons,* by Richard Boleslavsky, my favorite book about acting. I should nod off quick, as I've read it about a dozen times. It's well-worn, with coffee stains and peach juice on the pages, and there's a cigarette burn on the cover.

Talk to you later, when I'm sane again, or as sane as I get.

Thursday day

Well, *The First Six Lessons* worked. I woke up refreshed and ready to face my future with gusto. Dorie, our new nanny, made me a stack of pancakes. I devoured them.

I have a photo shoot at eleven, so I clean up real good and load a lot of pretty clothes into my Maserati and take off for Hollywood. I hate still photography sessions. Hey, I'm a movie actor; I need to move. By the time they put me in a chair and tell me to sit just so, and turn my head this way and smile, all they're getting is a photograph of a piece of meat. But this guy—Braden is his name—was cool. He rapped with me for a while about all kinds of stuff up on the roof of his Bohemian pad, then told me to forget about the camera and, you know, just made me feel good. Then he took me down to his studio and photographed me feeling good. He had me lean against the door to the balcony, for the daylight, and I just grooved on the pretty girls, fat guys, punks, and weirdos walking by on Larchmont Street. We shot two rolls of 35 mm and then I took Braden and his assistants downstairs to the Starbucks for cappuccinos. We sat at a table on the sidewalk talking philosophy and movies and watched the girls go by at closer range. Larchmont is a very cool, largely unknown strip of sweet boutiques and cute restaurants with a street life that feels like, well, not the South of France, but maybe Portugal. An old Chinese guy gave me a kung fu salute as he passed: Black Tiger style. Very impressive. I gave him a thumbs-up. The two assistants took off, and Braden and I went back up and shot a third roll by ourselves with a whole new outlook on life. The last few shots we did with me wearing a leather jacket with no shirt, to show the great shape these months of training have put me in. Well, okay. Why not?

While I was stuffing all my stuff into the Maser, a muscular black dude in a tank top and a huge white guy came up. The black dude stared at my abs and kept saying, "You . . . you . . . you . . . Wow! You de man! I'm great. I mean, I'm right there! But, you're it! Everything I am is because of you, man. I got my black belt and I'm perfect, but you are . . . I mean, you changed my life!" The usual thing. Happens every day. Sly Stallone has bodyguards to keep such people away; but you can't call this stuff "getting hassled." Then the huge white guy stepped in. He said he was a judo instructor and he was forty years into it. That means he predates me. It's refreshing when I meet a martial artist who didn't get into it because of watching me on TV. Come to think of it, that means he would predate the Bruce Lee craze, too. This guy was not a media product. He was the real thing! No artificial ingredients, no sweeteners.

This evening we had dinner with my brother Keith and his sweet Hayley, at Capriccio, a really great Italian place on Ventura Boulevard. We sat outside so we could smoke, and Keith charmed the owners with his fluent Italian. Not just fluent! He does the whole ethnic bit, with not just a perfect accent—he does the gestures, the shrug, and the lip thing, like a native Roman. He had just got back from shooting a Western in Calgary, Canada, with Tom Selleck and Brother Bobby. I would have been in it too but for *Kill Bill*'s constantly changing schedule. Would have been sweet. Riding horses and hanging out with the bros. We haven't done that since *The Long Riders*. And Tom Selleck is a great guy. Well, I'm not complaining. We traded stories about China, Calgary, and my four new kids, and laughed our heads off at Hayley's humor. She has a funny remark or a fall-down-laughing gesture for every situation. And she's an excellent mimic. You should hear her Meryl Streep. It's better than Meryl. And she's beautiful to boot. Keith is a very lucky guy. Well, so am I. Annie spreads goodness around her like a pebble in a pond spreads ripples.

"Priceless" is too cheap a word to describe these ladies. I'll sleep easily and dream sweetly tonight.

Saturday, September 7

Six-thirty A.M. Woke up from another heavy dream—not a bad one, though; a very good one, I *think*. Scary, yes, but just super. It was sort of like being one of the *Men in Black*, but not battling anyone really—*Men in Black* in the sense that we were being recruited for some higher purpose and subjected to accelerated training, and had to dodge the regular authorities, who could never possibly understand our "mission."

Quentin told me once that some really deep thinker of some kind, one of those people who can "see" things, had told him that he had this mission he had to perform, his mission in life, and that there was actually no way he could fuck it up; it was a given. I think there *are* absolutes like that. Incontrovertible elements of Fate, if you will, which will unfold, no matter what we mortals try to do to screw them up. And, for sure, there are some people who are "chosen." I'm sure it's possible for such people to blow it, but only by getting in their own way, not from outside forces, not easily. Anyway, thinking that way about himself for just a day or two, he said, had changed his whole life. Well, I've always believed in these missions from God, and that there are special beings who are not part of the regular mix, and, of course, I hoped I was one of them. Quentin is definitely a higher being, and without any Hindu gobbledygook or Science of Mind bullshit. He's gotten most of his perceptions of the eternal and the beyond, his model of the universe, from comic books, I think, more than movies. Same with me. When I was a little kid I read a comic book called *Supersnipe.* This maybe six-year-old kid was the world's biggest comic fan, and he dressed up in baggy red long johns with the window in the back, plus a cape and a little black mask, and went around trying to fight crime and stuff. But in a couple of the stories, he actually *became* SuperSnipe, over six feet tall, with lots of muscles and skintight long johns, but still with this tiny six-year-old head on top of it all. And it wasn't exactly a dream in the stories; the daring deeds really did get done.

Well, I *was* the world's greatest comic fan, and I got my grandmother to sew me a superhero costume and tried to fly in it, off the garage roof. I really believed in this stuff, and I'm not even embarrassed to say I still do.

Okay, I can't fly, not when I'm awake anyway—at least not so far. I believe wholeheartedly in King Arthur and Merlin too, and in the Shroud of Turin; I don't care what the experts say. I don't buy fairies, though, or goblins. So, it's totally reasonable, especially after this epic power dream, for me to wonder: Could Quentin be an agent of some higher powers himself, like Tommy Lee Jones in *Men in Black*, and is he recruiting me? Pulling me out of the humdrum to activate me for a higher purpose? (Whether he knows it or not, come to think of it, though maybe he does.) I sure would dig it. I definitely feel as though I've been reenergized, like Frankenstein when Dracula zaps the anode and cathode in his neck with his ring of power.

Superhuman abilities are a lot of fun. Rarely in the comic books do they get into the price. It's heavy, as I remember. But, hey, you live only an infinite number of times, so why not make yourself useful.

I'm going back to bed.

September 11

I hear through the grapevine, which is in my case e-mail, that everyone out there is betting on whether *Kill Bill* is in trouble—behind schedule, over budget, all that. Does Harvey Weinstein still love Quentin? Can Quentin still deliver? Will the picture get back on track? Such total bullshit! This picture could not be more on track. Quentin and Lawrence are doing exactly what they set out to do, on exactly the schedule they set for themselves. Way back there on Academy Award Sunday, Quentin told me it was a six-month shoot, and that's what it's turning out to be, Miramax's efforts at condensing the schedule notwithstanding. That's what is called artistic integrity. They're making the movie they set out to do. And it's going to be a killer. I had lunch recently with one of my favorite A-list directors, and he said Quentin has totally blown his reputation for shooting fast. I said, "Yes. Deliberately."

The director replied (I sort of have to keep his name out of it; you know, protect the innocent . . . and the guilty, of course), "Well, I like seeing him spend as much of Miramax's money as he can."

"Yeah, sure," I said. "But, apparently, so does Miramax. They're letting him run."

"As well they should," said my to-remain-anonymous director friend. Damn right. Harvey Weinstein himself calls Miramax "The House That Tarantino Built."

Tuesday, September 17

Meeting with Scott Melrose at Endeavor in the afternoon. Endeavor is my dream choice of the moment for an agency. Their reputation is they're young, hip, tough, and no nonsense, with a small but great client list. Just what I need; what anyone needs, actually. Gayle pitched them, and, after some deliberation among themselves, they turned us down. How that happens is, out of the legion of agents who work in the firm, three will give a bad rap on me, though they have probably never met me. Even if all the other agents are huge fans, that lack of solidarity will not create a "maybe," it will ensure a "no." That's just the way it is.

So Gayle called Scott, one of the vice presidents, and said, "Look, David is the coolest. He's straight-ahead, cooperative, loyal. He's been sober for six years. He looks great. He's in incredible condition. He doesn't have a six-pack; he has an *eight*-pack. Plus, he's a fucking Icon. When this Tarantino movie comes out, with David in the title role, he's going to be so hot that you're going to be begging me to have him. And, just on principle, I'm going to have to turn you down. Not only that, but every time he gets a big studio picture, you're going to be the first person I call, even before I call David. And I'm going to keep doing that for the rest of your life." You have to love this lady.

Scott laughed. "Okay," he said, "I'll take a meeting." Today was the day. He wanted to meet with me alone, without Gayle. One-on-one. All I had to do was knock him dead with my personality. I went in and actually did that. As a side effect, I charmed everybody else in the agency too, on the way in and out. He called Gayle up right away and told her everybody was flipped out by me and by the way I looked. Thanks to kung fu, vitamins, herbs, my father's amazing constitution, and my mother's tough pioneer genes, not to mention my six years of being off dope and booze, plus of course, the three months of Quentin's grueling training for *Kill Bill*, I really did look pretty great. And not even just for sixty-six years: simply great. We were on. Next case.

Wednesday, September 18

Gayle's been telling me for a few weeks that I have to have a publicist. She's been pitching Rogers & Cowan, the legendary outfit that took care of Liz Taylor and other Icons back in the golden days. I've had some experience with them. About twenty years ago or so, when I was superhot, I hired them. For two thousand a month or so, they got me little blips in newspaper columns. Hell, I can do that myself. I can call up Army Archer and tell him a story, and he'll say, "Write it up and fax it to me. I'll print it." Disgusted with these screws, I fired them and hired a young girl named Allison Brennan. She introduced me to Charles Champlin, who became a lifelong friend, hooked me up with AFI, and put me together with the president of United Artists, who came to a screening of the rough cut of *Americana* and bought the picture for distribution. Well, Gayle was all but adamant about me taking a meeting with these guys. "They've changed," she said. "And they have all the contacts to do the job for us." Okay. I took a meeting with a lady named Julie, a vice president at Rogers & Cowan.

Annie was off on some errand in the morning, so I had to make sure I got there on time all by myself. I ended up arriving at the place an hour early. Weird. I called Gayle, who hadn't left her house yet, and she said I could take the meeting without her, if I wanted. I said, "No. We're in this together. I'll go get a cup of coffee." I took this young English guy, James, who was staring at me while I talked to Gayle, down to the Starbucks next door. I hate Starbucks. They have poor service and weak coffee, and they've run all the really good espresso bars out of business by opening up a franchise across the street from every one of them.

We rapped for a while, the Englishman and I, about everything. Very cool dude, as it turned out. That still doesn't prove anything, though. Back in the office, he turned out to be the man who would be handling my account, with this lady Julie overseeing. Julie got me from "Hello." She strode in, her long red hair flowing, exuding confidence and expertise from every pore, along with a lot of very attractive pheromones. Gayle showed up, looking absolutely beautiful. I could have sworn she must be in love. Her hair was a new color, and she was wearing a decidedly non-business dress, with a jade Zen thing on a black velvet choker around her neck. I aired my objections to "the old" Rogers & Cowan. I also made my feelings known about various outlets. Julie agreed with me that *People* magazine was just a tabloid on slick paper. She also agreed that *Premiere* contained a literate film commentary, while *Entertainment Weekly* was just another Time-Life rag. However, she said, *Premiere* is a monthly, and *Entertainment* is a weekly. We have twelve chances in a year to get on the cover of *Premiere*, and fifty-two with *Entertainment Weekly*. Every opinion I had, every idea, she seemed to have the real and precise scoop on. Then she outlined what they would do, and how it would benefit me. I was falling in love, or, at least, in like. Gayle was just beaming.

We went down the elevator together in a state of glee. We spent another twenty minutes walking each other to our cars and talking about it all. "This is going to work, no doubt about it," was the mood. We'll see.

Thursday, September 19

The Serpent's Egg, the movie I did with Ingmar Bergman, is about to be released on DVD, and the people at United Artists wanted me to do the commentary on it. I'd never done one of these before, and there was no money for it, of course, but I wasn't about to pass this one up. I saddled up the Maserati and cruised down to the recording studio in Santa Monica. When I got inside, I realized I'd been there before, for a beer commercial. They have a great espresso bar, with lots of cookies and stuff.

After I loaded up on cappuccino and chocolate chips, they took me into a room and did an interview on camera. They wanted to know all about Ingmar and Liv Ullmann, my costar in the picture. I told them what I could. Both of them are very private people, so what I said had to be pretty superficial, but they all seemed to be pleased with how it went down. Then they took me downstairs to a room with a big screen and showed me the movie, while I sipped coffee and just said whatever came to mind. It was pretty cool. With the sound turned down, I wasn't hit so hard with the "angst" of the thing. I could just feast on the beautiful photography, the wonderful lighting by Sven Nykvist on the close-ups of Liv, so lovely, and myself. God, I was so young. The Serpent's Egg is a difficult movie, a hard one to watch twice. But this time I could just cruise through it, reminiscing on those days in Munich in the winter of '76.

It took a long afternoon to get all this done, and then I had to rush to make it to Bobbie Shaw Chance's acting workshop. My daughter Kansas, coming from a day of shooting on the little movie she's starring in, and Annie would meet me there. Bobbie's an old friend, dating back to when I directed her in You and Me, in 1972. She wanted me to meet a couple of directors, and the vice president of Rogers & Cowan. That interested me, since I was thinking of signing up with them. She introduced me to the class, and Kansas too, going on about how great we are as artists to the point of embarrassment. But, Bobbie's like that. I expect it every time I go there, and accept it. She loves me; what the hell, you can't get enough of that.

What I wasn't prepared for was for her to make me get up on stage and lead an exercise. Well, she's been trying to get me to teach a class there for years. I did that chore and then tried to run, but she caught me outside and introduced me to the guy from Rogers & Cowan, a young Chinese man. I wasn't impressed. He was totally unlike the people I'd talked to the day before. It turned out that Mr. Rogers and Mr. Cowan had split up a few years back, and this guy was with the other half. I could tell, right off, that the vibe I remembered from the old days had gone with the old dude—I guess that's Cowan. He had represented people like Liz Taylor, and was famous, and old-fashioned to the point of backwardness, while the other half was hip, young, vital, all that.

I was as polite as I could stand, and then I split next door, with Annie and Kansas, to the Casa Vega for some enchiladas.

Friday, September 20

Gayle, knowing I hate doing interviews, has devised a way to root out the unimportant ones: She demands payment for them. Not a lot, but any charge at all is unheard of. She tells them "Take it or leave it; it's the only way David will do it." This ploy definitely eliminates the chaff from the wheat. Today, I had one with a talk show from the Netherlands. It was to take place in a suite at The Sofitel, a five-star hotel near the Beverly Center. It paid a thousand dollars—chicken feed, but, hey, I've got chickens to feed. I wasn't looking forward to it, or to the long, hot drive. On the way, I got a call from Gayle saying they wanted to photograph me driving up in my Maserati. Okay.

I arrived, and saw a group of young Dutchmen hanging out in front of the hotel. Netherlanders are easy to spot—they reek of European hip. They had me circle and come in again for the camera, and then asked if I would mind posing for a Polaroid with a pretty young girl, who was introduced as the editor, as a favor to her. They shot me being photographed with her in the circular driveway, then panned with me as I accompanied a couple of the young fellows into the lobby. Inside, the place smelled strongly of good coffee. I asked if they would mind if I relaxed with an espresso. They eagerly agreed. Later, I would understand their eagerness.

We sat at a table in an alcove of the sumptuous lobby lounge, and talked for about a half hour (no one seemed in a hurry) about my many visits to Holland, mostly for the filming of *Mata Hari*, the movie I've been making with my daughter since 1977.

I should explain that: We shoot for a few days every year or so, and the result will be to watch the actors age naturally in their parts. Someone said, "Carradine doesn't use makeup, he uses decades." The extended schedule also makes it possible for me to finance it with my own personal cash flow, so I don't have to deal with bossy backers. I hate being told what to do. The creation of Art, which is what I'm trying to get at here, does not lend itself well to committees. If van Gogh had backers he had to answer to, he might have sold a painting, but we'd probably never have heard of him.

After close to a half hour of this kaffee klatsch, I started to look at my watch, so we went up to the suite.

I stepped into the room to find a funny-looking young Japanese girl—very pretty, but with buck teeth and big round glasses—sitting in an easy chair and an older Japanese gentleman in a suit on a couch to the side. Two cameras were set up and ready to go. Seemed weird, but it was their money. The girl—I think her name was Sushi—brought out a little toy hamster which, when you pressed its front paw, twirled a numchuck and sang "Kung Fu Fighting." Then she proceeded to give a very strange interview, peering nearsightedly at her notes on a big clipboard held up to her nose, and asking very bizarre questions, starting out with why I had trouble with women, why I couldn't stay married, and if the sex was good. Well, Amsterdam is known for its preoccupation with sexual freedom.

Sushi seemed to understand very little English. Occasionally, she would confer with the Asian gentleman in Japanese. He was, apparently, a famous martial artist, and a big fan. At one point, he insisted on clearing away the coffee table and sparring with me for the camera. This could have gone on for quite a while, I think, except that I got him in a hammerlock to put an end to it.

Sushi seemed to be completely insane. It was like talking to Peter Sellers in one of his ethnic comic portrayals. I thought of his classic performance as a brainless Hindu airhead in Hollywood in *The Party*. I wondered how in hell she got the job, but I flowed with it easily, if perplexed, for about an hour.

Near the end, she asked if I preferred blondes or brunettes. I told her I had had serious relationships with only two blondes in my life, and both had been nothing but trouble. Then she asked if I would give her a picture. I said I didn't have one with me but I could send her one. She then said she wanted to give *me* a picture, and handed me the Polaroid from the driveway, which was signed over to me with best wishes from her.

I said, "But this isn't you. It's your editor." Whereupon "Sushi" ripped off her black wig and glasses and removed her buck teeth to reveal the blonde girl in the photo. Ah so! The whole thing suddenly was becoming clear. I actually *had* been interviewed by something like one of Peter Sellers' characters.

These Cartesian interviews with celebrities were a regular feature of this blonde lady's very popular talk show in Amsterdam. The gag apparently no longer worked with Dutch subjects, because everyone there knew the joke, so she was now branching out with *Sushi Does the U.S.A.* The director and the quite sizable crew, who had been hiding in the bedroom, now sat around and had a good laugh with me. They explained that they had been relieved when I'd requested that espresso break, as "Sushi" needed the time to get into makeup and wardrobe.

On the way home, I couldn't wait to call Gayle and tell her about the mad tea party. It turned out she'd been in on the joke all along.

Monday, September 23

This was going to be my first day on the film in L.A. I had been told my pickup time would be 5 A.M., unless I wanted to stay in Lancaster Sunday night. No point in that. I knew I wouldn't see anybody; they'd all be in their rooms. Sunday, the good news came that the call had been moved back. Surprise, surprise. There would be a car standing by at the house at 10 A.M. Everyone knew, though, that I wouldn't really be leaving then. I had done a little packing the night before, but still had a lot to do, and we had to pick up some cleaning to complete the job—all my Hawaiian shirts and one of the shirts from the movie, which they might need.

Around nine-thirty, Annie woke me with the news that "Dawn in Production" had called and they wouldn't need me to leave until eleven-thirty. The Lincoln showed up right on the dot at ten. Annie sent the driver, a sweet young thing from New Zealand named Jessica, to the Coffee Junction just down the street to hang out and get wired. At eleven-fifteen, I was all packed and ready to go, but hadn't had *my* coffee yet. We called Dawn in Production and were told the blastoff was now noon. So, I sat down with Annie to a leisurely breakfast.

Jessica came down the driveway again, and we loaded up: my big suitcase full of Hawaiian shirts and jeans, a carry-on full of magazines, my laptop and the portable printer, a bunch of flutes, my old Gibson, the two-gun rig with the rubber practice pistols, and a single-action .357 to twirl in my spare time. A .357 spins better than a .45, as the cylinder is a little heavier, making it more center-weighted, like a mid-engine sports car. (They spin easier, too.) At about twelve-fifteen, we took off. The rule of thumb as I've learned it, from forty years in the trade, is that if you're called to the set after 10 A.M., you won't work till after lunch. If your call is after lunch, you may not work at all. I predicted I'd be in the last shot of the day, mainly because a director likes to know he's at least started the scene.

The trip to the location took about an hour and a half. I worked on my lines for a while, and then Jessica and I talked about movies for the rest of the trip. The set was way out in the desert, in the middle of absolutely nowhere. Well, not nowhere, really—more accurately, the place where we used to make all the Westerns. I kept looking for horses along the way, but never saw one. Things change.

You could see the base camp from a mile or so away. It looked like a circus, with all the trucks and the big tent for lunch. We pulled in and unloaded the stuff into the biggest mobile home I've ever seen, with an expansion section on both sides. Inside was slightly more space and a good deal more opulence than I was going to find in my hotel suite at the Desert Inn.

Lunch was just over—a good sign, by my rule of thumb, that I wouldn't work for a while, if at all. I ran into Samuel L. Jackson at the caterer's wagon. We said "Hi" as though we'd known each other for years and had seen each other just yesterday, though, actually, it was the first time we'd ever met. I wondered what he was doing there, but didn't ask. I got hold of some teriyaki swordfish and settled down in the motor home with the script; gotta get it letter-perfect. Someone banged on the door and told me makeup and hair were ready for me. Manny was as voluble and funny as ever. Heba seemed truly glad to see me. She said the picture hadn't been the same without me. Well, I'm a really friendly guy.

Some people have tunnel vision. You can't get much out of them except the work. I am what you might call voluble. I gave Manny the whole story, well rehearsed by now, of the "Sushi" interview. He got a big kick out of it. I asked him what Samuel L. was doing here. He said he was playing a cameo as the wedding organist. Hot. That would mean I'd get to gun down a Jedi Master, sure to increase my standing in the rankings of contemporary action heroes, a field in which I had already reached rare status. I love this job.

I went back to my Mobile Mansion and read the *L.A. Times,* immersing myself in serial killers and rumors of war. Just about the time I started on the crossword, an AD stuck her head in the door and said, "Fifteen minutes." Well, I knew better. Movie companies are notoriously optimistic about when they're going to get to the next scene. I aced the crossword, read all the comics, then took out my pen again and circled houses for sale that looked good, until, after about an hour, the same AD stuck her head in and said, "They're ready for you." Music, sweet music, to my ears.

Quentin seemed . . . I don't know: subdued, I guess. Preoccupied. I hate to see him like that. But, today, the kid with his train set was sort of missing. He was on his game, directing Uma through a difficult moment for her character. He just didn't seem happy about it. I wished I could help him with it. Well, I would, when I got my chance.

Uma was playing a side of her character we'd never seen in the picture before. It's the afternoon before her wedding day. She's in her white bridal gown, and she's happy, giggly, and just having a great time. But the truth is it's all an act. She's really fooling everyone, pretending to be someone she's not; and she's about to marry a big, dumb guy whom she doesn't love. You have to see a little of that, but not too much of it, just a hint.

Now, a few minutes later in the movie, this whole wedding party is going to get blown away, and all the actors know that. Quentin's problem is to keep them from telegraphing it, get them to act as though everything is extremely right with the world. Then Uma hears a flute playing, and her face must undergo a change. It's got to make a little shiver go through the audience.

Quentin always knows what he wants. Nothing escapes his notice. His genius is obvious every moment he's working. The really extraordinary thing about his method is that he never stops until he has extracted the very best from everybody: the actors, the camera, the sound, the script, and, most of all, from himself. If anything is not working, he'll tweak it until it does. He plays the entire crew like a symphony conductor, and at the same time like a basketball coach. I could have said like a football coach, but the pace of his game is too fast for that. He's a very regular guy, and at the same time totally autocratic, like a king; no, like an emperor. And every minute he's having fun. One of the reasons his set works so smoothly is because that playful style of his is infectious. Everybody else is having as much fun as he is.

Today, his entire game was exactly as it always is, but his voice had a little less snap to it. His usual boyish enthusiasm wasn't there. He wasn't having fun. He just didn't seem happy. And this was unique in my experience with him. Quentin usually laughs about something roughly every ninety seconds. He wasn't doing that today. He was just moving ahead methodically and very seriously.

Of course, it was a Monday.

The other hairdresser, who was there to handle things on the set for Uma, came up to Manny and said, "I thought you were going to put the wig on David." Manny said, "You're kidding, right?" She said, "No. Didn't you say you were going to put the wig on him?" Manny said, "You *are* kidding." She said, "What. I don't understand. That isn't what you said?" Manny said, "He's wearing it." She was standing about four feet from me. Her mouth just sort of hung open. Manny is good. No one is going to see through this thing. They're all going to think I just grew my hair long for the part. Even Jessica, my driver, didn't know it was a wig, and she'd just seen me a couple of hours ago with my own short hair.

In the back of the beautiful Santa Fe–style chapel with beam ceilings that our people had created by gutting and rebuilding an old, originally very plain and run-down desert church, the wedding party milled around. Samuel L. sat at the organ in a sharp suit over a gold shirt, with a black drug dealer–style fedora hat and shades. Okay, I thought. Samuel L. as Ray Charles. That works.

Finally, I was called to play my flute off-camera for Uma's close-up. I showed Quentin the collection of flutes I'd brought for him to choose from: the Silent Flute; the other bamboo one I'd made for *Kung Fu: The Movie,* the picture I'd done with Brandon Lee; my silver concert flute; and an antique ebony example with silver keys that had been a gift from Mike Vendrell. I would have brought the alto, which I had used in Canada on *Kung Fu, The Legend Continues*, but it's having problems. He chose the Silent Flute again, as I'd thought he would. Had to give him the choice, though. It turned out the Silent Flute wouldn't play, not one note. It had completely gone south. Become, in fact, a truly *silent* flute. I called for Jessica and asked her (quietly) to bring the one from *Kung Fu: The Movie,* and played that, leaning against a century stand in front of the church, surrounded by the crew, with the boom man holding a mike over my head. It was the thing to do. Quentin would never know the difference, I figured. It had all the same vibes, except for the extraordinary bottom note of the Silent Flute. After a few takes of that, they told me I was wrapped.

I said, "Huh? That's all? An off-stage flute?"

"Yeah. Lucky you. Get some sleep. Your scene is first up in the morning."

So, my work today was strictly as an off-stage sound effect, mostly to get Uma in the right mood, I guess. Putting me in wardrobe and makeup could have implied that Quentin had changed his mind about getting to my scene, because the light would be failing and we wouldn't be able to get in deep enough to make it worthwhile. It's just as likely, though, that they dressed me and made me up simply because no one had told them that they didn't need to. I took off all the clothes and Manny carefully removed the wig. None of this, you understand, was ever on camera. Good practice, though.

Jessica drove me to the Desert Inn, a far cry from the St. Regis—or from my trailer, for that matter: It was minimal and mostly worn out, but there were two rooms, a double bed, and a sad little kitchen, good enough for a few days. I unpacked my shit, set up my laptop, spread some magazines around, took the old Gibson out of its case, tuned it up, and lit a candle. It felt pretty damn homey, and I was too deadbeat to care anyway. I called Annie, getting all the news from home and exchanging a few sweet thoughts. Then I twirled my rubber six-shooters a few times, took a disappointingly tepid shower (the hot water and the cold were exactly the same temperature), and went to bed with a car magazine.

Tuesday, September 24

Well, I didn't get more than an hour's sleep. I lay awake for hours, after staring at pictures of auto show prototypes and new totally boring Japanese sedans. Finally, I turned on the TV and watched Al Gore on C-SPAN criticizing President Bush's proposals regarding a war with Iraq. He really got me. He was not boring, not stiff, and didn't have the embarrassed glaze that sort of looked like guilt which he used to have. He was still full of endless minute statistics and laboriously researched points of fact, but it was fascinating, and all seemed right on. I could see the slim possibility of another run for president. Well, why not? It's funny. At the beginning of Dubya's reign, it didn't look like he was going to make it to a second term. Then, after September 11, his popularity, maybe deservedly, went through the old roof, as a result of his "quick, firm response" to those terrorists of whom we've become so weary. It was obvious, both to his supporters and his detractors, that if things didn't fall apart for him, we were in for another four years of cowboy politics. He wouldn't need his brother or the Supreme Court to fix the fight for him this time. Now, we're beginning to weary of his cowboy rhetoric, or at least I have.

And Al's plodding exactitude is almost a relief, especially since it's not boring anymore. Then there's the silent minority out there—the greens, the lefties, and the libbies—who are scared of Dubya's aggressiveness; who always were, actually. Of course, Gore reminded us of the $100 billion surplus that turned into a $200 billion deficit more or less overnight. Rich sons of Texas millionaires can be real loose with their credit cards. Al didn't bring it up, but everybody's aware of how the economy plummeted as soon as they got the accursed liberals out of the White House. All this could go anywhere by November 2004.

I finally fell asleep, while Gore was signing autographs, only to be brought out of it with a wake-up call at 4 A.M., when I'd left it for 5:45. The guy at the desk apologized, but the damage was done. I got up and did some stuff on the laptop (this stuff) until Jessica knocked on my door at 6:15, then hustled to get out the door, after downing a handful of three kinds of ginseng and some guarana root, hoping it would get me through at least the morning.

No need. The work today was going to be so stimulating, I wouldn't even be able to think about being tired. Quentin took me inside the chapel, and we sat in a pew and discussed the fine points of the scene. He mentioned that he thought this might be my best scene in the movie. I said it might be the best scene in my entire career. He thanked me for that. Thank *me*? We went out onto the porch, where the first part of the scene would be played. The light was remarkable. There was a forest fire in the mountains to the south, and the cloud overcast from that gave a soft, pastel touch to the day. Uma rehearsed wearing a pair of hip-hugging jeans and a little top that showed her creamy tanned midriff and her cute belly button. For the takes she changed into a floor-length white wedding dress, with a basketball or something inside it to stand in for the baby she was supposed to be pregnant with. She looked adorable. This was essentially a love scene, at least for the first five pages (minutes) or so: old lovers saying farewell for the last time; it would end, though, with a massacre of the wedding party.

Uma was terrific, and Quentin was on fire. His malaise of the day before was just gone. He was jumping and dancing in his usual manner, joking with the crew, and the laugh was back.

I started out sitting on the bench playing a flute obbligato, which was to be what would draw The Bride outside from her wedding rehearsal. "How'd you find me?" she says. "I'm The Man," Bill replies. Then we just sailed through the scene. Quentin had us start out a great distance from each other, and then, in little baby steps, almost without volition, move closer to each other throughout the exchange until we were almost nose to nose. Bob Richardson, our sainted cameraman, was pumping diffused light from a couple of 5Ks through big silks. We did it about forty times. It just got better. Could have done it another forty times. The whole company was totally jacked up by the tenderness of the day. A beautiful day, too. The light on Uma's face was heavenly: her lips and eyes sparkling, her skin like a shaved peach.

I had an interesting conversation in between takes with Lawrence Bender regarding how I felt about the fact that in a moment I (as Bill— let's keep that straight) was going to blow away seven members of a wedding party in cold blood, and then shoot the bride in the head. I said, "Well, she pissed me off." We got into an analysis of bad guys that the audience loves, a case in point being Bruce Willis in *Pulp Fiction:* a cheater and a killer, a little dense, certainly crude, and not very nice to his women. I thought about it for a while. I came up with three very good reasons why we root for him. One, he scams the scammers. Cheats the bad guys out of their crooked money. And he won't throw the fight. That's one and a half. Two, he's willing to risk his life to retrieve his father's watch. And, three, he doesn't walk out on Ving Rhames, whom the kinky cop is fucking in the ass behind the pawnshop. Instead, he goes back and whacks away at the pervert with a samurai sword. And, actually, he is kind of easy on his French girlfriend, apparently aware of her timid sensitivity and willing to drop his macho down a notch to make her comfortable. That would be four. He acts the gentleman with the lady. And he seems to forgive her totally for leaving the watch behind. All those antiheroes have a certain nobility. My Bill has his.

When we got to the nose-to-nose part, Bob took me aside and asked if I might want to be leveled off with Uma. I said something like, "Huh?" He explained that I was looking up at her, and that didn't seem right. Well, she's over six feet tall, a Valkyrie, and I'm just about six feet even, like Jesus of Nazareth. (Not that I have a Jesus complex. I did, way back when, but I gave it up when I turned thirty-four without being crucified.) Would I like to stand on an apple box, he asked. I agreed, though I could understand his pulling me aside to ask me that. Some actors would be humiliated to be told in public that they were too short to stand toe-to-toe with an amazon female costar. Alan Ladd, I've heard, was obsessive about it. He wouldn't stand on a box. Instead, he'd make them dig a hole for the actress. That's how Veronica Lake got her career; she was short enough so they didn't have to dig a hole for her. I told Bob I'd thought of the problem and would have worn the high-heeled black cherry Luschese boots they had for me if they'd been laid out in the trailer. Someone ran and got them. They proved to be too small for me. I said, "Well, I do just happen to have an identical pair in my closet at the motel." They sent a driver to fetch them. While we waited, someone cranked up the ghetto blaster with salsa music, and the company took a break. I relaxed in the back of the church with a Dr Pepper and rapped with Bo Svenson, there to play the Pastor and get shot, always a pleasure (talking to Bo, not getting shot).

When the boots arrived, I put them on and stood up to Uma, eye to eye. It's weird I had those with me. They're almost thirty years old, sacred relics from the original San Antonio factory, in perfect new condition, as they've never seen the inside of a barn or the outside of a horse. I rarely wear them, except with a tux. I own about a dozen pairs of boots. There was no reason whatsoever to bring these babies out here to this remote dusty, desert location.

Destiny always prevails, don't it?

At the end of the day, we tried different ways to break up the intimacy of the moment so we could get on to the rest of the scene: the part where I meet the potential bridegroom, while masquerading as the father of the bride. None of it would work, so after several tries, Quentin apologized for wasting our energies and wrapped us for the night, to come back to it fresh tomorrow morning. I should have been physically and emotionally drained, but, though I was grateful for the long days coming to an end, I could have gone another fifteen rounds. As I said, I love this job.

Wednesday, September 25

Six o'clock call. I managed to get *some* sleep—not much, though, after watching the last half of *The African Queen,* much more fun than Al Gore. I'd like to make a movie like that. Well, who wouldn't? Pretty much the best work of Bogart, Hepburn, and Huston. Stands up to the years like a Botticelli painting or a Greek sculpture. The footage of the *Queen* shooting the rapids is awesome, especially considering that there weren't any special effects involved; they just did it.

Today promised to be a good one. We would finish up the scene with Uma, then go on to the sequence inside the chapel, where I would meet the groom.

First we had to do over that ending. Quentin had decided that, since it had proved so difficult to cut out of our intimate moment, he would just let us stay in it, and let it be simply broken finally by the arrival of the groom. Chris, the special effects makeup guy, who was playing the part, looked hilarious in the role. A shiny, obviously rented tux that almost fit his big frame, fake bow tie hanging sideways, big worker's boots with a lot

Quentin grooms the groom ANDREW COOPER/MIRAMAX FILMS

of dusty mud on them, and, of course his canary yellow hair and a matching four-day growth of canary yellow beard. Chris was nervous as hell, and wanted my help. I told him he'd do fine, though I did try to give him some pointers from my vast experience as a secretly nervous actor myself.

Long before I ever encountered kung fu, I developed my own meditational tricks to put myself at ease. One effective exercise to calm the heart is to unfocus. I would imagine I was having a flying dream and looking down upon the action I was in, an unbiased observer. A more physiological solution for those whose imaginations are not as accessible as mine is remembering to breathe. When you're tense, you tend to hold your breath. Take a deep one, let it out all the way till you've emptied your lungs, and start over. Whatever you do, don't go over your lines in your head. If you don't have it down by now, it's too late.

I had great fun with this scene, having the opportunity to kind of overact as the character of Bill faking it as the "father" of the bride. Sort of a Daddy Warbucks act. When it came time for Chris' close-up, I told him, "This is the most important moment of your career. If you blow this, you'll probably never work again. So, whatever you do, *don't get nervous!*" It seemed to help. Took the onus off the moment. Humor—great stuff: healing. Meanwhile, at the back of the church, Bo was towering over everybody, doing his thing as the Reverend Harmony, his voice like thunder, as big as his frame. Great. Just simply right on.

Suddenly, I got a great idea, one that had nothing whatsoever to do with the scene. I went over to the prop guys and asked them if they had any lacquer. They said if they didn't, they would get some. My idea was to treat the Silent Flute, recover its lost timbre by filling the cracks with lacquer. I'd done this before, years ago, and it had worked then. But lacquer shrinks, and the cracks had reasserted themselves.

A little later, the guys showed up with what passes for the right stuff in California these days. Real microcellulose lacquer is forbidden—something about its effect on the environment. No matter. I poured the stuff, whatever it was, down inside the flute and twirled it around. Then we hung it on a pole with a wire hanger through the blowhole, and I did the outside with a brush. I was ecstatic. Every time now that I played the sucker, at home or in concert, I would remember that it had recovered its voice on the set of *Kill Bill,* beside a little chapel in the middle of the Mojave Desert.

We went to lunch while the flute hung out to dry. I hoped we weren't due for a sandstorm.

Then, after lunch, there was a sweet moment when Uma says good-bye, on her way to rehearse saying "I do" to her redneck. She cried and gave me a kiss. I cried too. None of this was in the script. On the third take, Quentin told her to ask me if she was pretty. He told me to tell her she was, in my own words—whatever. Uma kissed me on the lips and, with a tear running down her cheek, placed her veil on her head, adjusting it carefully, and said, like a little girl, "Am I pretty?" I stared at her for a moment, very level, and said, my throat kind of choked up, "Oh, yeah." I wasn't faking it. Then she started to kiss me again, but changed her mind. She walked away, looking back once. I never took my eyes off her. Quentin jumped up and down. *"Yes,"* he shouted. *"Yes!"* Then something surprising happened. I had undone the button of my jacket, and the script supervisor came up and objected. "You would see the gun," he said.

"What?" Quentin said. "I don't see it. I don't see any gun. And, anyway, he doesn't kill anyone anymore." Huh? This was news to me. What was going on?

It all became clearer when, at the end of the day, they began to rehearse the arrival of the Viper Squad, using their doubles. There was going to be an awesome steadycam shot which would end up with the operator stepping on the crane and going up and over the chapel. The vipers would advance on the church and go inside, armed with Uzis and M16s. You would hear all the gunfire while seeing the tranquil church against the desert sky, lit up inside by the explosions. This was all new, out of nowhere—or, rather, out of Quentin's fertile and never-resting imagination. I wondered if I had been kept out of some loop, but, no; Quentin had thought it up right on the spot. He wanted to do a steadycam shot that would rival, or maybe even beat out, the one in *Bound for Glory,* which, though it had been the first one ever, had yet to be matched.

Hal Ashby had the steadycam operator stand on the platform of the Chapman Titan crane, which put him eighteen feet above the action. I'm standing below, surrounded by the migrant workers' camp. In the back-

But then . . . *ANDREW COOPER/MIRAMAX FILMS*

ground, a mob of the migrants is nearly rioting at the gates until the company goons disperse them with bats and clubs. The crane majestically swoops down and the operator steps off and follows me as I walk through a big tent, out the other side, and through the crowd to the fence, where I have a conversation with Randy Quaid about the injustices of the Depression. The effect was as though the crane itself (a vehicle, actually, about the size of an eighteen-wheeler semi) had performed the operation—an obvious impossibility. You could have done a shot sort of like this before the invention of the steadycam, using a handheld camera, but it would have been bumpy, and you couldn't have had synch sound. On the first take, one of the extras walked up to me as I was approaching Randy and started talking about how he'd met me before on another movie. I had to tell him we were in the middle of a take. That's how unobtrusive the steadycam is. That take circulated around for a while on TV as a famous movie blooper, along with the time I had my nose broken on film during one of the fight scenes in the movie *The Silent Flute*.

This was cool for me. I mean, always being the subject of the best is pretty okay. I stopped Quentin in the middle of a run and asked him, "Do I still shoot Uma in the head?"

"Oh, yeah," he said.

Now, the ladies were gathering. Daryl looked incredible in a black skintight jumpsuit, with high boots and very high heels, making her legs look even longer than they are. There was a black patch over her left eye, which Pai Mei had plucked out just before she'd poisoned him. Vivica had her hair in long cornrows, and her skintight stuff was equally sexy, making her look like a panther. Lucy was almost conservatively dressed, with tight pants and a crew-neck sweater. Michael Madsen was really the cutest of all, in the rumpled black suit from *Reservoir Dogs*, his tie crooked, turquoise rings on about eight of his fingers, and one scruffy black boot with a silver tip and one totally unmatching scuffed-up lizard boot.

Michael had brought his wife and kids with him, and he took them out across the road, where the gun crew let him fire off about thirty rounds from his M16: ostensibly to test the weapon, but really for the kids.

As the time to shoot the scene approached, people kept coming around passing out earplugs to all the actors. I had my own rock & roll earplugs. You can hear everything but it can't hurt your ears. Great invention. I've discovered over the years that I can't act (or sing) if I can't hear myself. Before these things were invented, I was progressively destroyng my hearing. Anything for art. Then, in they came, guns blazing. Four automatic weapons blasting away in a little wooden church. The sound was deafening—yes, even with the plugs. The concussion was so great I could feel it battering at me where I stood against the wall. Brass flying everywhere. We did about five takes of that. The floor was littered with spent cartridges.

Then we wrapped. We were told we'd do one more of those in the morning, for the different light, I guess. Riding back to Lancaster to my spartan suite at the Desert Inn, I was tired, certainly, but not beat, and certainly not the least bit dusty or dirty. I laid my head back on the seat. This is okay, I thought. This is really okay. My only regret was, that I didn't, after all, get to shoot the shit out of a Jedi Master.

Thursday, September 26

Bright and early, like six or so, we all showed up. One more take of the great steadycam shot was not the case—several, as it turned out. But it kept getting better. Thank God for my rock & roll earplugs, huh?

I gave a call to Annie, and told her she'd better get down here or she'd miss it all. She was real disappointed that she wasn't going to get to see me blow away the wedding party with a 9mm.

Annie loves firearms.

They were shooting an extreme low-angle group shot of the Viper Squad, spread out in a semicircle, supposedly Uma's point of view, from the floor of the church. I stood out on the porch, watching the road for Annie. I got to talk to Bo for a while. He had a great idea (Bo is full of great ideas) for a documentary—covering me, not as an actor, but as a guy. All the real-life stuff, with pictures from the past and cutaways to footage of some of my escapades. I've been filmed in many situations that most people lived through in anonymity. Only the Kennedys have been as well documented on film and tape.

Then Annie arrived, with Thunder, my giant Bernese mountain dog. Everybody fawned over him, except Quentin and Bob. They were seriously concentrated on the game. Then I got my chance to stand over Uma. My scene was a little different from all the others. It takes place after the Viper Squad has beaten the crap out of her. The camera is on her bashed-up face on the floor. All you see of me is my hand, coming into frame and wiping a little of the blood off Uma's pretty face, with a monogrammed handkerchief, just so you know who's responsible. But I strapped on the two-gun rig anyway, to give everybody something to look at.

As they were setting up the shot, I twirled the guns a little. These are great pieces—cute little nickel-plated single-action things, with pearl bird's-beak grips—and the gun belt, a copy of my old Andy Anderson rig in black, is a true work of art. I look down at Uma, all cut up and bleeding, in her ripped-up wedding gown. "Do you find me sadistic?" I say. She's not in any shape to answer. I go on to tell her, "No, this is the most masochistic moment of my life." Then I shoot her in the head. (Love hurts.) Fake blood shoots out of her golden tresses, getting all over her bridal veil. Quintessential Tarantino. He just loves to put Uma Thurman through really tough shit.

We did this a few times. Between each take, there would be a big delay while they cleaned up Uma's hair and such, and recharged the blood shooter thing. I hung out with Annie, who was having a great time watching me pretend to be mean. She thinks she knows better.

Quentin, more than any other director I've ever worked with, even with all the stunts and special effects shots, never stops till he's got it right: in this case, until we had almost run out of clean handkerchiefs. I was having a ball. I love the next take. Don't really ever want to stop. Quentin is the same way. We are a great team.

Then we got down to the individual shots of the Viper Squad. Each member got her or his close-up shot from the floor, looking up, intended as another point of view from Uma, who would theoretically be lying on the floor with the shit beaten out of her. These would be used as flashback memory sequences. Every time she catches up with one of her tormentors five years later, she will look into their eyes, remembering how they fucked with her, and then kill them. That's pretty much how the whole movie goes. Finally it was my turn: a close-up of the reverse of the shot I'd done earlier. I could see myself reflected in the matte box, so I knew just what the camera was seeing. I flipped the pretty little single-action out of the holster with an underhand twirl, one of my signature moves (I have many), pointed it at the camera, pulled back the hammer, and fired: a quarter-load.

Quentin said, "What?! That was supposed to be loud? I wore earplugs for that? Broke my fucking record for that?" The prop department hurriedly loaded the gun with full loads for the next take.

I said, "You can get a flash, too, if you grease the barrel. Would you like that?"

Quentin said, "Yeah, yeah!"

We did it again, same drill: fancy draw, pull back the hammer, *BLAM!* I don't know if there was a flash, because the space in front of me was solid smoke. My image in the matte box just disappeared. I waited till the smoke cleared, and then did my reverse twirl and slid the pistol back in the holster. Quentin loved it and did a few more. Then we spent a half hour or so doing a shot of my vintage black cherry Lucchese boots (with my feet in them) walking ominously across the boards of the church, kicking spent cartridges out of the way. End of day.

End of one hell of a day. And my swan song at the church.

I bid my good-byes to everybody. Some of the girls I wouldn't see again on the picture. It was heartbreaking. We've all become family.

We could have gone home right then, but Annie and I elected to stay in Lancaster for the night rather than buck the traffic for two hours. We had a beautiful dinner at the Desert Inn. Totally unexpectedly, the restaurant there is an absolutely first-class gourmet affair. We went to bed happy and fulfilled. With the lights off, and a couple of Our Lady of Guadalupe votive candles I'd picked up at the liquor store, our room was acceptably romantic.

Friday, September 27

It turns out Annie's grandmother lives in an old folks' home out here just a few blocks from the hotel, so we visited her. Her husband died years ago and left her totally comfortable, it seems, but she was talked into mortgaging her house to invest in some scheme, and lost it all. Now, in the home, she's living in what amounts to a cheap hotel room and eating in a cafeteria, and without her piano. I wonder if that's one of Samuel Goldwyn's eight possible movie plots. It sounds very familiar. She pointed at the pictures on the wall and talked about all her relatives, living and dead.

We took her to lunch. She is, of course, a sweet lady. Most old people are. What else do they have to do? She couldn't read the menu, as she'd forgotten her glasses. I loaned her my brown-tinted drugstore cheaters. She looked incredibly hip. We talked about music.

After we dropped Granny back at the home, Annie and I swung by the set, as I wanted to catch a glimpse of Michael Parks playing the crusty Texas Ranger who investigates the massacre and discovers that Uma is still alive, the only survivor. Michael would have to be classified as one of my mentors. He was the star of *Bus Riley's Back in Town*, also starring Ann-Margret, the movie in which I had my first part, one day's work as Michael's old high school buddy. I had three lines. Our paths have crossed many times since then.

All the members of the deadly Viper Squad were gone. It was as though we were in a different movie. Samuel L. was missing, too. Another guy was hunched across the piano, dressed up in Sam's bloody threads. The floor of the church was littered with actors, playing dead. The walls of

Chris and I really got along *ANDREW COOPER/MIRAMAX FILMS*

the church were riddled with bullet holes, which the crew had created with drilling and feathering. They looked very real. So did all the dead people. I had a little talk with Uma, who was there on her back on the floor in her trashed wedding dress, wearing her fake blood and fake gashes and bruises. I think I cheered her up. Bo was propped up in a corner with a big hole in his white shirt, in front of a smear of blood on the wall where he would have slid down after he was shot. He was in great spirits, though. I had a short conversation with what I suddenly then realized was a dummy, of Chris, the bridegroom.

The dummy was a remarkable likeness. The only thing that gave it away was that half of its head was blown off.

There was Michael, decked out in Western khakis and a cowboy hat, with a Silver Star pinned to his shirt. We watched him, and his son as the deputy, do a master of the scene. Michael is very cool, a fine actor, and totally his own man. He walked through the carnage they had laid out for him like it was his kingdom, and had the dumb old ranger down perfectly, talking country and being careful not to dirty his boots.

I collected my shit from the prop department (my excuse for dropping by), taking with me the can of fake lacquer and a good brush they threw in (you never know), and bid my farewells to everyone. We'd meet up in another ten days or so, if the schedule stayed firm.

Wednesday, October 9

Went to see *Red Dragon,* which was okay. Edward Norton was great, totally real; well, he's one of our young Masters, isn't he? Ralph Fiennes was remarkable. Anthony Hopkins was good, I guess. Annie liked him, but I think he should have stopped playing this character at least one movie ago. He's using tricks that are beneath him: my opinion. Hannibal is becoming a caricature, if he wasn't already. Anthony is one of the best actors we've got, but this was not one of his truly great moments. The critics loved him, but I've learned that they're suckers for excess, particularly from the British. I hope he got paid a lot for it.

We stopped by P.F. Chang's for coffee, and were hailed by a woman sitting there on the terrace with three black chicks. People are always calling out to me on the street: people I don't know. I responded politely, though distantly, until I saw that it was Deedee, the associate producer from Beijing who had been so instrumental in putting the campers together for party times. What on earth was she doing out here in the West Valley at a mall restaurant?

Then I realized that the cute little black girl under the Walter Matthau gardening hat was none other than Vivica A. Fox, and the other two girls were her support group—her personal makeup and hair technicians, I believe, whom I'd met at the chapel in Lancaster. I leaped to embrace her, and we hugged each other for a long second, just giggling. Vivica is such a happy trip. She had just finished her last day on the picture. She was high on the feeling, and we had a great talk, about all that we had suffered through, and how awful and great it had been. I was really pissed that she was wrapped. I had absolutely wanted to get down to the set and see her work, but they had cut her shoot short (removing a few elements of the scene—notably, apparently, the stuff for the animation sequence) and finished her off early. Saved themselves about a million dollars, according to Quentin. I wondered if that meant the whole cartoon idea was out.

Vivica's scene with Uma contains the toughest fight scene in the whole movie. Down and dirty. Those two ladies just rip each other, street fight–style, tearing Vivica's suburban rumpus room to pieces. I would have liked to have seen that go down. Vivica said she was bruised all over her body from doing her own stunts. I could believe it. She wouldn't show them to us, though. After it was all over, she said, she had stood in front of the mirror in her trailer, with tears running down her cheeks. But then, she soldiered up and said to her reflection, "I did it! I fucking got through it! And now, I've *done* Tarantino! Yow!"

We spent about two hours together, maybe more. It was a volatile conversation, to say just the least. Deedee had a lot to say about the unnecessary expenses and delays, which, according to her, had contributed to all the changes. She blamed everybody in the administration of the picture, though carefully excluding the folks at Miramax. That, obviously, is where her loyalties lie. She also talked about how expensive it was to shoot in L.A. relative to China: a hundred sixty-five thousand a day, as compared to seventy in Beijing, she said.

"Rightly so," I said. In a democracy, people get paid living wages. And they're worth it. L.A. film crews can't be beat; they're the best. Deedee also defended at length Yuen Wu Ping, whom she referred to in hushed gushy tones as "The Master," over and over. I never had bought that stuff. Hey, I've known some Masters. Wu Ping is an artist, for sure, and he certainly knows what he's doing, but *Master*? This guy runs a business. He's not on top of a mountain, drinking tea and dispensing wisdom, and he's a little too arrogant to ever get my vote. He treats his people like minions, and everybody else like members of a lesser species. As far as I had been able to determine, what Wu Ping was a master of was not looking at people. He'd stare right through you. Especially when anyone tried to be friendly to him.

Deedee said that a lot of the problem was the language barrier, and

This is your Vivica A. Fox *DAVID CARRADINE*   This is your Vivica A. Fox on Tarantino
DAVID CARRADINE

that his interpreter, Fish, was somewhat creative in his translations of what "The Master" said. Yeah, maybe so. Still, it took me a month to get a simple nod out of him when I said "Good morning," and that was after a hundred or so smoke breaks with him outside the gym, where he would studiously keep his eyes elsewhere. His trainers, who were full of smiles, had the same language problem, probably more so. No, his problem was pretense. And the darkness in the man is as obvious as the nose on his face from which he looks down. Maybe Wu Ping can kick some ass and maybe he can't, but he has none of the humility and the gentleness with lesser beings that distinguish a True Master. I've dealt, after all, with Indian chiefs and medicine men, the monks at the Shaolin Monastery, including the abbot, a definite guru or two, and a few real geniuses. A Master doesn't need an act.

I said all that, or most of it anyway, in between Vivica's hilarious and spirited blow-by-blow of the whole glorious fiasco, from the beginning of the training back in April till now: The Good; yes, The Bad; and with great fervor, The *Ugly* of it all.

At the end, as we said good night, Vivica oh-so-sweetly melted in my arms, and came real close to tears. She reminded me that at breakfast one morning at the St. Regis in Beijing, when she had been suffering from matters of the heart, I had told her, "Just be happy." She said that's what she was doing now: being happy. Well, I could see it. She was glowing, *shining*; looking about seventeen years old. I sure hope I get to work with her again someday. I love the bitch.

Thursday, October 10

The schedule did not remain firm. I don't know when I'm going back to work. It's okay—at this end, I mean. More time to get the mountain of words down. At the back end, though, it's a problem. The last day of shooting will get pushed off again. I can't accept any new work, and I'll go off salary in a week. I'm going to be scraping bottom.

Monday, October 21

The schedule has changed yet again. Now it looks as though the picture won't be finished until the middle of December. That's two months over. And I'm in it till the end, with no more bread for the extra weeks. It's going to be a lean Christmas, unless my new agents come up with something.

Tuesday, October 22

I had a meeting with Endeavor today. About eight agents gathered in Scott Melrose's little office. Gayle was there, looking New York chic. A whole bunch of young, eager workers. I'll never remember their names. I brought along the proof sheets for the stills from *Kill Bill.* They were a big hit: filled up the gaps, and showed them that we really are making a movie here. They're mostly 2¼s from Andrew's Hasselblad, so they're big, even in proofs, and very impressive. Everybody remarked on how good Uma looked. Nobody said anything about me. I took the opportunity to give Gayle her belated birthday present: a bracelet from Tiffany. She rates it. The whole meeting was a romp. I think this is going to work out. I just hope something happens *soon*—before the wolves show up.

I said, at the end of the meeting, "This is only a small beginning." Everybody said, "Yeah! Yeah!" I said, "I was talking about the bracelet."

Thursday, October 24

Larry McConkey, the steadycam operator, drove up in a big truck with the last increment of our Beijing purchases, a huge ceramic fishbowl from the Qing Dynasty, about 150 years old, decorated with carved and painted dragons. Annie's gardeners showed up to move it into the backyard. It weighs around four hundred pounds. I don't know why Larry was driving the truck, but it was great to see him. We had coffee together and talked about the movie. He's seen some of it cut together, with computer effects and music. He says the action stuff makes *The Matrix* look tame. But he's been on every one of Quentin's movies. He's a true believer.

Wednesday, October 30

A couple of people showed up today from wardrobe to raid my closet again. Looking for stuff for the new version of the "Mexico" shoot, which is no longer going to be shot in Mexico. It was originally written for a tuxedo. Now, the sequence is more casual. They brought a few designer pieces with them. Hugo Boss, Issey Miyake, Prada. Stuff I'm told is supposed to be *the* thing. It's all just hype to me, bits of cloth priced on a par with semiprecious gems. But some of it was really beautiful. And perfect for dressing me up to be a billionaire international assassin. Of course, it's all up to Quentin.

The shooting schedule continues to change . . . and lengthen. I expected to leave for Barstow for the scene with Michael Madsen Sunday, but now it looks like Wednesday, or Thursday even. That pushes back the hacienda stuff with Uma, and delays the Mexico shoot as well. This movie is turning into a lifetime project.

A big residual came from SAG, from a cartoon I worked on three years ago or so, *Balto II* or *III*. I play the voice of a wise old wolf in it. When I saw it on the big screen, I was blown away.

Annie and I drove around depositing money in various banks, and then celebrated with an early dinner at Dan Tana's. We were going to go to a movie at the Beverly Center, the huge mall-like thing across the street from Cedars-Sinai, but there wasn't much worth seeing. Instead, we window-shopped a little. Had to buy *something,* though.

Picked up some perfume for Annie.

Monday, November 18

Time to go back to work on the film. Barstow: my scene with Michael Madsen, who's playing my brother, Budd. A car picked me up late at night. I had spent the evening at the Skirball Center, hosting a charity function, something about trees, mostly giant redwoods. I'd never hosted one of these things before, but I have a lot to say about trees, so I nailed it. Got my laughs and made some money for them.

Barstow has absolutely nothing going for it, except a speed trap. It is the bottom of some barrel or another, which was exactly what we wanted. We pulled up to The Ramada Inn about 2 A.M., and try as I might, there was no hope of sleeping. I arrived on the set in a perfect trance. Michael's character's trailer, too funky even for white trash, sat in a box canyon, surrounded by spectacularly strange

ANDREW COOPER/MIRAMAX FILMS

The main men yuk it up *ANDREW COOPER/MIRAMAX FILMS*

rock formations. Around it was spread the usual piles of junk that gather around such hovels, and his character's sad pickup truck. Outside all that were the many trucks of the production company, and all around the site, men were hustling with lights and equipment. Over it all, hanging on a cable from a giant yellow crane arm, was a silk the size of a doubles tennis court, stretched over a frame of aluminum girders.

At this point of the film, Budd is looking up from the bottom of a bottle of Viking schnapps, combined with snuff behind his bottom lip, which he periodically spits into a coffee can. Quentin asked Michael how the combination tasted. Michael replied that it was a pretty powerful mixture. That made me wonder if the schnapps might be real. I didn't ask; I knew the snuff was. Quentin had to do some of that himself, of course. I passed. Been there, back when I was working at Lucky Lager Brewery, where you can't smoke, but can spit. Didn't dig it in the least.

We worked the scene all day, hurrying a little as the shadows ran across the canyon. That shot must have been something. Me, in my Western garb, with my two nickel-plated six-shooters, and the gunmetal gray De Thomaso Mangusta, the car they'd picked out for Bill after Cadillac told production they could have the Cien prototype for a million bucks, crouched in the background, like John Wayne's trusty steed brought up to date. All this set against the red rocks, with the shadows creeping across the car as I had my long speech. Awesome. Michael was fantastic, so good I couldn't possibly keep up with him. He had this guy totally down. Doing all the shtick he could muster, much more than anyone else could ever get away with. But it all seemed totally real and unmannered.

Early on, Quentin told me, "Don't fall into what Michael is doing." I said, "Are you kidding? I wouldn't dare. I'm not moving a muscle!" And I didn't. Apparently, though, I still gave a decent performance. Everybody was flipping over me. But Michael: the best! In between setups, he got me aside and asked me if I believed in God, and wondered about the world his children were being handed, and about the meaning of it all. I tried to answer sincerely. Those are tough questions. I told Michael I just put one foot in front of the other and try to remember to walk softly on the Earth

It's not all laughs, though *ANDREW COOPER/MIRAMAX FILMS*

ANDREW COOPER/MIRAMAX FILMS

and replace my divots. He just nodded, and then he hunkered down in the dilapidated doorway of the trailer and turned back into the scroungy redneck drunk who's a bouncer in a titty bar.

Finally, the day quit on us, and I was told we'd pick up the pieces tomorrow afternoon. In the morning, they'd be concentrating on Daryl, who would slay Michael by feeding him to a black mamba while I was sleeping in.

I skipped dinner, as I do most of the time, and snacked on 7-Eleven junk food, while I watched movies on TV until I passed out.

Tuesday, November 19

An even better day. Now that we had most of the scene in the can, and with all the nuances that Quentin had drilled into us now part of our natures, we barreled through the close-ups, gaining on what we'd built. Funnier, deeper, more focused. Well, *better*.

We repeated our sunset trick again at the end of the day, this time on Michael's long speech, and I wrapped with a super sense of being a great part of a great movie. I'm going broke sticking with this endless shoot, but who cares? It was never about money. This shit is why I quit my job at the brewery to become an actor.

Tuesday, November 26

I got a pretty much last-minute call to go back to Barstow on Monday for a wide shot of me driving up to Budd's trailer in my De Thomaso Mangusta. This meant I'd have to leave Sunday night after Norby Walters' annual pre-Christmas party at the Friars Club.

Norby gives this thing every year. Cocktails and turkey with a hundred or so of Norby's friends. Norby has got to have the best Rolodex in town. Everybody on his list was there, old folks like Sid Caesar, whom I used to play poker with. Bless his heart, he can hardly stand on his own these days. Then there'd be some young stud whose name I'm supposed to recognize, but don't. Beautiful women of various ages and with various degrees of cosmetic surgery dressed for action and quaffed for battle. Old stars, new stars, has-beens, and wannabes. I counted at least a dozen Best Supporting Oscars, and at least one Best Actor nominee. All of them having a great time. The Friars is a really old place. I love going there. It's the only place in town where they still call me "Kid."

I got in the Town Car about 1 A.M., and tried to sleep, while Frank I think his name was handled the two-hour drive. Got about an hour's sleep at the Ramada Inn, and was in the makeup chair at 6:30. Then we waited for the sun to make it up from behind the mountain. It was as cold as you'd want it, and sand was blowing in our faces. The Santa Ana winds had arrived; that was clear. It happens every year about this time, blowing across the desert, bringing weird vibes and lots of brush fires every time.

The camera was up the shale slope about a hundred feet on a promontory that looked almost secure. I could see Bob Richardson's mane of snowy hair blowing in the wind. Budd's trailer sat there in the middle of the box canyon, now cleared of all the moviemaking equipment, surrounded by broken appliances and rotten upholstered couches and chairs. The Mangusta looked deliciously out of place, like a UFO had landed. The whole scene looked like one of those hip TV commercials.

Quentin marched in with his cadre, bundled up in a big parka, bigger because Quentin is so big himself.

I said, "Are you still on this picture?" He laughed, as he does at almost everything, and we gave each other a big hug. He explained the shot to me, which was just me getting out of the car (a feat in itself—the Mangusta is low, the steering wheel is in your chest, and the door is weird) and walking up to the trailer. Someone from props handed me my gun belt. I strapped it on and shoehorned myself into the driver's seat.

Quentin climbed up the mountainside to the camera and we did about five takes of one version and two or three of another for backup, Quentin shouting his directions from above. "You can hear me, right?" Are you kidding? Quentin's voice will cut through solid rock.

I kept hearing his laugh echoing through the canyon. And that was it. I was on the call sheet for tomorrow, but was told that was off; it was only in case we didn't get to it today, because of weather or whatever. This, as the Santa Anas were starting to blow Pepsi cans and small pieces of equipment down the rocky slopes and across the ravine. Back in the Lincoln to base camp, off with the wig, and we hit the road. I'd be home for lunch. We took an alternate route to avoid the traffic. As we passed Burbank, we went through a red cloud that reminded me of the dust storm we'd created for *Bound for Glory*. The wind was sweeping over the hills, newly denuded by the forest fire, and picking up the meager topsoil to carry it to L.A.

Another week off and then we'll start on the final sequence of the movie. I'll be working almost every day from then until the end of the shoot, which now looks as though it will be just before Christmas, though there's a rumor that some people are being asked about their availability in January.

Sunday, December 1

Manhattan Beach, where the soundstages that will serve for our Mexican hacienda are, is just too far away for a daily commute. Traveling back and forth would add three hours to my workday. I've made a deal with the company to put me up at the Marriott for the duration. A Lincoln Town Car, driven by a bloke from Australia named Blair, stands by from about 11 P.M., to drive me down. I load my shit into the car: my Mossman guitar, my alto flute, the Silent Flute, a sword, my laptop, lots of magazines and books, a dozen bottles of vitamins and herbs, some trail food, enough shirts for a week, the several different versions of my lines I've typed up and printed out, just as an exercise to help bolt them into my head. The car is really packed full. I get it together around one, and we take off.

At this time of night, it's only a half hour to get there. I don't sleep, though, which is no surprise to me. I never do, the night before a shoot. This doesn't worry me, as I've been told the first day will be a rehearsal, which won't happen until the afternoon, so I'm okay to go to sleep at dawn as usual, with impunity. That's what I do. I turn out the light around five, after going over the script in bed one more time. I've got it just about letter-perfect.

Monday, December 2

At eight-thirty, the phone rings and Dawn, the AD, informs me that Quentin has decided to do the rehearsal in the morning. Ah, well. Not a problem. I don't get my energy from sleep, anyway. I get it from being inspired, which I'm surely about to be.

So, I'm driven around the corner and down the street about three blocks to Raleigh Studios, a more or less spanking-new facility with . . . can it be . . . twenty-six or so soundstages! After a silly wait at the gate, while we suffer through a security check that would seem excessive up the road at NASA, and takes much longer than it took to get here from the hotel, I'm dropped off at my palace-trailer.

I don't wait to be called to the set. Shit, I'm eager to trot. I find my way to stage 26, and enter a world apart. A huge cyclorama of black night encompasses a very convincing resort compound. Lush landscaping with real palm trees surrounds a Mexican hacienda, built on four levels, fit for a drug lord or an Aztec emperor.

As I'm marveling at the exterior of the building—walls a foot thick, real beams, real stucco, real tile, real everything—one of the set decorators asks me how I like it. He tells me that the architect (David Wasco, the art director, I guess he meant) had designed it with me in mind, trying to build a house I'd want to live in. It's not far off. It's painted a pinky orange, like a Mexican whorehouse, with Prussian blue accents—not exactly the colors I would have chosen, but I suppose it all fits with my radical mystique, and it feels just right for the temporary home of a billionaire assassin with a four-year-old baby girl. Everything is real here. If the house were not built on a soundstage (and if there were bathrooms), I could move in.

Quentin is in the garden (the grass is real, too: about a quarter-acre of fresh turf, delightfully moist from the morning watering). He has several of the various two-hundred-or-so-page scripts, versions going back to over a year ago, spread out on a designer teak picnic table. He jumps up immediately and insists on taking me on a tour. There's a living room with a forty-foot ceiling, where most of the action will take place. Another sitting room up a couple of steps leads out to a covered patio, the main purpose for which, it will turn out, will be for Uma to lounge in with her knitting—yes, knitting—between takes. Off to the other side, there's a very sweet little bedroom, with a mosquito net over a big bed that gives a *Night of the Iguana* effect to the place. We won't shoot anything in either of these rooms, just see them in the background. Even so, they're thoroughly furnished and accessorized. But where is all my stuff? At first I see none of the ninety-six items that Sandy commandeered from my storage.

Reason being, I'm told, that Bill no longer lives in his own palatial villa, surrounded by bodyguards, as the first draft of the script had it. Quentin decided a world famous international assassin had to stay on the move, so instead he's living in the most extravagant hotel suite on the planet. We continue the tour up a sweeping, cantilevered, circular staircase that hangs in the air, and along a hallway with arches overlooking the main room, to the child's bedroom, cute as all getout, with horsies and a doll house and all the stuff you'd expect for a warlord's little girl. Across the hall is a terrace, overlooking the garden. This spot, also, we will never shoot, perhaps never see on film, even in the background. It will be a great place, though, to hang out and smoke between scenes. There are signs everywhere about not smoking, but Uma and I are automatically excepted. Noblesse oblige. Quentin shows me all this with great excitement. Then he leaves me to myself for a bit while he confers with somebody about something or other.

I wander on my own, and do find a few of my artifacts: a Mayan sculpture on an end table, a little balsa wood donkey. Inside a cupboard, where no one will ever see them, are some antique books of mine, held up by my Egyptian bookends.

On two of the side tables are a couple of elegant leather folders, a phone book–sized one for the room service menu, etc., and another slim one with monogrammed stationery inside, with big tooled "Qs" on the covers, for the Villa Quatro, the actual name of the real location in Baja California where we'll be shooting the exteriors. When production is over, these will, of course, become Quentin's. The big one is the perfect size for another of his epic screenplays. A nice touch, one which underlines the decorating crew's complete attention to detail, is a room key, attached to a big leather "Q," tossed onto a coffee table, alongside my own leather cigar case.

Back in the garden, Uma sails in, dressed very casually, though fetchingly, and changes the whole atmosphere just by her presence, like the muse she is. Then Quentin orders lunch; we have a choice of three local restaurants. We go for Italian. I order a carpaccio, raw meat always being my favorite drug of choice.

Then we get down to this rehearsal—no, not a rehearsal, yet. First, the explanation of Quentin's new plan. Whole new ball game. The biggest change being that the final fight to the death is no longer on a beach in Mexico. It's going to be done right here, in the garden of the hacienda. The script I have so laboriously drilled into my head is going to completely change. Some of the new stuff will stay in, some of the old-new stuff will be reinstated, and some of the original, or aboriginal, dialogue from way back in February will find its way in again, plus some brand-new-new stuff, needed as connective tissue, to hold the whole thing together. We start, reading the new (now old) script, then we go on to the old-now-new stuff. My head is spinning, of course, but it's all good.

Lunch arrives, and we break for that. Then we go through some blocking, trying to decide where in the hacienda we're going to say and do what. In the script, most of the action happens at a banquet table, with Bill in a tuxedo, but all that's gone. Quentin has decided that will all take place at the wet bar, where I'll be making sandwiches while giving what amounts to a two-page monologue on the subject of Uma's daughter BB's learning about life and death as a result of stomping on Emilio. (Emilio was her goldfish.) After that, I'll continue the monologue while carrying BB up the cantilevered stairs to her bedroom. That will be a great shot, with the crane tracking us up the stairs and along the balconied hallway. Then, I will leave Uma and BB alone together to watch a Disney movie (if we can get the rights for it).

When Uma has put the kid to sleep, she'll come back out on the balcony to find me downstairs, watching a Roy Rogers picture on the big TV. We work out the private scene between Uma and me, almost a love scene, if you discount the fact that we're about to attack each other with samurai swords. Uma looks delicious leaning out over the banister, gazing down on me. This whole process feels very sweet, like rehearsing a play on Broadway.

When we finish going through it all, I chime in with a few piddling suggestions. I've brought some things with me which I thought might add to the atmosphere. First off, I throw onto the picnic table a pack of Mexican Delicado cigarettes that I've been saving since the *Warden of Red Rock* shoot for Showtime in Durango three years ago. I do hang on to stuff. Then, I truck out the Silent Flute. "Yeah, great," Quentin says. "Definitely that should be here." I show him my "Sword of the Day Warrior," a comic book superhero thing I picked up at an autograph convention. Quentin flips over it. "Let's put it in the set somewhere," he says. I reply, "Sure, that, or Bill's samurai sword." Q says, "Yeah! Great idea. But where? Find a place for the sword," he says to anyone who hears, which is everyone. Quentin never mumbles. That's one of the great things about working with him. With my ruined hearing, from guns and rock & roll, it's delightful to work for someone who always speaks so I can hear him. I never have to say, "What?"

People start looking all over for a good place. I say, "How about at the front door?"

Quentin's not sure. "Maybe too much," he says.

"I don't know," I say. "First thing she sees, when she comes busting in?"

"Okay," he says. "I dig it."

I donate the display stand for the "Day Warrior" sword to sit it on. I would suggest laying out Bill's two-gun belt somewhere, but Scotty, the prop wrangler, already has it set prominently on a side table in the garden. I suggest to Scotty that he might want to place my guitar somewhere, since they're all trying to make Bill as much like me as possible. There's no way I'd be living anywhere without a good guitar in evidence. I break open the gnarly hard-shell case I inherited from Brother Mike, with Harley stickers and Native American mandala decals all over it, and pull out the axe I've chosen from my collection.

I could have come with a vintage Gibson, or the priceless Manuel Contreras Classical, but I chose the Mossman Golden Era Custom, which I designed for myself back in '73, for its looks; there's an ornate abalone vine snaking up the fretboard and a mother-of-pearl Kansas wheat straw inlaid into the peghead. A really beautiful instrument. Quentin, who misses nothing, overhears us. "Yeah," he says, "I think I might even have you play it." That, as it would turn out, would never happen. You can't have it all, I guess.

Quentin has decided I should smoke a cigar at one point in the scene, so Scotty asks me what kind of cigar I want. I say, "Why, do they make cigars anyplace but Cuba?" That gets a chuckle out of him. Then I say, "Hey, anything will do. It's only a movie, right?" But he insists. I say, "Well, I happen to have a few with me." And I haul out my portable hermetically sealed humidor: "Road Warrior," it's called. It looks like something you'd find on the space shuttle, absolutely airtight when you want it to be, which means watertight as well. If the *Titanic* went down with it aboard, it would find its way back to the surface, with its contents as good as new. It holds about twenty cigars. I've got a little of everything in it, from little dinky things to foot-long Lanceros. "Okay," I say. "For myself, a Cuban Montecito or Partagas would do just fine. A Dominican would be okay. But, for *Bill* . . . Well, the standard for Billionaire Assassins is a Cohiba. It's supposed to be what Castro smokes." Scotty says, "Great! We'll try to find some. But just in case we can't, give me a band from one and we'll copy off a few, and put them on Dominican cigars." That sounds okay to me. I carefully slip the band off a panatela and leave it with him.

Finally, Quentin calls for the camera crew to come in, and he explains what he's going to do, sort of. The first shot, Quentin says, will be Uma coming through the front door, ready to kill Bill. Okay. There are a few questions from the various departments. Then Quentin goes on to describe the whole sequence, while he walks, or runs, with the crew hustling to keep up with him, up the stairs, into the kid's bedroom, back down to the living room, over to the fireplace, describing everything we'd worked out, up to the point where, in a kind of cliff-hanger, I say, "It just so happens I have a solution." Then Quentin, with an expansive gesture, says, "And that's what we're doing for the next few days. I'll tell you the rest of it Wednesday."

Everybody jumps to effect the changes in strategy that will be required—not the least of which being that someone has to assemble a new script. Quentin runs Bob Richardson through an outline of what we'll shoot first. Boy, it's great to see Bob hop to it. That guy is totally unflappable. Always smiling, eager to move ahead to a future he has no doubt will be better than the present. All that established, Quentin sends us home. Tomorrow (early, of course) we'll start the shooting.

We meet *ANDREW COOPER/MIRAMAX FILMS*

Not by chance *ANDREW COOPER/MIRAMAX FILMS*

t's a love story *ANDREW COOPER/MIRAMAX FILMS*

eally *ANDREW COOPER/MIRAMAX FILMS*

Quentin's a lot of fun *ANDREW COOPER/MIRAMAX FILMS*

Bill attacks *ANDREW COOPER/MIRAMAX FILMS*

he bride defends *ANDREW COOPER/MIRAMAX FILMS*

uentin shows us how *ANDREW COOPER/MIRAMAX FILMS*

Bob loves his job *ANDREW COOPER/MIRAMAX FILMS*

Here's why *ANDREW COOPER/MIRAMAX FILMS*

We go to a mad tea party *ANDREW COOPER/MIRAMAX FILMS*

Annie's found a good spot *ANDREW COOPER/MIRAMAX FILMS*

"**S**huffle off to Buffalo"
kung-fu style *ANNIE BIERMAN*

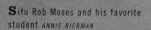

Sifu Rob Moses and his favorite
student *ANNIE BIERMAN*

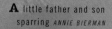

A little father and son
sparring *ANNIE BIERMAN*

功 夫

t looked so easy on paper *DAVID CARRADINE*

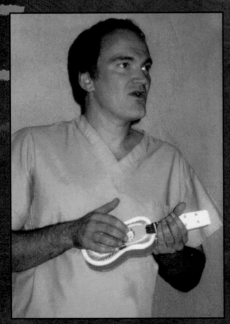

ever mind! I'm not gonna let this ruin my day.
DAVID CARRADINE

Tuesday, December 3

The set is transformed, and now full of people — "Abuzz" would be a good word for it. Strewn around the patio are a bunch of child's toys; the Silent Flute lies across some kid stuff, including my vintage copy of *The Patchwork Girl of Oz*, on the picnic table. The pack of Mexican Delicados which I've been saving for a decade or so for just such an occasion is there, too. Propped up in one of the chairs is the Mossman Golden Era. The effect is a frozen moment during a late morning daddy-daughter play session.

This is when I meet Perla Haney-Jardine, the kid who will play BB, the five-year-old girl who is our daughter in the script, whom The Bride (Uma) has never seen, since she's been in a coma since before the kid was born. Perla is a sweetie. A very pretty little girl, given to shy smiles that could melt glaciers. I can perceive none of the alien-creature elements that dominate the personalities of most child actors. With her long blonde hair, she's physically a fine choice to play Uma's daughter; though, actually, her looks are remarkably reminiscent of Daryl. It remains to be seen what kind of an actress she is, but that smile will take her a long way.

Uma picks up the copy of *The Patchwork Girl of Oz,* and begins rhapsodizing over the brilliance of the set decorators. Not to take anything away from these worthies, but I tell her it's my personal copy. She gives me a very deep look. I guess I don't look the type to be collecting *Oz* books. Shows you what she knows. Uma has a five-year-old girl of her own, so, what the hell! I pick up the book and write an inscription inside it to her daughter, Maya. I collar Scott, the prop man, and tell him that when the set is wrapped he should give it to her.

Quentin now tells everyone the first increment of his new plan. He's very excited. Uma will come bursting through the door, he says, brandishing a 9mm in one hand, with her samurai sword in the other, expecting armed response. She'll make her way cautiously through the big room onto the patio, where Perla, as BB, and I will greet her with the water pistol game from the first draft of the script, then pretend to have a shootout where we all fall down and play dead.

The crew sets up for Uma to come busting through the front door. Uma goes off to makeup and wardrobe to transform herself into the vengeful bride.

I go check out the "Hanzo" sword. It looks great cradled in its ebony stand facing the front door. I pull it out and swing it around a little. They've put one of the real ones in the scabbard, so this is especially fun. There are several levels of these swords on hand. There are two of the real steel ones, with blunt edges; one with a really sharp blade; several aluminum ones; and a whole slew of wooden ones with shiny aluminum tape over the blades. Past experience tells me we'll break a lot of them when we get around to the fight. I can't wait. I sure love swordplay. Someone points out that the lighting crew is trying to line up on the sword, so I stop twirling it and put it back in its cradle.

I go off to perform my own makeup and wardrobe chores. Manny and Heba are glad to see me again. We have a great reunion.

Back in my trailer, I set up a little table to display my "Day Warrior" sword and my short hara-kiri-style samurai blade, just to keep me in the mood of the movie. I set up housekeeping, pulling out the trail snacks and the foot-high stack of magazines, the new

A gift for Maya, Uma's five year-old *DAVID CARRADINE*

Tony Hillerman novel, *The Wailing Wind*, and *The Annotated Wizard of Oz*, all of which I assembled to keep me occupied during the anticipated inevitable endless hours of waiting around.

Knowing how important the moment of Uma's entrance, her vengeful homecoming, is to the movie, and also knowing how careful Q and Bob are with their setups, and how many takes and angles they're bound to go through, I don't really expect to work till after lunch. There are pages they've copied out for the day's work, garbled compilations from the various scripts, that bear little resemblance to what we're actually going to do. It's hard for anyone to keep up with Quentin's constant re-creating.

Halfway through the first chapter of *The Wailing Wind*, I lay back and took a snooze. I have no idea how long I was out before Heather, a perky young crew member, knocked on my door. "They're ready for you," she said.

On the way to the set, Scotty stopped me and told me they had obtained a box of real Cohiba panatelas, and gave me back my cigar band.

"Boy, that was fast," I said.

"We aim to please," he replied. Hollywood crews are the *best*.

Things were being set up on the patio for our water pistol fight. This was the first I'd seen of Uma's costume: a skintight leather jerkin over tight pants, with the Hanzo sword on her back. She looked like a super-hero (heroine). Tough, and oh, so sexy. We played around with the scene for a while, getting just the right positions, with Quentin and Bob debating the angles they would use.

Marty, the script supervisor, was totally out of the loop, as was everyone, regarding what script we were using. I filled him in on how it was going to go, as far as I knew. Perla and I started to have fun with the pistols. As it turns out, they aren't water pistols after all. Perla has a green thing the same shape as Uma's 9mm. I have a red Flash Gordon Ray Gun. It would make noises and flash lights, perhaps shoot sparks, but the batteries are (wisely) not loaded. Perla starts out by practicing falling down and dying, while the stage father, actually a pretty nice guy, drills the new (old) dialogue into her. Meanwhile, Bob does his considerable lighting magic with his big silks.

Finally, *"Action!"* Uma comes around the corner, her eyes blazing, her gun ready, to find Perla and me sitting on the steps pointing our toys at her. "Bang!" I say. Uma just stares. So, I say, "Oh, Mommy got us! Fall down, Baby. We're dead!" Something like that. We both fall down, gasping and groaning. Then, from beyond the grave, I assume the voice of an announcer, droning on about "Fast-Draw Kiddo" (that's Uma), and we lure her into the game. The "announcer" explains how BB is not really dead, "due to the fact that she is impervious to bullets." So Perla shoots Uma, and she acts out a very corny death rattle and falls down. Then she and Perla hug and stuff, while I look on beaming.

This sweet little scene, you understand, takes place toward the end of the movie, after Uma has killed or maimed a little over a hundred people with a samurai sword, a Marine combat knife, or her bare hands (lots and lots of fake blood and severed rubber arms and heads). And right when the audience is expecting the final huge battle between us, we start acting as though we're in a Disney movie. We shoot this scene for the rest of the day, at lots of different angles, though always from Uma's point of view. We wrap very late, almost eleven. We'll come back tomorrow and do it all over again for Uma's coverage, with the camera facing in the other direction. Bill, the first AD, very apologetically asks if I will forgo the twelve-hour turnaround guaranteed me by the Screen Actors Guild. I say, "Of course."

There's a parlor grand piano in the lobby of the hotel, and I think about playing it, but, at the moment, a very old man is picking out familiar melodies with one finger. I order a cappuccino and determine to wait him out. He's really bad. I wonder how a guy who's as old as he is, who has any interest in the piano at all, could have lived so long without learning how to play a little better. Finally, I can no longer stand the noise. I walk over and hover behind him like a hungry condor until he gets the message and relinquishes the bench. I sit down, thinking, I'm going to blow this cat's mind. But I don't actually play that well tonight. The old guy likes it anyway. I give it about fifteen minutes and call it a night, though I won't sleep much.

Wednesday, December 4

We continue to play the water pistol game, this time favoring Uma throughout. Gayle Max, my manager, shows up with Scott Melrose, my new agent. They don't get to see me work, only off-camera. Gayle would like to stay and watch, but Scott is ready to split. He gets antsy when there's no deal to be made, while Gayle just wants to bathe in the reflected glory. That's the difference between a manager and an agent: The manager loves the client; the agent loves the deal. Finally, we're finished with the scene, and we go inside to the wet bar. It's all set up for making lunch. Quentin sits on a bar stool and says, "Okay. Make me a sandwich. Make it like you would for BB, and one for Uma, and one for yourself."

I pull out a couple of slices of bread from the package, which has an appropriately Spanish language label, select a knife, and reach for the mayonnaise jar. "I don't like mayonnaise," Quentin says. Okay. I put back the mayonnaise jar and pick up the mustard. Then he says, "I don't want a squeeze bottle for the mustard, I want a jar, so I can see the knife go in." After a bit of scurrying, we realize there is no jar of mustard.

"Why can't I get what I want?" he says. "Why do they always give me the wrong thing? Why don't they just ask me, instead of sticking me with stuff?"

Somebody suggests they could fake it for the moment with a jar of plaster of Paris. Quentin says, "No way! I'm not having David Carradine make sandwiches for me with plaster of Paris, which I might want to eat later. So, we'll just wait." He turns to me. "So, David, go have a cup of coffee and a smoke, for five or ten or twenty minutes, until they get their shit together around here."

And that we do. It does take about twenty minutes for someone to go out and buy mustard. They come back with a jar of French's and some Grey Poupon. Quentin goes for the French's. So I start making a sandwich. Quentin nixes the lettuce; he doesn't like the color.

Uma shows up then, amid a discussion about what they will shoot first, while I pile bologna, smoked turkey, and two kinds of cheese on the bread. When it comes time to cut the bread (I always cut my sandwiches in half), I mention that I have a short samurai blade we could do that with instead of the table knife they've provided, which won't do the job very well, anyway. Quentin thinks about that, but opts instead for a chef's knife with a two-inch-wide blade. I'll get to wave that around while I drone on about dead goldfish, as a reminder to the audience that there is some menace underlying this sweet little domestic scene.

There is a problem about what to shoot right now. Perla's day, by order of the California State Child Labor Laws, is finished. We could shoot me over the shoulder of Perla's stand-in/body double, but we have to avoid Uma as well, as she's out of makeup and wardrobe. She volunteers that she could run over right now and get it all back on, and probably be back before they're ready to shoot.

Quentin says, "Well, maybe we can shoot over your shoulder. We'll just see your hair." Uma doesn't do anything with her hair for the movie, just lets it fly. Quentin and Bob circle the set, discussing angles. It seems that over Uma, we'd need to see Perla, and over Perla, we'd need to see Uma. And they can't shoot over my shoulder, because you'd have to see at least one of them head-on.

Finally, Quentin says, "Look, there's nothing here we can shoot that we'll want to be in the movie, so let's wrap." Behind him, the whole room lights up with rows of white teeth, as the faces of the crew break into big grins. We get to go home, after a mere fourteen-hour day. I guess I should point out that almost everyone else in the production is commuting from their homes every morning and driving back every night. Our late wraps make going home easy, but in the morning, it's got to be an hour and a half on the road for most of them.

I, on the other hand, have a five-minute ride to the hotel. I get there in time to order a cappuccino, and do an hour on the grand piano, playing much better tonight. Back in my little room, overlooking the golf course, I work on the monologue for tomorrow. Around ten-thirty or so, I get on the phone with Annie, and we coo at each other for about an hour. I'm starting to really miss her, and the kids, and Thunder, of course. I had thought about bringing him along. He would have loved it, but I need to concentrate on my game.

I get a little sleep—not much, though.

Thursday, December 5

Today I made about a hundred sandwiches, while at the same time reeling out a five-minute Tarantino rap about life and death as illustrated by a stomped goldfish named Emilio. This is the beginning of Bill's domination of the film, prior to his long-anticipated demise. Which means it's my very long moment in Quentin Tarantino's spotlight. I'm supposed to show them in this scene why I was hired for the part. This is a moment coming at the end of the picture, if I don't captivate the audience with what Quentin's given me to say, they're going to fall asleep on us.

Quentin goes at it with a mixture of total abandon and minute exactitude. It had already become clear that he was in no particular hurry. We're obviously going to stay here and work at it until it sings.

A lot of this is going to be on my hands, making the sandwiches. I look at my grubby, short, broken fingernails, and remark that Bill would definitely have a manicure. I go on to say to no one in particular that if they wanted manicured nails, they hired the wrong actor. Within seconds, Heba, the makeup artist, shows up with a whole little manicure set, and Quentin says, "Heba is ready to give you anything you need." I say, "Well, my nails are so short, there's nothing much she can do. Mostly, what I need is to wash my hands." I repair to the men's room to do that: get them squeaky clean. And we start. Making sandwiches, and rapping away to Uma and Perla. It seems Perla likes the crusts cut off, so that gives me something else to do with the big knife. We try to curb Perla's desire to wolf down every one of the things, knowing that later on she's going to have to eat them on camera.

We do this all morning. There's got to be a huge pile of half-eaten bologna sandwiches building up somewhere behind the scenes. I wonder if there's any way to get them to homeless people or something. I pass on lunch.

In the afternoon, we continue with the coverage of the scene: on Perla, until the teacher tells us it's time for her to quit, and then on Uma. I'm still making sandwiches, still rapping away, right into the late evening.

Friday, December 6

I've got a day off! While they shoot some pickup stuff with Pai Mei's dou-ble (easy to do; his makeup is so extreme, like that of an evil Santa Claus, anyone can double him) and Uma. It seems sort of odd that they would stuff this fast food right in the middle of the huge entrèe we're in the mid-dle of. What that's about, though, I think, is that Quentin has been busy at night again. There will be some changes when we go back in. This guy is determined to get it right. He won't stop thinking until it's exactly what he wants. Whatever that takes.

Anyway, I get to go home. It's great to see Annie. She cooks me a great dinner, and the kids and dogs are all over me.

Monday, December 9

Great to be back on the shoot. Quentin told me once that when he was conceiving this movie, he thought how he didn't want to just make a movie, he wanted to live it. To make it his life, his whole universe, for however long it took. To lose himself in it. Well, we've all done that with him. *Kill Bill* and Supércool Manchu have become our lives.

The crew had moved upstairs to Perla's bedroom. A beautiful set. A perfect little girl's happy place, with stuffed animals and murals on the walls. A doll house, a rocking horse. All that good stuff. Not a hint that BB's father is an international assassin.

As the first shot of the day was being set up, I realized that something was missing. A whole scene had disappeared, to be replaced by something else. I had been ready to do another chunk of monologue while carrying Perla up the stairs. That was now gone. We would start with us already in her room, me tucking her into bed. I thought, What a pity. The crane following us going up the stairs would have been a great shot. Of course, however, Quentin had an answer for that, which I would find out later. He would follow Uma *down* the stairs with the crane, in yet another new piece of writing. And, yes, it would be better.

So, meanwhile, the three of us—Uma, Perla, and I—played out this very sweet domestic scene: a father and mother putting their kid to bed, prior to the two adults' going after each other with samurai swords. That's assuming Quentin wasn't going to throw yet another curve at us and change the whole ending. In between shots, I hung out on the terrace, having a smoke and maybe a sip of good coffee. I had to continually remind myself that I wasn't really outside overlooking a south-of-the-border garden, next to a beach in Baja California; the whole ambience was so realistic. Just to confuse us further, between setups there was mariachi music coming in over the sound system.

I started paying a lot of attention to Perla's work. Quentin and Uma were giving her a lot of help, making a game out of the whole thing. Perla was eating it up, and giving a performance that was so natural, so real, that I was actually envious of her skill. This from a five-year-old. One of my favorite days in Show Business.

Tuesday, December 10

We're back upstairs in Perla's little room again. She and Uma "watch a video together before bedtime" is how the call sheet reads. In the script it's written as *The Aristocats,* but it turns out Disney won't let them use it, so that's been replaced with *Samurai Jack.* I have a couple of lines and then leave them alone together. There's a thing about a plastic toy gun. Then, for half a day I hang out in the trailer, while the ladies snuggle up in Perla's bed and Quentin shoots the scene from every possible angle.

After lunch, the changes that Quentin thought up over the weekend become apparent. He starts out with me lounging barefoot on a big sofa, watching the Roy Rogers movie. The script supervisor or someone points out that my feet are black on the bottom, from walking around the really filthy soundstage. Quentin likes it. He says they look like David Carradine's feet to him. What happened to Bill?

Uma is going to come out of Perla's room and talk to me over the rail of the balcony. Suddenly, I pull out my six-shooter and put four rounds into the stucco just beside her head. No more Mr. Nice Guy. Now they do that crane shot following her down the stairs. I'm getting a real kick out of just watching Uma walk, all six-feet-one of her, her eyes smoldering.

At gunpoint, I make her sit on the couch while I try to get it straight between us, see to it that before we start slashing each other up with samurai swords, we tell each other the truth for once. She tries to make a lunge for Bill's sword, which is tantalizingly near her, causing me to draw my other six-gun and place a couple of shots in the couch. I tell her if she doesn't sit still, I'll put one in her kneecap. Then I blow away the papaya in the fruit bowl, just for kicks.

All this, you understand, is brand-new stuff. I'm loving it. So are the prop guys. So will the audience. This is totally unexpected, and pure vintage Tarantino. Shooting the shit out of the place and talking endlessly about something completely unrelated. I'm starting to feel like Samuel L. Jackson—except that Sam had to put up with an argumentative John Travolta with greasy hair as his audience. I get a little over six feet of a beautiful blonde bombshell.

At one point, Scott mentions how beautiful Uma is. Yes, she is. I think I made that clear a hundred pages or so ago. Absolutely stunning. I was crazy about her when she was "Poison Ivy," but she's got something else going now. All the fire is there, and the long legs and the tight body, but the new baby did something to her. There's an inner softness, an Earth Mother thing added to the mix that increases her voltage about threefold.

Scott goes on to say that he has to stop himself from staring at her, so she won't start treating him like a stalker. I tell him, "Well, I get to stare at her all I want. It's what I'm supposed to do."

He says I'm lucky. Yeah. I am. I'm lucky. Definitely.

The blobs are chunks of papaya; the black spots are bullet holes *DAVID CARRADINE*

Wednesday, December 11

Today is supposed to be Perla's last day. We go back up to her room and do a little improvisation of her showing all her stuff to Uma. It turns out Perla has names for all the stuffed animals, knows how to work all the gadgets, and is ready to totally unself-consciously talk a blue streak. Quentin sits there grinning, just eating it up. Every now and then he says something like, "Go over to the horse now," calling it by name. Perla responds without skipping a beat. We shoot a whole lot of this.

Thursday, December 12

When I get to the set, I'm handed five pages of xeroxed dialogue, parts of it in Quentin's handwriting, mixed in with bits and pieces of the typed script. And, it says at the top of the page, "Part One"! I gulp and go to my trailer to study up. But it's great stuff. Wonderful stuff. He's solved problems I didn't know we had. Every change he's made has enriched the picture.

The sequence starts out with me pouring two glasses of Sauza Tres Generactiones tequila, remarking to Uma that she's a lot more fun with a couple of shots in her. I down my shot, and . . . it's *real*! And I've swallowed it straight down. Too late to spit it out. My reaction gets a laugh from the crew. Yeah. Very funny. Who do they think I am, Michael Madsen? Well, there was a time, but this is not it, after almost seven years, and with more words than *Hamlet* looking at me. I wait while they replace it with a bottle of watered-down Coke.

I get to do some more fast draws. Quentin sets up a shot just for that, and I show him my best stuff. I'm really up against it, as the gun has a futuristic silencer on it that makes it a bitch to pull out fast, and a hassle to get it back in. Then there's doing it left-handed. This is all compounded by the disconcerting fact that Quentin has gone on and on to the whole cast and crew, periodically, since the first table read back in May, about how good I am at this. Ranking me up there with Sammy Davis Jr. and the legendary Rod Redwing. Now, they're all waiting to see "The Master" work.

I do okay, though. For one thing, Scott and his prop crew made a two-gun holster set copied from the Andy Anderson–designed gun belt that Smiley Burnette gave me to practice with when he taught me the fast draw and all the fancy stuff for my role in the TV series *Shane,* and I'm really used to pulling leather with that rig, having been doing so off and on since 1966.

We shoot up about a hundred rounds. The gun gets real hot. Feels great. Then he has me pull out a dart gun from behind the wet bar and shoot Uma in the leg with a truth serum. These are all, of course, new pages. I'm having the time of my life. When the camera turns around on Uma, I get to do it all over again, to give her something to react to and for the smoke.

Uma is a model of professional cool throughout all this. She just flows, smiling and joking, with her deep, sexy voice. In between shots, she goes back to her knitting.

At one point, Bob is setting up to do a shot of her lying back on the couch, with her feet up on the coffee table. He's going to start close on her feet, and pan all the way up her body to her face. With Uma's toes pointed, that's close to seven feet.

Uma watches the process for a while, and then says matter-of-factly, "Sometimes it frightens me how far away my feet are."

Friday, December 13

At the bottom of every call sheet, there's an item: "Quote of the Day." Uma's line about her feet made it in today.

I now tackle my eight-page monologue, which Quentin cribbed from our cigar-bar talk in Beijing a couple of centuries ago. "Part Two" of the handwritten new script. I'm sweating bullets (and firing off a few) to get the words right. Funny: Later on, I'm going to hear people remark how amazing I was at getting all the way through it every time, like it was a piece of cake, never breaking character. At the time, it seemed to me I was screwing up all over the place, barely pulling it off. During one of the breaks, while they were reloading the guns or the camera, I don't remember which, I said, to no one in particular: "Sometimes it scares me how far away my *brain* is."

Saturday, December 14

My line about my brain is the "Quote of the Day."

Bob Richardson is extremely agitated. We have to do a shot over because it was out of focus. He's mortified. We fool around with that for a while, and then go back to the Superman monologue. We are doing many angles of this, and many takes. Each time, Quentin gives me some more to work with. The whole thing is being fine-tuned to something really excellent. And then, he also comes up with alternate versions for me. "Okay," he says. "We've got that. Now try this."

Bill thinks it's funny ANDREW COOPER/MIRAMAX FILMS

Coiled and ready to strike. Isn't she sweet, though? *ANDREW COOPER/MIRAMAX FILMS*

At one point, he says, "Now, give me one where you don't do anything you've ever done before." This after refining the thing to the point where every moment is just perfect. What else can I do? How can I step away from the perfection he's nudged me into? But I give it my best shot. I remark to him that this is like being on Broadway. It feels like Theater, with a capital "T." I show up every day, get into makeup and wardrobe, and then work at making this day better than what I did the day before. That's Broadway.

Finally we have it, in as many ways and from as many angles as seems possible, and then Quentin, with an impish grin, says, "Okay, David. Now, this is your final performance on Broadway. It's the last chance you'll ever have to play the scene. Give it your 'Good-bye to Broadway' take." Out o' sight! I give it my all.

We move outside to start the scene that will lead up to our final fight. A new (blue instead of black) cyclorama has been unreeled around the whole garden set. It's dawn now. Quentin has me sitting at the picnic table, finishing off the bottle of tequila, my Hanzo sword beside me. I check the tequila carefully, to make sure they're not dosing me again, before I down a shot. Uma comes over with her sword in hand and takes a chair. We start the scene. It's going to be great.

Sunday, December 15

It seemed Annie and I needed a little break this weekend. We found someone to take care of two of the kids, and invited Amanda, the recently turned teenager, and Max, the four-year-old future NBA star, to join us for a day in Santa Barbara. I love that drive. We had lunch in a cavernous restaurant, with couches for the college crowd, I guess it was, to lounge on. I ordered a super red-eye (coffee plus three shots of espresso) to get me kick-started. Then I took a smoke break on the street. This place had tables outside, but almost nowhere in Santa Barbara will they let you light up, even at an outdoor table. California is so uncivilized.

I sneaked down the road to look at some rings for a possible birthday present for Annie, but found nothing that worked. When I got back, we wolfed down the food and I had another one of those caffeine depth bombs. Max was starting to climb the walls (literally) by then, so we got out of there and wandered around State Street, looking at the shops. With Christmas so near, we needed to pick up some gifts, which we definitely did.

At one point, we separated, the unspoken mission being to look for presents for each other. Annie gave me the choice of taking Max or Amanda. I opted for Amanda, and we hung out until Annie was out of sight, little Max jumping around her as they disappeared down the promenade. Then, with Amanda as an eager accomplice, I popped into Victoria's Secret, to find something in red, and into a jewelry store, where I found some beautiful turquoise baubles that I thought Annie would love. No ring, though. I guess that will have to wait.

Annie took the wheel of the Yukon on the way back. I slept most of the way, but I did get an eyeful of some of the great coastline. I was hoping to see a whale maybe, but no such luck. Back home, I built a fire and we had dinner by it. Then someone from the studio picked me up a little after midnight to drive me down to Manhattan Beach. A lovely weekend. The outing made the one short Sunday seem like a long weekend.

I was refreshed and ready to kick ass all week.

Monday, December 16

We start the day with a pickup of Uma reacting to the exploding papaya. It seems we had shot this angle before we did the insert where we loaded papayas up with napalm, and there weren't enough splatters to match. At this point, you could find blotches of dried papaya as high as twenty feet up the walls. This meant I got to fire off the gun again.

Quentin had partied over the weekend, and he was still feeling the effects. He was cheerful and alert, but definitely needed a few cups of coffee, and maybe a new head. The gunfire didn't help.

Q: "I get really drunk on Sunday, so it will last into Monday."

Suddenly, Uma realized that Quentin had changed the angle.

UMA: "This is not a papaya shot. There's no papaya here. You're just making me do it over to pass the time till you sober up."

Q: "Are you accusing me of doing busywork?"

UMA: "No, I'm accusing you of making *me* do busywork."

Tuesday, December 17

When I walk on the set, Wu Ping's boys are there, to teach me the sword-fight. I'm scared. It's really complicated, and I have to learn it all right now, and we're supposed to shoot it today. Weird. The fight with Michael Jai White I rehearsed for three months, and now I've got a few minutes to learn the one that sells the picture.

I get it into my head in a fuzzy fashion, and then we sidestep to do a shot of me watching the Roy Rogers movie from a new angle. Kansas visits the set to wish me a belated happy birthday. She got the part she was trying out for.

We start the fight. Kansas gets to watch. Somehow, I've got the first part of it down well enough so as not to disgrace myself.

These days Uma is fond of telling me that it's time for me to die. *"You're going down"* is how she puts it. It's not that she doesn't like me. She's been on this picture in one way or another for about three years now, and she's really eager to see the end of it. I guess I am too. Though I kind of dread acting out the dying thing—not because it's distasteful to me, but because I don't know if I'll do it well. This is just pretend that we're doing here, but I think if it were for real, I'd still be concerned with dying well. Like a warrior would or should.

Coming back from the trailer, I come upon Quentin, Uma, and about a dozen of the crew engaged in one of those roughhouses where everybody piles on top of each other. Back in my repertory days, we used to call the person on the bottom "Lucky Pierre," but that's another story. I sometimes wish I could involve myself in stuff like that. I'm always a watcher. I'm too hung up on dignity, I guess. I know that sounds silly coming from me.

Gayle called to tell me I have the chance to play a character on the superhot TV Series *Six Feet Under*, but there's no way I could get loose from *Kill Bill* long enough to do it. Some other time.

Wednesday, December 18

More swordfighting. I walked on the set to some great rock & roll. Off in the distance I could hear Quentin's signature laugh. He sure has fun. Uma was in good spirits; lots of jokes abounded. At one point, as I was preparing for a shot where I was supposed to disarm Uma, I heard Quentin, from behind the camera, singing, *"Some enchanted evening . . . You may kill a stranger . . ."* Almost immediately, the in-house Muzak came on with Perry Como's version of the song.

Quentin kept saying, "Mo' speed! Mo' powah!" I was swinging (the real Hanzo sword: I kept breaking the wooden ones) as hard as I could. It was pulling my arm out of its socket. All worth it. I love this shit.

The "wire guys" from Wu Ping's outfit were on hand, as we were also pulling some special effects tricks, which I won't spoil everyone's fun by describing here.

For today's festivities, they also brought in stunt personnel, wearing wigs and costumes to pretend to be Uma and me. The idea being, when I'm swinging a tempered-steel samurai sword at Uma's head with all the speed and power I can muster, and when she's returning the compliment with equal vigor, either the attacker or the intended target will be a photo double, depending on whose face needs to be in the camera. That way, they are only risking one principal actor at a time. If the double gets whacked, they can still go on shooting the movie. Sounds cold, and it is, but that's always been the way they've done it.

It's okay with me; I'm the main aggressor in this fight. I'm not likely to get whacked, but I definitely don't want to be the one who whacks Uma. I've fallen in love with her. Chris, my stuntman, is thinking about only the move, while at least half of my brain is concerned with giving a performance, acting like Bill, at the same time. I could make a mistake. At those moments, I'm happy to watch.

Then, in the two-shots, where we both had to be seen on screen, we discovered that the wooden swords tended to flex, like...well, like wood, when they were worked as fast as we were going. The thing would whip wildly at the end of a swing, almost slapping Uma in the cheek, or the eye, or the lip. Not good. So, we had to switch to cold steel. It's rare that you do that in a movie, but it was actually safer.

There's a rumor, or maybe it's just a suspicion, that Quentin will shoot this whole fight over again on the beach in Mexico, next year: that this whole week is just a delaying tactic, and a sop for Miramax. Everybody knows that Quentin, given a three-week vacation, is bound to come up with new ideas, not to mention the ones he already has that he's just not telling us about. Well, maybe so, but the way this is working out, so small, so contained, and so intense within that small space, and then, so charged with emotion, I think maybe this rendition will hold. After all, we've all seen duels to the death on deserted beaches at dawn before, if only in our minds or imagined off the pages of books. It's a classic image, and Quentin is all about veering away from all that. And he is giving his all to this very specifically "his" rendition of it.

I'd find it hard to believe he is not totally committed to this really wild departure from the blatant bravura of the old-new version of the script.

Just as I'm about to leave, Scotty whispers in my ear, "Stick around. We're going to hang that reporter today." This is the kid who hung around us at the White Lotus Temple in Beijing. In his article he had made fun of Bill, the AD. Okay for us, but not for outsiders. So the wire crew was going to string him up from the flies and let him dangle there for a while as a lesson. I decided to stay and watch. They hoisted the kid up and spun him around till he almost threw up, while everybody cheered. I thought about whacking him with one of the wooden swords, but he was mortified enough. I tried to get a shot of him with my Leica, but without a flash I doubted if I could stop the spinning action.

Then they let the kid down and everybody went back to work, while he staggered around the soundstage like an old drunk. I think he learned his lesson. How we treat the ones we love is our business. Don't presume to take the same liberties if you're not one of the gang. He got off lucky. When you're down in the hood, you better not call a spade a spade unless you're a spade.

An early wrap for me (9:30 P.M.). For the first time in many days, Bill didn't have to ask me to forgo my twelve-hour turn around. Maybe I'll get some good sleep tonight.

Thursday, December 19

Well, I got a *little* sleep. More than usual. Anyway, I went to work feeling plenty chipper. Today I'm going to have to face up to dying. For most of the day that's what I'll be doing, over and over again. And then, tomorrow, I'll have to do it some more, so it's good that I've got some cheerful energy going. Or maybe the reason I have that energy is because I know I'll need it.

The way the fight works, I never give Uma an opportunity to launch an offensive of her own. She never even gets the chance to get her sword out of the scabbard. I keep her on the defensive with lightning slashes of my Hanzo sword, and she's hard put to keep up, while every move I make is an attempt to cut her in half, all of which she barely escapes. Finally, I disarm her and her sword sails across the garden, helped out by a little wire-pulling on the part of Scott and his crew. Uma's left defenseless. With great regret, I prepare to deliver the killing blow.

Quentin tells me to stop time here, stretch out the moment. The result is a quantum space, when time just ceases to exist. Then, after a small eternity, the Universe starts up again, and Bill thrusts home, aiming for her heart, his own heart breaking; but that's how it is with warriors, I guess.

Uma avoids death in the neatest way, which I won't tell you here. I want you to go see the movie, if you haven't already. And then, she does me in, almost delicately, with hardly any effort, in sharp contrast to the all-out slashing blades that preceded the moment.

We did all this I can't tell you how many times, from many different angles. Uma delivers the death blow (Pai Mei's "Five-point-palm explod-

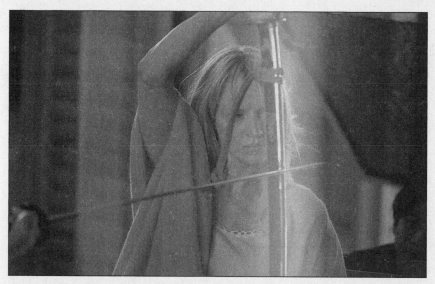

Uma wields a sword of light *DAVID CARRADINE*

ing heart technique." I can tell you that: It's been in so many magazines, and on the Web). Tap-tap-tap-tap-tap, and, at the fifth tap, I'm supposed to lose it. The first couple of takes, as I'm reacting, I inhale some of the movie blood I'm holding in my mouth. I actually choke. The camera keeps rolling, while I go through a paroxysm of a coughing fit. I must look like I'm dying for real. It takes a minute or two before I can talk, and then only with great effort. Quentin talks me through it, in between coughs, encouraging me, with great tenderness, to go on: careful to avoid stepping on my gasps and choking spells. These are great takes.

Finally, though, I figure out how to avoid actually strangling on the blood, and we do a few more with me under better control. The fifth time, or sixth (or twentieth, I can't really remember; it all runs together in my mind, as I'm now *acting* as though I'm choking my lungs out), Quentin says, "Now, get it together. Wipe the blood off your mouth." I do that. "Give me that smile," he says. "*That* smile." I don't know what that is, but people have been asking for it for years, and I sometimes seem to be able to deliver it. Not always, because I can't really smile on cue. If I try to fake a smile, it looks a little like I'm trying to be cheerful at a funeral.

So, I give it my best. Maybe it'll work. After all, this *is* a funeral. It's a strange moment: eerie, and beautiful. It's all very beautiful, this dance of death we're doing.

And that's the day. Mercifully, Quentin calls a wrap, and I go wash up. Hell of a day. *Great* day.

Friday, December 20

The last day? Well, yes. It looks like we're going to make it. No one can see how we have more work left than we can get done in one long day. Of course, no one can predict Quentin. He could come up with a whole new scenario. Uma and I report to our stations. We will sit in our big teak chairs opposite each other, and she will administer the Five-point-palm exploding heart technique to me perhaps twenty, or forty times more. My chest over my heart is a little sore, but fittingly so. I can't walk away from this scene without some pain; it wouldn't be right. Bob's camera circles around us, shooting from every possible angle, including overhead, while Uma pokes me and I spit up blood. And then, in a sort of ultimate fatal calm, we exchange our last words, before I stand up and walk to my—well, Bill's death. It's a love scene. No doubt about that. I always knew it would be. Uma is just fantastic. Her intensity is total, her compassion enormous. And then, she laughs, like a teenage girl. Captivating. Quentin is so happy with what's unfolding that he is quiet, his usual exuberance overcome by the gravity of the scene, and maybe by the realization of his three-year-old dream's rushing to its conclusion. At one point, as I'm squeezing out my last words, my own real emotions in turmoil—between love, regret, courage, elegance, all kinds of conflicting stuff, plus choking on the fake blood—Uma reaches out and touches my hand. Quentin jumps on that. He orders up an insert of our hands, and we play out a heartbreaking little story with our fingertips. Quentin calls it "a whole other movie."

He tells me I will stand, straighten my jacket—"a gentleman to the end"—and then walk away and simply keel over in the grass. He demonstrates, doing a fall like a soft oak tree, if you can imagine such a thing. I spend the rest of the day trying to match that fall. Each time I hit the grass . . . and hold still, trying not to breathe, while behind me, Uma as The Bride gathers herself together to go on living . . . I experience an enormous sense of peace. It's very sweet, lying there, my nose in the wet grass. Then Quentin says, "Cut," and we do it again. And again. And then, that was it. We'd killed Bill.

Suddenly, everybody gathers around. The entire crew, including people I've never seen before, come drifting in. Like animals before an earthquake, they know. Quentin stands in the center of it all, and yells, "This is a wrap on the picture for David Carradine!" Thunderous applause ensues, and some comments from the gallery, which are drowned out by the clapping and shouting that is going on. When the noise dies down a little, just a little, I yell out, "A likely story!" And Quentin says, "Well, maybe there'll be a couple of pickups." The applause starts again, mingled with a lot of laughter. Then he grabs me and whispers something in my ear, something so sweet it makes me blush. I stumble away, and bump into Daryl, with a big scar on her forehead. I hope it's makeup.

Yes, they have some other stuff to do tonight. A valiant effort to kill this location in time for Christmas. I go back to my palatial trailer—or try to, well-wishers stopping me every few feet to . . . well, wish me well. I get out of my costume—hardly a costume anymore, really. These are my own clothes now. Almost worn out already.

I wander back in to find the crew shooting a samurai sword flying through the air on a wire. I seek out Scotty, the property man, and recover my guitar. He tells me he's going to put a box in the trunk of the car with some goodies. I thank him, but that scarcely expresses how I feel about *all* of this. I find Manny, and we go back out to get the wig off. We talk as we perform this ritual for (perhaps) the last time. Reliving some of the times we've had together. I stash away the jewelry I bought yesterday for Annie. (I know. This sounds like we're running down here, but we are, aren't we?)

Manny asks me if I'm going back in. I say, "Of course, for a little bit." So, I do. I light up a Cuban Montecristo No. 5 (my favorite), figuring I'll stay as long as the cigar lasts. The shooting has ended. There's a cocktail party going on with about fifty people. Music blares. The lights are turned low, and a neon Christmas tree hangs blinking up above the sky cyclorama, alternating with a shimmering martini glass. Very disco. I find myself a root beer and circulate with my stogie. Quentin is over by the open bar, talking and talking to some people I don't know. Uma has vanished. Oh, there's Daryl. She sure is pretty. Everybody wants to shake my hand. That's cool. Blair finds me and asks when I want to leave. I say anytime. He takes that to mean "later," and walks off. Not what I meant at all. Cocktail parties don't hold much appeal for me. And when a movie is over, it's over. But I don't want to squash Blair's fun, either. As I notice the Montecristo getting short and tasting harsh (the root beer is long gone), I get an idea. I track Blair down among the revelers, and say, "How about you drive me to the hotel, drop me off, come back here, and pick me up in about an hour. I still have to pack."

That's what we do. In my room, I put The Red Shoe Diary DVD into my laptop and watch that, more or less, while I stuff all my shit into the bags. Blair shows up with one of those luggage gurneys just at the right time. "They're still boppin' in there," he says, with his down-under brogue. I tell him I couldn't handle it, no way. He says neither could he. So we're in synch. We pack it all in the car. There's a lot. Plus, Scotty has slipped into the backseat the fabulous two-gun rig; a real, honest-to-God, *sharp,* steel Hanzo samurai sword; and all the copies of the Silent Flute that he made in case we were going to do the fight with it.

So that's it. I'm off to home. Picture in the can. The point being, a great picture, I think. Maybe my best work to date. On film, anyway. Probably nothing will ever beat *The Royal Hunt of the Sun* on Broadway, but I knew that back then, didn't I? And that was on a different planet. Theater can't compare with movies, in spite of what all the dilettantes say. Parading around in front of an audience is fun and all that, but carving something in stone for future generations, with a camera looking right through you to your fucking bare soul is something else entirely. Hey, I'm jazzed. I could lie down right now and die happy, if I didn't have Annie to go home to.

I'm outta here.

December 31

Q,

My head is still spinning. After spending a small eternity waiting to be killed, and finally released back into my own mad, though humdrum by comparison, "real" life, I am nothing but pining for those days with the Band Apart. Well, that's predictable. You told me, in our first meeting— well, not our first, but the first about this movie—in that fifties rock & roll Thai restaurant, that there has to be a romance between a director and his actor. Well, yes, Quentin, my friend, I love you.

Your act, Maestro, is the best yet, in my book. All your ego trips and personal prejudices aside, strip away all the poses, all the routines, and even the truly hip aspects of your *band-apartness:* Your genius, and that's what it's got to be, has, apparently, no bounds. I hate the idea of seeming to be one of the foolishly dedicated worshippers who surround your amazing energy, and, I hastily add, I'm not; but I've got you under my skin, like a teenage girl with her favorite pop star. Oh, where is my cynical, or at least objective, perspective when I need it? You know, I have my own kingdom to run, and it's huge, and equally worshipful, and filled with syco-phants and *Troll people,* and among the millions, at least thousands and thousands of whom are into me for all the wrong reasons. The point being, I really don't want to seem to be one of those of yours; but I just can't find anything wrong with how you do it.

I'm called, by most of the dilettante critical mafia, those that don't hate me, a "great instinctive actor." Well, that just shows I'm actually bet-ter at it than they think, because, as I'm sure you've figured out by now, as a performer I'm like a cabinetmaker, totally analytical, and actually hide-bound to my techniques, invisible though they may be to observers of the final product. It's actually a bummer to me, though editors love it, that I can't help but match what I did on the last take, or the other angle, that my sense of order takes precedence over my love of Chaos. You stripped away some of that, and shoved me over the edge into unknown territory. Delicious, I'd have to say the experience was.

I, for sure, gave you all I've got in this movie. I wish I could have given you more. I fervently wish for another chance someday. Make that someday soon.

And while we're on the subject of falling in love, I am absolutely smitten with, and by, Uma. No one needs to tell you that you have found, and released, a monster actress. Awesome. Some dumb young journalist who crossed the great water and climbed the stairs at the White Lotus Temple to hang out with us there was gushing at me in between takes about her (and you, of course). He wondered how you two did it. I told him that, well, you both have very big brains. That wasn't enough for him. He sort of said, *"Duh."* So I told him, "Well, intelligence is a handy thing to have, if you're into wanting to be a genius."

So, enough of this shameless adoration shit. I can't wait to see some of this epic we collaborated on. Please bring me around anytime you want to show any of it.

Oh, lest I forget, there's Bob. Boy, you sure can find them. I've worked with some of the best cameramen, from Tacky Fujimoto to Hassle Wexler. Those guys, even Sven Nykvist, are, by comparison with little Bobby, old farts, and probably always were.

This little bag of supércool warrior coffee is a gift from Rob Moses, who, you will be at least a little glad to hear, is doing exceptionally well on the big island of Hawaii, where his status as one of the truly great kung fu masters of our time is being recognized, and where his massive humility is swept aside, while gorgeous Wahinas and Big Kahunas alike pay him the adoration which is his due. I miss the dude. For twenty years(!), I've walked beside him, laughing and learning. God knows where I'll ever find a replacement for him. Probably won't. He is one of a kind.

Here now, as the smallest token to repay you for one of the sweetest (though most interminable) episodes of my life, something that will interest you. A friend of mine, a very good friend, has in his possession some footage you would surely be interested in seeing. It would be as much a gift to me as to you, and you should meet this guy anyway. He's another unsung hero, and I know you revere such people. The only catch (and it's not really much of a hitch; it actually makes the thing more juicy): It's a *secret*. You can't tell anyone about it.

What he has is a considerable amount of cut footage, both on tape and in 35 mm, of *The Other Side of the Wind,* Orson Welles' unfinished multileveled murder mystery starring John Huston. I viewed some of it, years ago, when the fat guy was still with us, and the little I saw was deliciously mad awesome Orson. If you want (am I kidding?), I could arrange a private screening in your "church."

Good-bye now, for now.

Please finish this *Bill* thing up quickly, and get started on another one.

Love, Baby. I miss you all.

Your

David

Tarzana

December 31, 2002

Sometime in January 2003— It's not over yet!

I've lost track.

Well, Quentin was right: A few pickups were in order. I got a garbled set of instructions, but it was clear that I was to show up at a little movie lot in Culver City today for some stuff. Blair showed up in a Ford SUV. I guess at the end of the shoot Town Cars are no longer in the budget.

I climbed into the makeup trailer, but there was nobody there. Then Dawn, the AD, popped her head in and told me that they were only interested in me from the neck down today. Okay. So I checked out the set to see what that was all about.

Inserts were what they were doing. My hands, pouring a shot of tequila, for starters. Then me picking up a toy gun from the floor. It had to be the right floor. They had built a section of hacienda veranda just for this purpose.

Then we got down to the good stuff. I had to load my single-action Colt .45. I'm very good at that. Where does this stuff go into the movie? I asked, interested in matching. But it doesn't fit into anything we've done. It's all new. These are cutaways of Uma driving to our final meeting, of my preparations for her arrival. Pour a shot, load my gun. Then we did a series of holstering the gun.

Quentin wasn't sure which fancy return I showed him was his favorite, so we would shoot them all. I stood on my mark and practiced while Quentin went off to do something. Did about thirty tries, maybe more. Some of them were great. Some of them were not great. A few of them were pure magic—just a very few, though.

I said to Bob, who was still at the camera throughout this, "Well, we're going to have to do a lot of takes."

He said, "I shot all of those."

"Huh?"

"Yeah, it's all on film. We'll have to do it again for Quentin, but it's in the camera."

Cool. That meant the pressure was off; I could relax. Quentin came back and I gave him a bunch more. Some great ones. And it was a wrap. I wore the costume home. Helen, the costumer, wasn't too sure about that, but I assured her that if the clothes were needed again, they were safer with me than anyplace else.

I hang on to stuff. Back in '85, when we were putting together *Kung Fu: The Movie* at Warner Brothers, they asked me how Caine should be costumed. I said, "Just like always—the funny hat, the leather coat with the fur down the front, the work shirt with the mandarin collar, the bag over my shoulder, the bamboo flute." They said, "We don't have any of that stuff anymore." I said, "I know. Not a problem. I have a set."

A couple of years later, the Smithsonian talked to me about displaying the outfit. It would have been a nice tax write-off. I hung on to it, though. Sure enough, it came in handy again on *Kung Fu, The Legend Continues,* when we did a flashback to the Old West. I still have it all. The Smithsonian will get it when I can't jump anymore.

Monday, January 6

This was to be my true last day on the picture.

Well, we would see.

I had a late call, which kept being revised. Finally, Blair showed up at one. On the way, creeping along the 405 Freeway, we got a call from production. Quentin was restless, saying, "Let's shoot something!" Fine, talk to the traffic about it. I remarked to Blair that they should have just called me in early; the set is a great place to hang out. We rolled into the studio at three, right on time for our call. This was yet another tucked-away movie lot. They'd built a few half-assed sets for these pickups.

First up was a room with yellow art-deco wallpaper, for a telephone conversation with Daryl. In the script it had been a scene with Daryl hovering over Uma's comatose form in the hospital room, contemplating pulling the plug on her. She gets a call from Bill, ordering her to abort the mission. But you don't hear or see Bill. While Quentin was on hiatus, he'd written the other side of the scene. You will hear my voice, but all you see of me is my hand caressing the hilt of a Hanzo sword and my knee, viewed around the corner of a wingback leather chair.

I remarked to Quentin that this shot paid homage to about a hundred film noirs, from *Citizen Kane* and on down. Like the guy with the cat in his lap in one of the James Bonds. He said, "Yeah! Yeah! You're right!"

They dialed up Daryl at home, to do the other side of the conversation. I said, "Hi," and she said, "I thought I was wrapped on this picture." I said, "Yeah, it's *The Never-Ending Story,* isn't it?" We tried a couple of takes, Quentin directing me to play upon the sword with my fingers, pull it out of the sheath slightly, and then slap it back in at an appropriate moment. He added that it would be good if the sound of the sword hitting home came over the dialogue.

"You know," I said, "there's a sword somewhere with a devil's head [Bill's symbol] engraved into the blade. Wouldn't that be good here?"

"Yeah," Quentin said. "Let's get it." There followed a flurry of activity, ending with, "It can't be found." Bummer.

"I'm sorry I brought it up," I said.

"No, no," Quentin said. "We should have it."

"Well," I said, "it's never been seen, and this is our last chance." Someone came up to me and said, "You took a sword home. Was that the one?"

"No. I checked the blade this morning." (Examining the sharpening I had given it the night before: pretty keen it was.) "I don't have it."

"So, where is it?" Quentin asked, pretty loud. "Find it!"

We took a break. I chatted with Daryl for a while on the phone. She was about to leave with my brother Keith to drive up to Telluride, Colorado. They had to be there for a hearing to try to block a road from going through their properties there. They own two hundred acres or so each of pristine wilderness, with a lake—a private lake—between them. Wouldn't be anything like private anymore if they put that road in. Developers were sure to follow, like jackals. I hope they succeed in blocking it.

Then I wandered over to props to talk to Scotty about the sword. He had been gone, working on another picture in the interim. He said a bunch of stuff was missing. Oh, oh. The scavengers have started in.

Someone came up to me, a big lion of a man with hair to his shoulders. He had a piece of sculpture, a bas-relief that my dad had done in 1951. I remembered it. The subject was my big stepbrother, Mike. I'd watched Dad working on it in his garage. It was probably the last thing he did; the arthritis in his hands was really bad by then. This guy had found it in a house he'd bought, so he gave it to me. I'll maybe ransom it to Mike. Maybe not. Finders keepers?

They called us back. No sword. "We're going with the one we've got," Quentin said. "You can still see the devil's head that's on the scabbard. That's enough."

We do a few takes. Quentin says, "I want you to do this sort of like John Wayne." He laughs. "Not . . . totally. I don't mean . . . Well, you know what I mean."

"Sure," I say. I give him as perfect an imitation of The Duke as I know how, which is pretty good. Everybody laughs. Quentin especially. "I didn't mean ex*act*ly!" Of course he didn't. But I could see now how it would work. I give him a few more takes, with just a hint of The Duke, Quentin tweaking me all the time. I love being tweaked by him. You understand, all this care is going into a shot of my hand, with Daryl on the phone long-distance, and they're not recording her.

Finally, Quentin calls it quits. There's a pretty blonde girl sitting behind him with a big smile on her lovely face. I say, "It must have been good. She's grinning."

"Who?" Quentin says.

"Her." Pointing.

He turns and looks behind him. The girl smiles again. So sweet. "Oh, her!" And he laughs again. "Yeah. You must be good."

I said good-bye to Daryl, told her it was great talking to her. Bill, the AD, got on to tell her she was (again) officially wrapped on the picture. The crew gave her an accolade over the phone.

Then we moved on to a close-up of Uma, in her sleeping bag, with a little piece of the campfire set from my very first day in Beijing. She had turned back into a teenager again, giggling, with her hair in that cute ponytail.

The guys who were handling the campfire were special effects dudes I'd worked with a few times in the past. One of them went all the way back to *Shane.* That would be about thirty-seven years. I remarked that he must have been about ten years old.

There was a debate about how much of Uma's breast had been exposed in Beijing. Then another question arose about exactly when in the scene I had bopped her in the head with the Silent Flute. Quentin was irritated that the information was not readily available. "Well," he asked, "where's the video then?" "Not here," someone said. "Get it."

"Kill the campfire," someone yelled. The special effects men turned down the gas. We all took a break. I stood up and stretched. I was feeling really kinky.

Uma was thinking. After looking over my script, she volunteered her idea of when in the scene she thought the action had happened.

"That's not the point," Quentin said patiently. "It should be here."

After a pause, the info arrived. Uma had been right on. Well, of course. Her pretty blonde head remembered perfectly well what I was saying when it had been repeatedly whacked with a bamboo pole.

The special effects guys started up the fire again, and we started shooting. I was off-camera, retelling the five-page bedtime story and playing the Silent Flute while Uma reacted and threw a couple of lines. I had the script in my lap, but after the first take it all came back to me and I never referred to the pages.

The flute was working much better since I'd relacquered it in Lancaster. The sound department put a mike right on it. I hope they use some of it.

After it was over, I collected some of my things from wardrobe and props. I almost got away with another Hanzo sword, but Lawrence Bender walked into the prop truck and put a damper on that. I gave him my pitch about how my house was the safest place for this stuff, but he stayed firm. He told me to tag what I wanted, and I'd see it when the movie was finished. That would be after Mexico. I'll never see that sword. Things disappear at the end of a movie, particularly in Mexico.

Out on the tarmac, I ran into Quentin. He was very excited about a new idea he and Harvey Weinstein have come up with. Since everyone's afraid the movie will be too long, coming in at 160 minutes only if Quentin cuts the shit out of it, the mind-bending solution they've postulated is to release it as two 90-minute movies, the second to be released five weeks or so after the first.

This would be awesome! After all, this movie is a paean to exploitation revenge flicks of all kinds—kung fu, samurai, spaghetti Western, Japanese anime; I think that covers it (oh, well: love story, yeah). And ninety minutes is how all of those genres tend to run, except for the Sergio Leone masterpiece *Once Upon a Time in the West,* which runs to three hours, and we could go that way, too.

But to release two short pictures, the second one right on the heels of the first—that's hot! Everyone would come to the first one, and they'd all be back for seconds, and bring their friends.

Quentin also told me about a scene he'd always wanted to shoot between Daryl and me, but which didn't fit into the one-big-movie format.

That would be so cool! Except for the phone conversation I did today, I never got to work with Daryl on this picture. And in that conversation, it had been revealed (sort of) that we are lovers, so a scene between us would be a natural. And it would deal with just that: how we became lovers. Well, I figured, we'll see what happens.

I hung around while the crew ate dinner, just because I hated to leave. I love Hollywood crews. Finally, after many hugs, we pulled out.

I'm waiting now for the Cannes Film Festival. I can't imagine how Quentin could have the picture (or pictures) finished by then. No. No way. It's just two months away, and he's still shooting. But the presence will be there for sure. And so will I, the gods being willing and my schedule permitting.

Tuesday, February 18

Well, Annie and I just got back from a very sweet weekend in San Francisco, celebrating St. Valentine's Day, where we narrowly avoided getting caught up in the 200,000-strong rally to protest the proposed invasion of Iraq. We went window-shopping instead at Neiman Marcus, and had a caviar snack at the St. Francis Hotel. I suppose that blows my public image, but an antiwar protest march is not my idea of how to spend Valentine's Day, or any other day, for that matter.

In my fax machine was today's call sheet, outlining what they're shooting right now in Costa Careyes, Mexico. So, the saga continues.

volume
two

功夫

Thursday, February 27

Have been informed that the picture officially wrapped yesterday—155 days, 840,300 feet of film, by official count, though I've been told it was actually only a mere 740,300; I don't know how the discrepancy comes about. Even so, with the "frugal" three-perf process we used, according to my calculations, that would be the equivalent of 983,733 feet of regular-ass 35 mm, or about 23,629,582 separate images, and 6,564 minutes. Quentin has to get rid of just under 106 hours to get it down to a 3-hour movie. (Can that be right?)

None of this would be a record, but I suspect it's probably in the top ten or so. I think the all-time record is probably held by *Roar*, a wild animal epic starring Tippi Hedrin, her daughter Melanie Griffith, and lots of beasts that filmed for several years and was never to my knowledge released anywhere. They shot almost a million and a half feet of film. I had an editing suite at MGM while it was being made, and boxes marked "ROAR" were everywhere. All the hallways were lined with stacks of them. For sheer volume, it beat even *Heaven's Gate,* but we won't go into that.

I had a telephone interview with my old friend Marilyn Beck, the syndicated columnist, yesterday. I haven't talked to her for years. She bailed me out of trouble a couple of times in the past.

This time, though, she got me *into* trouble. I blabbed to her about the idea for the two ninety-minute movies. When the article appeared—*syndicated* in five hundred newspapers across the country—the folks at Miramax went ballistic. Hey, nobody said it was supposed to be a secret. But the problem was the way I said it. We were talking about how the script is two hundred pages, and how long the shoot was, and how I was finally wrapped a month or two over schedule, and I said, "I probably shouldn't say this, but, what the hell, they can't fire me," and blurted out the little secret. And she printed it, just like that. So, the folks at Miramax could see that I at least guessed I shouldn't be talking about it. And the "can't fire me" bit sounded like a "fuck you" to them. I just hope this doesn't make them back off from using me to publicize the picture. I don't want to miss out on the fun.

I got a message from Lawrence Bender to call him at home. I did so, with great trepidation. He was cool, though. I told him about my ancient relationship with Marilyn, and how she'd saved my ass once or twice. And it wasn't like she's a tabloid queen. She's the real thing, with a big heart. Lawrence said, "Yeah, yeah. Look, I know you love Quentin, and everybody loves him, but they're always ready to trash him, too. And if he decides not to do the two-part thing, he'll look bad." I was now part of Quentin's family, and the media is *not* part of that family, he pointed out. "I know you were just kidding around, but you just can't say stuff like that," he said, as though he were talking to a child.

Well, I qualify.

I said, "Okay, I'll be more guarded." He jumped on that. "No! We don't want you to be guarded. You've got a great way of saying what you feel. We want that! Just don't get into that stuff. Talk about the shoot, and Quentin, and how much fun it was, or how hard it was, if you want to. Look, Quentin won't care; he's his own loose cannon, and he says what he thinks. It's Miramax. They're flipping over there. Anybody asks you about it again, tell them you were just kidding around."

Well, okay, folks. I was just kidding around.

March 3

Harvey Weinstein

Miramax

Dear Harvey,

Please accept my apologies for any uneasiness I may have caused you. I certainly understand your concern, and please believe I have nothing but goodwill toward the project. My long relationship with Marilyn Beck put me off my guard, I guess. I think of her as an old friend, who has been very kind to me. I felt I wanted to throw her something good, and my enthusiasm for the picture is difficult to contain. Lawrence has pointed out to me that the media . . . is the media.

I only regret that I was not informed of the need for secrecy. Trust me to be more cautious in the future.

Your supporter as always,

David Carradine

Somehow, the letter kicked around the house for almost a week before it went out. I hope it does the trick. Harvey's not someone you want to be mad at you. Not because he's scary, which he is, but because he can be a good friend.

Saturday, March 8

Found a notice in my fax machine on Thursday. There will be a wrap party for the cast and crew tonight. This bash had been put together at the last minute. I was eager to go. Be great to see everybody. I envisioned an over-the-top performance by Quentin, and some cool moves by Lawrence. And to see Uma and Daryl, and Michael Madsen, if he deigned to show, would be very sweet.

Trying to figure out what to wear, I pulled out the pale beige pinstripe Kenzo cotton suit I'd bought in Hong Kong, which looks like Paris in the twenties. Annie accidentally matched my act with a soft off-white outfit.

The gala was at a hotel in downtown L.A., an old structure built like a hacienda, with an inner courtyard surrounding a pool, next to an outside bar. It felt just like a Mexican resort. And the weather helped. Los Angeles was putting on its best winter face. I wondered how this place could survive down here in the inner city, until I remembered all the artists with studios in the warehouse buildings.

We ran into Bo Svenson outside having a smoke, and talked to him for a while before we went in. He has become the nicest guy. I guess underneath the booze-fighter facade, he always was. He had another idea for a documentary that he pitched to us, a very fresh idea that could work.

Inside, madness prevailed. There wasn't much food, which was a disappointment for Annie, who is always hungry, but I remarked to myself, and to a few others, that it was nice to be at a party where I knew some of the people. Right away, we ran into Scott, the prop man, and then Heba, the genius makeup artist. We found Lawrence in the midst of the crowd, being very smooth and friendly as always, and Daryl.

We turned out to be the best-dressed couple at the party, and the only ones in bright outfits except for Daryl, who was blissfully the worst-dressed, in a baggy yellow jumpsuit with huge pockets everywhere, looking like an incredibly sexy highway worker.

Michael Madsen gave me a hug so big and long it left me breathless. Michael Jai White, looking extremely handsome, had as his date a six-foot black lady, who was absolutely stunning—a very large being, with an aura that filled the room. We circled around several times and had a few smokes outside, until we discovered the inner room, where everyone was defying the law. It was full of tough-looking guys. That's where we found Mike Bowen (of course). He walked up to me and said, "Where's the men's room?" I waved my arm toward the collection of bad-asses there and said, "This is it, Bro." When he didn't laugh, I took pity on him and pointed the way. The reason for his seriousness was that he was looking for Christen, his angel of a wife. We were recruited to tell her he had gone to the restroom.

Bill, the AD, came up about then, grinning, as he always is. I always introduce him as "the real Bill."

There was a rumor that there would be a video presentation of outtakes, so we hung around in anticipation of that. They were waiting for Quentin to arrive. But at around 1 A.M. he still hadn't shown up, so we thought about going home. We ran into Bo again, and he told us there was also a problem with the video, so it might not happen at all. I thought, It would if Quentin were here. He'd just say, "Fix it!" We split, though. I heard later from someone that he had shown up at 4 A.M. No way we could have lasted that long, unless we'd reserved a room. The bummer about all these evening obligations is that they interfere with our love life.

Monday, March 17

Great night. Showed up at the ArcLight, formerly the Cinerama Dome, to see the premiere of a new movie: *Spun*. Did the red carpet thing with a wild northeast wind kicking up around Annie and me. Totally un-Southern California in character. Those are going to be some wild-haired pictures.

The movie was brilliant, and awful. No-holds-barred, cutting edge, all that. Moments that were almost transcendental and others that shook you by the balls. Ugly, gross, scary. Took no prisoners. Then sometimes almost sweet. The sexy parts were handled in a mundane way that made them seem even kinkier. One moment, and one only, of incredible beauty. "Spun" means, apparently, "high on crank," the amphetamine that's cooked up out of diet pills.

Every performance was right on, but Mickey Rourke walked away with the picture. He was magnificent and hilarious as the Crank Cooker. Played an absolute prick and did it with the power and majesty of a lion, and went out in, literally, a blaze of glory at the end.

The whole thing left everyone in a very hyper state. In front of the theater, we all hung out while the limos collected the stars. No one could just walk away; the movie had grabbed them all. This was a predominantly young crowd with, I suspect, a personal attachment to the material. We stood there in the midst with James, my publicist, and talked with several people we knew and some we didn't. I have many admirers in this age group, largely because of my outlaw pose, I think. Then Maria Ferrara whipped around the corner in a Lincoln Town Car, looking hot with her Cherokee-influenced cheekbones. I've heard it said that the reason there are so many part-Cherokee people in Oklahoma is because the Cherokee women were of remarkable beauty. I'd have to agree (and so did my great-great-grandfather, or so I'm told). Maria whisked us away to an after-party being given by the superhip magazine *Flaunt* (well, superhip for some—you have to be interested in smoky photographs of naked guys) at the Ivar Club, a place we'd been to before for one of these things. Very young-cool-hip, of course, and loud.

I found Francis Coppola in a quiet corner amid the rock & roll madness. You don't see the old master at many of these things, but this was a special occasion for him: His nephew was the star of the picture. I hadn't spoken to Francis in almost thirty years. Had a long chat with him. We talked about children and houses. He asked me how I was doing. I said, "Great," of course. Told him I'd had some slings and arrows, but now was good. He's got to know about *Kill Bill,* but we didn't talk about it. He asked me where I was living. I told him too far out, that I wanted to move into town. He said, "Here, or New York?" I said, "No, just over the hill, to where the lights are." Then he wanted to know how many children I had living with me. I said five. He said I needed a big place. I said, "No kidding, plus room for all my shit: music and art and movies." I said I'd read somewhere that he didn't want to direct anymore. He told me he'd never said that—never would. He promised me he wouldn't give up directing. Said he's writing. That would mean screenplays.

He's made movies that will last for generations. I told him so, told him how they get better with the years. Just sitting there in the bottle, they develop character and finish, like some of his fine vintages. I asked him how you do that. He said, "You don't. It just happens. You have the right people around you and it just comes together." I thought of all the troubles he had on *The Godfather* and *Apocalypse Now.* Cooperation doesn't seem to me to be Francis' big strength.

"So you can't do it on purpose," I said.

"No," he said. "I can't."

Bullshit, I would say (though I didn't). It's clear to me that when he's on his game, he just won't stop until he surpasses himself. Dragging everyone along with him, and hocking everything he owns to get to the end of it. No one else does that. Well, Cassavetes—his mentor—did. That figures, doesn't it? I should have told him how great *Godfather III* was. He took a lot of abuse about that picture, in spite of its getting nominated for Best Picture. But I didn't. Didn't tell him, damn it. Reason being right then Nicolas Cage came in to pay his respects, and my audience was pretty much over. Talia Shire was there, as was Francis' granddaughter and a few other obvious family members. They all radiated reverence for the old guy. He's a much nicer man than he used to be. Humble—maybe humbled. Not that I didn't love him back then. But he's more of a human now, like Marlon's Godfather in the last half hour of the movie.

Sunday, March 23

The Academy Awards are back. We did the obligatory "Night of a Hundred Stars" at the Beverly Hills Hotel, and then went to the *Vanity Fair* party. In past years I've crashed that one a couple of times. It's always the best party. For once, I was invited, thanks to James Selman of Rogers & Cowan. It was an absolute blast. Best party I've been to in years, maybe ever. Its only close competition would be the premiere of *The Empire Strikes Back* in London, which I attended with Brother Bobby on our way home from the Cannes festival, where we'd been for the premiere of *The Long Riders*. We were greeted by one of the princesses — Margaret, I think. Alec Guiness and Ringo were there. Dino De Laurentiis was sitting in a corner, with one of his daughters beside him. Many luminaries. It was a pretty great affair, but this one tonight was over the top. Everybody who'd won or been nominated, *ever,* was there. And it was a *smoking* party, in blatant defiance of the California Legislature and the whole New Age community. Ashtrays everywhere.

Harvey Weinstein was hosting his own party across town, but there can't have been anyone there — his people were all here: Lucy Liu, Daryl, a bunch of winners from *Chicago.* I lit a cigarette for Peter O'Toole, who had received a Lifetime Achievement Award that night, and he told me he knew my father, and Barbara. I told him that relationship, as soon as our son was grown, went up in smoke — and, as punctuation, did my fireball magic trick for him. He loved it; his jaw just hung open. Right then he must have decided I was okay, because he got very friendly and talked a blue streak, sitting on a bar stool, feeling very much at home, looking a lot like my dad: same pose, his legs crossed, elbow on the bar, head thrust forward, same painfully skinny frame and long face, same loud voice, pretty much the same Irish-English diction. I said something about *The Savage Innocents,* a movie by Nicholas Ray, with Peter as a Mountie in the Far Arctic coming after an Eskimo, played by Tony Quinn. Peter told me all that had been shot at Pinewood Studios, in London, at 100 degrees, and the snow was salt. Absolute hell, he said. Exactly the story I could have told him about Uma's samurai fight with Lucy Liu in Beijing: salt-snow on a soundstage, 100 degrees. Movies are movies, I guess. We stopped in at Harvey's party. He was holding court in the middle of a small crowd. He was sweet, and told me not to worry about the publicity thing. No big deal, you're great in the movie, we love you, etc. A good night.

May 18, 2003

So, to backtrack a little, the plans to premiere the picture at the Cannes festival are, of course, off. And, to boot, they haven't even prepared a promo reel. Miramax has Quentin locked up in the editing room to get the film ready for the Toronto festival in September. Even that will be a tough date to meet, with all the elements he has to wrangle together.

Very disappointing to Annie and me. Cannes would have been a gas. Of course, we could go on our own; I've certainly done that enough over the years, and it always works out. But until this damn renaissance gets rolling, money is pretty tight. Even more than usual, as no one in my camp wants to ruin the moment with any little exploitation films for the bucks.

I took a meeting with some French filmmakers, who have a picture about the "Rap Wars" they want me to do, which would shoot in L.A. That would be a new one for me: a European movie shot on my own turf. They gave me a treatment to read, and a brochure they'd made in the shape of a vinyl record. It all looked hot, and I liked the guys right away: a bunch of young dudes, kids really, Arab-French, what in Paris they call "Pied Noir": literally, "Black Feet." They're connected somehow with Luc Besson, which was what caught my attention in the first place. He's sort of a French Tarantino, the guy who made *La Femme Nikita,* which has become a cult classic in the United States. I actually prefer John Badham's American remake, *Point of No Return,* with Bridget Fonda, but no one else seems to share my opinion. Well, I'm hopelessly in love with Bridget, as, apparently, was John Badham, judging by the tenderness with which he photographed her.

The two Arab-French boys wanted me to participate in making a little teaser that they'd take to Cannes. They offered to bring Annie and me along as their guests. I jumped, of course, especially when they added in a few days in Paris as well. They found a couple of righteous black guys, authentic dudes from the rap scene, for me to work with, and we shot the promo in a Ferrari dealership near the house. That went, well, almost fairly well. I could see what these kids lacked in experience, they made up for in git-go. It might all work.

So, after three hot days and hot nights in Paris, Annie and I arrived in Cannes. Even though the film is not ready, and there's not even a promo reel, *Kill Bill* has a big presence here. Everyone knows about it, and the anticipation is electric.

At the big party for *Premiere* magazine, an exclusive bash on a three-story pleasure yacht parked behind the casino, I ran into Harvey, and he mentioned that if he could have hurried "Captain Q" to produce a forty-minute teaser, it would have swept the festival, especially this year, when the lineup is so wimpy. *The Hollywood Reporter* calls it "sluggish."

The last part is true enough, I guess, mainly because the clout and bravado of Hollywood is largely missing, though Nicole Kidman's performance in *Dogville* is enough sustenance for any red-blooded American male. She was just remarkable. A synthesis, or, no, an overpowering of the images of a handful of past icons: Ingrid Bergman, Grace Kelly, Merle Oberon, Ida Lupino; she knocked them all out. And for beauty: She actually made me forget about Kim Basinger and Michelle Pfeiffer. I'm hooked, I admit it. It's a strange movie, and a lot of people are not going to like it. There will undoubtedly be unfortunate wordplays on the "Dog" in the title. But no one will be anything but full of praise for Nicole. She carries the whole picture—*saves* it for me. And her presence at the screening in the Grand Palais was equally stunning: Tall as a tree, and wearing her elegant beauty as humbly as a girl at her junior prom, she gave a gracious nod to Annie, who was done up even more elegantly, and was actually the most striking lady at the event.

After the screening, in the middle of the huge, endless applause from her peers, Nicole looked over at Annie and rolled her eyes heavenward as though they were accomplices. And she gave me a special smile. That night, I received more media attention than ever before that I can remember, I think because they all took a second glance to identify the guy with that sensational gal on his arm.

Anyway, back to the *Premiere* party: Harvey went on to say that my performance in *Kill Bill* was super (I wish I could remember the exact words he used). He said, and I've remembered *these* words exactly, "It's a renaissance richly deserved." Then he walked away, raising his voice, so that everyone on the boat would hear, " Just you wait! After October, they'll be all over you. I just hope you remember my name!" Harvey's cool.

Saturday, May 24

A bunch of pictures of Annie and me from Cannes have shown up on the Web. We look great. You know, Quentin is going to love this, because, since the shoot, my hair has grown out to where it looks exactly the way it did in *Kill Bill*. Nobody who isn't reading this will be able to figure out that it's a wig.

Sunday, June 8

Okay, so here we go, yet again. After I got back from Cannes, there was a whole big to-do about my having said to someone, I think it was *The Hollywood Reporter,* that *Kill Bill* would premiere at the Toronto festival in September. This was called "revealing Miramax's market strategy," a no-no. It was cleared up fairly neatly, when I pointed out that this had been told me by one of Miramax's executives (who shall remain nameless) at a big party, within earshot of about a hundred exhibitors and at least a dozen members of the press.

Then, today, Gayle left a message on my cell phone that Miramax had faxed her in a brand-new huff because they had received a request for permission to use some photos in the release of a DVD version of my video instructional tapes.

Apparently, I must rely on Miramax to find their own outlets and distribute pictures as they alone see fit. Well, damned if I want some stranger deciding which photo is going to represent me to the media, etc. I'm not so photogenic that you can just shove any shot of me into somebody's hands, and, besides, I have spent many hours touching up the things in Photoshop on my laptop. My prints are a lot better than theirs.

Anyway, I'm in fucking Dutch with them again. This is becoming tiresome. And I'm getting just a little pissed off. I haven't been scolded like this since I got out of high school. Not even in the Army did I get this kind of high-handed treatment. I wanted to say, "Who the hell do you think you are? I'm an international icon, a legend, or so I'm told (fortunately, living), with a career spanning over forty years (almost fifty if you count the Little Theater and the Shakespearean repertories), and I'm twenty years older than any of you. And you're treating me like a schoolboy. Show me some goddamn respect!"

Well, I couldn't really say all that. Too strong, even for me. So, to get it out of my system, I sent off a much calmer letter to James at Rogers & Cowan—not to Miramax, you understand; to James, my handler at R&C. Just to get it off my chest. He can do with it what he wishes. Or not. But I feel a lot better for having written it. And it may serve to give friend James and those folks there at R&C a little backbone.

Here it is.

June 6, 2003

To whom it may concern,

So much static from Miramax. The latest being: David Nakahara, an old friend (1985), who is preparing a DVD version of some of my kung fu and tai chi instructional tapes, needs some pictures relating to my career. Regarding *Kill Bill,* I told him to get in touch with Miramax for permission. The flak I got back is that I am not permitted to give out any pictures. Well, I purchased those prints, through the company and with its approval, at a cost to me of around $1,300. They are mine. And they are, anyway, readily available on the Internet. I don't understand the problem, and I can't see how it can be said that I can't give them away. That's what they are for. Andrew Cooper was not hired and paid his princely fee so that the pictures will languish in archives or in my desk drawer. Their purpose and function, as I understand it, is to promote the film. Moreover, the DVD will not be released until after *Kill Bill*'s premiere. And a retrospective of my work should surely include something from the film. It seems that won't be the case. A pity.

If every time I make a move I am going to be scolded by someone at Miramax, perhaps it would be appropriate if I were given a specific list of what will be considered transgressions of the secrecy policies of the company. I certainly have no desire to upset the makers of a film of which I am so inordinately fond.

I must say that in my forty-some years in the industry I have never before encountered this degree of security on any of my 101 films. So, educate me. Tell me what it is you want, not after the fact of an interview, but prior. The last scolding I received was right after I had done a blitz of twenty-seven interviews. Chances are at least half of them got the information in question.

I can't very well simply refuse to talk to the media, though that's pretty much what I'm doing now. I tell interviewers that I can say very little about *Kill Bill* or they will have to be killed. This is cute, and they all enjoy it, but they are left dissatisfied. Well, who cares? They're just The Press. So, fill me in. What else is it that you don't want me to do that I don't know about?

It's a new experience for me to be scolded by employees of a company working for a movie in which I'm starring. I'm accustomed to direct conversation and discussion, collaboration and complicity, suggestions and requests, not edicts and condemnations forwarded to me through third parties. It's just not polite.

I'm easy to talk to (which seems to be our problem), so talk to me.

Fondly,

David Carradine

I cc'd the letter to Gayle Max, mainly for her amusement, though partly to have a witness. I especially like the "fondly." I think that was a nice touch.

I'm really sick of this shit.

Friday, June 13

Boy, this just keeps going on and on. Miramax is now crazed by the fact that some pictures showed up on the Web, for sale. They've traced them to me. And there are a couple with other people in them—Uma, Q, Michael Jai White—which they say haven't been approved. Yes, I'm guilty as charged, but I can't really get excited about it. The ones of Uma are exquisite. Michael Jai looks like a black Hercules. And when I got the contact sheets, most of the shots with Quentin had "X"s over them. I printed the ones that didn't.

Seems to me Quentin must have approved those.

I wrote a letter to the PR department, who were causing all the trouble, and cc'd it to Lawrence, to try to set things straight, but Gayle wouldn't let me send it. She said, "Let it lie."

Monday, June 23

Okay. Here we go again. On Saturday, there was a setup for Quentin and a bunch of the cast to make a splash at the San Diego ComiCon. A whole bunch of glitches conspired to make it another one of those opportunities for my nemesis in the Miramax publicity department to wipe the floor with me. So, I got a tirade from Gayle, describing the tirade from Miramax. Supposedly, the someone-who-shall-remain-nameless (I think the guilty should be protected along with the innocent) had complained to Q and Lawrence about it all, and they too were in a tirade. I wrote a couple more letters but didn't send them.

Then Friday, I think it was, I went down to Todd-AO to do the ADR (Automatic Dialogue Replacement) for *Kill Bill*. I love ADR. Most actors hate it, but I love it. I get to fix things: screwups by the sound people (rare), a glitch in the equipment, or ambient noise, such as an airplane. And, though it's hard to do in the sterile atmosphere of a looping stage, once in a while I can actually improve on my performance. This was one of those times. Well, Quentin is one of those directors. Actually, what he wanted me for was to throw in a new line he'd thought of. Something about Daryl Hannah's seeing something "with her beautiful blue eye," underlining and playing a joke off the fact that, in the movie, she has only one of those, the other having been plucked out by the evil Pai Mei. And Q was in a great good humor, as always. Our happy, funny, and, yes, intimate relationship seemed to be intact. I wondered if anyone actually talked to him at all, or if maybe he and Lawrence just brushed it off if anyone did. They're smart enough to see through all this crap.

Over the last week, it's come out in all the mags that the picture is going to be two movies, as I've known for months. At the end of the session, Quentin broke it to me that my face is not in Volume I. My hands, yes. And my voice, and maybe my boots. No face, though, until Volume II. Very tantalizing and mysterious; a trick that will be good for the movie, I'm sure. All that anticipation. Good for me, too, in the long run, but frustrating for me right now. People who have seen the trailer, with just four seconds of me in it, are already wondering if I'm really in this movie.

Well, they'll know, soon enough for my ultimate glory, though perhaps very late for the rent. One nicety that will result from splitting the film in two is I'll get another paycheck. Should be a lot. Could be a little. We'll see. They owe me, that's for sure, with all the work I did, and all the work I lost, over ten months of indentured slavery. Whatever it is, it's found money. Meanwhile, I've got a date for lunch next Friday with Scott Melrose, my new agent. Maybe we can whip up something in the meantime.

Not that there aren't a few rustlings in the bushes: the two pictures with the crazy guys from France. There's *Blaxploitation,* about the "Rap Wars," a very Bogart kind of role: I would be talking tough and shooting up the town, and there'd be a loose woman who needs protecting somewhere off to the side. And there's something called *Ali & Baba Against the Forty Thugs*: a comedy. They want me to play the chief of the Forty Thugs in that one. Having just seen *Pirates of the Caribbean,* I think I might have fun. Play it halfway between Johnny Depp and Geoffrey Rush. And another bunch of Europeans, very pretty ones, are doing a film about a real-life World War II double agent who was Ian Fleming's inspiration for James Bond. All of these are worth doing, if the movies actually get made. *Ali & Baba* is supposed to start shooting at the end of August. We'll see.

Thursday, August 14

Today I did a phone interview with *Vogue* magazine; they're doing a piece on Uma. I had lots of good words about her to give to the guy. He was cool: a Tarantino freak. Meanwhile the carpets were being cleaned. I read the rest of *The Dark Knight Strikes Again,* the very intense graphic novel by the master, Frank Miller, about Batman and his SWAT team of juvenile delinquents taking on the whole world, even to the point of kicking the crap out of Superman. Very radical stuff. Manages to stomp all over a whole lot of sacred cows. Superman is regenerated by an aerial coupling with Wonder Woman, which results in a baby girl who combines the powers of Krypton and the Amazons. The girl then kicks a whole lot of ass. That doesn't begin to tell the story, but it'll have to do for now.

Tonight was the director's screening of *Kill Bill, Volume 1* at Studio One on "The Lot," what used to be Warner Hollywood, and before that Goldwyn Studios: a traditional secret screening place. Last time I was there was for the cast-and-crew screening of *Bound for Glory.* That was a glorious event. Hal's cut was three hours and forty minutes. It was a rhapsody. Every one of Woody's songs was there in its entirety, and Haskell Wexler's extra handheld stuff—shots of trains and migrant workers, old cars and '30s skylines—flowed like cream. Hal had invited the hot young editor of the moment, who had just finished *The Exorcist,* to the screening, and after the film he asked the kid what he should do. The kid said, "Make it longer." Later on, after he'd cut it down to two hours and twenty minutes, Hal sent it to United Artists. Mike Medavoy sent it back to Hal and asked him to put in another twenty minutes. Rare.

I got out of the house a little early; no way I was going to miss any of this. On the way, the Maserati decided to heat up, and the ammeter was showing a discharge. Damn! Well, I was not going to miss this screening. I turned off the lights to save the battery and screamed down the 101 in silhouette, like Batman, switching on now and then, whenever the situation seemed to be approaching life-threatening. Going down Laurel Canyon, I shifted into neutral and coasted, to cool the engine. The brakes were good. Made it with some minutes to spare. In the parking lot, I ran into Lawrence Bender. We greeted each other with glee, both of us supercharged with anticipation. He told me I was going to be blown away. I told him I didn't think so, as my expectations were so high that there was no way I could be surprised. I was wrong. No one is ready for *Kill Bill*. No matter how much you think you know about Tarantino or me, or martial arts movies, this one is beyond anything you've ever dreamed of. Take the idea of kung fu fighting, samurai swordplay, a spaghetti Western revenge story, a gangster picture, a tragic love story, with a certain amount of Japanese anime thrown in, and add to that, sort of as an adverb, the word "Tarantino," and you'll have some idea, but you still won't be ready for what you'll see.

I stood on the balcony having a smoke while the theater filled up with Quentin's staff of worshippers: Sally, the editor; Bumble, Quentin's publicist; a whole passel of video store junkies, just like Quentin, though undoubtedly lacking the genius. No actors. I expected to see some of the girls and Michael Madsen, maybe Michael Parks, and I thought I saw Mike Bowen, but it was someone else: some other really tough-looking Aryan biker dude, with hair down to his knees. The only actor whom I recognized was Michael (boy, this movie is just rife with Mikes) Jai White, freshly back from Japan, where he'd been working on his Chinese martial arts movie and training someone to fight KI style, tomorrow at the Bellagio Hotel in Vegas, pay-per-view.

Quentin arrived just a little late, as always, and in great spirits as always: laughing and dancing. I remarked that I wished he'd loosen up and have a little fun once in a while. He came straight for me with a big laughing bear hug (Quentin is almost always laughing; it's what he does instead of clearing his throat), and told me, "The reason you're invited is because of your status as a director. That's why you're here." Another big laugh.

But I realized he meant it. He said to Sally, the editor, "Just make sure it's LOUD," and danced up to the front, where he gave an excited little speech, mentioning the test screening in Boston a few days ago, which was a triumph. Then the lights went down.

Quentin is a genius, we all know that; and though he's a creature from outer space (like me) he's a very regular guy, with endless energy and enthusiasm, and with a great understanding of what is fun to watch on a movie screen. And Uma. Uma Thurman has become my favorite actress. As good as she's been in the past, she outdoes herself (and anyone else) in this film. She's like a female Clint Eastwood. As tough as his beard. And yet, like Clint, she's occasionally heartbreakingly sweet. And scarier than any guy I've seen in a fight. When she starts swinging that sword, she's just awesome. Daryl Hannah, in a nurse's uniform, a white patch with a red cross on it over her supposedly missing eye, her other one like a baby blue laser rifle. Lucy Liu, the ice queen; Vivica A. Fox (a great lady), just down-home and totally lovable; Julie Dreyfus, a total aristocratic beauty in three languages: The deadly Viper Squad, Bill's team of beautiful assassins. They're all great. Michael Parks is just unbelievable. Funny as hell. I had to remind myself that I know the guy, and that he's not really a good ol' boy El Paso sheriff. And Muck! My little brother, Mike Bowen. He is just totally himself, and some other guy at the same time. Incredibly bad-ass . . . and funny! Like a mean bunny rabbit on steroids.

Meanwhile, I'm dazzled by the production design, the sweep of the film, the fabulous sets we built (and utterly destroyed): all this captured magnificently on film by the award-winning cinematographer Bob Richardson (*Platoon, JFK, Snow Falling on Cedars*, to name just a few). Bob is probably the most creative movie cameraman alive today. Am I gushing enough? I could say more, and that's, *literally,* only the half of it! There's more to come: much more. This picture (*these* pictures) are going to explode.

From the first moment of funky "Shaw Brothers" credits, and a luscious song from the past by Sonny Bono about how "my baby shot me," nothing whatsoever like *I Got You Babe,* sung with great feeling by Nancy Sinatra! Then the first image hit with a slam, Uma's incredibly torn and bloody face on the floor, her bloodstained bridal veil framing her head, terrified, almost unconscious, printed in high contrast black and white. Cut to a pair of black lizard boots approaching across a rough wood floor, kicking spent cartridges out of the way. Back to Uma's frightened eyes. Then Bill's voice cuts through—low, distinguished, and gravelly: "I suppose you think this is sadistic of me." A hand, looking as though it could crush concrete, reaches in and wipes off some of the blood with a monogrammed "Bill" handkerchief.

On the soundtrack we hear the unmistakable four clicks of a Colt single-action six-shooter being cocked. Uma says, "Bill, it's your baby," trying to get it in fast. She's cut off by a big *bang* and the screen goes black. From there, the movie just takes off, not giving a moment's rest for about forty minutes. Full of surprises, jumping all over the place and back and forth in time, as is Quentin's practice. Fast, gratuitously violent in the extreme, and outrageously funny most of the time. There's a quiet, very dramatic, almost solemn space in the middle, with Sonny Chiba acting his ass off, first as a funny, bumbling sushi chef, until his true identity is revealed—that of Hittori Hanzo, the legendary master samurai swordmaker, with Uma as the sweet, innocent American tourist who's there to buy a sword from him so she can rip Bill's heart out.

Then, after a harrowing visit to Lucy Liu's troubled childhood, done in hard-core Japanese anime, we get another forty minutes of incredible action, some of it very funny, some heartbreakingly beautiful. The pretty-well-full house would laugh a lot, then be utterly silent—"hushed" is the word. Every fifteen minutes, like a commercial, Bill's hands show up, with his voice like fingernails on a blackboard played at quarter-speed. My voice used to be a trumpet. The years have turned it into a grand piano. The effect is hot. The way Patrick Culliton, the Irish sage and renowned Houdini expert, put it: "I betcha I looked at you like I've looked at the greatest magicians in the world when they have fooled the hell out of me, when they've really *done* it." He pointed out that in this movie, I'm Harry Lime in *The Third Man*. Yeah, that's it. Orson! Well, as close as I come, anyway. About a hundred people fall to Uma's Hanzo sword, and then we're treated to a totally gorgeous battle in a Japanese garden, with snow softly falling on the cedars, and before anyone is ready for it, a cliff-hanger nonending. Cut to black, and it's over.

When the lights came up, everybody was very excited, bubbling, and sort of stunned at the same time. I got a little time with Quentin—only a moment or two, as he was surrounded—but quality time, and made it back to my car, to face how I was going to get home. I called Annie right away, and told her my predicament. She came up with the solution: Stash the car at Celebrity Center, right down the street, and hitch a ride home. No way, she said, was I to drive thirty miles with my lights off.

While I was doing this, Quentin passed by with his crowd, and flipped over the Maserati. I didn't realize he'd never seen it before; hell, it was always around when we were training. Tunnel vision. I spared him the knowledge that the car was giving me problems. After everyone was gone, I fired it up and made it to the Chevron station at the corner of Laurel Canyon and Sunset, famous to me as the epicenter of the Sunset curfew rebellion of the sixties, among other things. Treated the beast to a big dose of antifreeze and a quart of oil. There was a guy there with a classic BMW, and we had a conversation about Weber carburetors. I was not liable to overheat now, and the ammeter was reading better, so I called Annie and told her I was going to try getting over the hill on my own power. I said, "It's working, I don't know why." She said, "I do." And I laughed. "Oh. Right. Of course." Annie has a way, even over the phone, with electricity. I raced the BMW over the canyon, then put my foot in it once I was on the highway, and left him far behind. Well, I have two more cylinders than he does. Made it back without incident, the car purring all the way.

And that's my day. Tomorrow, we'll get down to serious negotiations for the extra bread I hope to get for the second movie. That will be fun, I guess. I mean they can't walk away. They have to make a deal. They can't say, "Screw it, we'll hire someone cheaper," like, say, Warren Beatty. The movie's already in the can.

Damn it! Up all night again.

Monday, August 18

Today I was called in for another ADR session. When I showed up, my little brother Mike Bowen was there working on his sequence as the intern in the hospital who as an avocation sells Uma's comatose body. We all hugged and slapped each others' backs. I said, "You don't think you can improve on this sequence, do you?" Quentin laughed (of course). "Nah, we're just cleaning up something."

I watch Mike nail a difficult synch problem in three takes, and then Quentin put me up. I watch some unfamiliar stuff fast-forwarding on the big screen: flashes of Uma on a plane, Daryl glaring into the camera with her one good eye, and a big profile close-up of Michael Madsen in a cowboy hat. "What?" I say. "Are you working on the second movie?"

"No," Quentin says. "This is the teaser. For Volume Two." No shit! "Here, go back to the beginning," he says. "Let's see the whole thing." The film stops in the middle of a shot of Julie Dreyfus and rewinds, past all those new images. Quentin says, "I've recorded this line for you, just to get the timing right. It's kind of critical." And the sound editor hands me a sheet of paper.

The film starts forward, with sound now. A little piece of the end of Volume One plays out. It cuts to black, and on the screen appears, almost demurely, the legend "Directed by Quentin Tarantino." There's a heartbreakingly sweet phrase played on a bamboo flute, which breaks into a pure Sergio Leone spaghetti Western theme—could be straight out of *The Good, the Bad and the Ugly*. And, in about two minutes or so, Volume Two is presaged by shots of Uma on the airplane writing down in a notebook her hit list. Every time a name is circled, the film cuts to a mysterious one-liner from each of the players.

When it gets to the end, after we've seen Uma write in big capitals "BILL," it cuts to Julie's tearful close-up from the hospital scene, my hand caressing her shoulder, and I hear Quentin doing me. "One more question, Sofie. Does she know her baby is alive?" And the screen goes black. I'm stoked! Suddenly, the movie makes a lot more sense. And, though this is a preview of coming attractions, it doesn't feel like that. It becomes the real end of Volume One. And it knocks it home. Tells you that Volume Two is going to be something else entirely.

Wednesday, August 27

Party for the Japanese distributors of *Kill Bill* tonight, poolside at the Beverly Wilshire. That should be cool. The bash is being given by Quentin and Lawrence, not Miramax. James thinks the two of them may be putting up the money for it themselves. If that's true, then Quentin might actually show up before 2 A.M. In any case, a pool party at the Beverly Wilshire is a very hip way to go. Lawrence and Quentin have a little more style than the Miramax juggernaut: They're sending a Town Car for me. Supposedly, a majority of the cast will be there as well. Unfortunately, Annie is out of town, as is Kansas, so I won't have a date. Well, I didn't have a date for a lot of things in my life that turned out very fine. Stag is cool. I just have to look good.

Well, fellas, this party was *alive*! James met me as I stepped out of the Lincoln. We tarried for a smoke together, and as we gabbed, a lady showed up to usher us into the party. The screening for the distributors, around the corner at the Charles Aidikoff Screening Room, was running late, she said. Jim hadn't seen any of the movie, so we opted to catch the end of it.

We walked in just as Uma, sword in hand and covered with the Crazy 88's blood, was pushing open the paper doors of the "House of Blue Leaves" to reveal the tranquil meditation garden with snow drifting down (actually salt, and actually about 110 degrees, as I remember). This would be where Uma would have her samurai battle with Lucy Liu, as O-Ren Ishii, the big boss of the Tokyo gangs. This is probably my favorite sequence in the whole film, an utterly harmonious combination of serenity and blazing action. The pace, the style, point out the huge similarity between Japanese samurai and Italian Western—all the beauty and all the violence of both genres. Added to that is the extra fun of watching two beautiful women act it out.

With aching slowness, the two ladies prepared to battle. Then when, finally, the first blow was struck, Quentin's mad genius threw a wild flamenco score onto the soundtrack. It all worked. Jim was knocked dead by the images, as, I could tell, was the packed house of Japanese distributors. These folk are too refined to yell and cheer. You could instead hear, in the silences, your own heartbeat. I'd love to see this sequence in a theater in East L.A. It would be pandemonium. The movie rushed on to its cliffhanger ending, and on to the "teaser," where Quentin had laid in a surprise for me. Uma says, "How did you find me?" and it cuts to a bitchin' close-up of Bill, my only shot in the picture. Bill says, simply, "I'm the man." And you believe it. Awesome, if I do say so myself. Thanks, Quentin.

Outside, we ran into Lawrence, with Daryl, looking as pretty as humans get. We talked nicely on the way in to the party, where the Band Apart had set up a very elegant to-do. Sushi was served, of course.

It was clear the Japanese were flipped over this picture. I helped their enthusiasm along, and did some interview stuff. Manny and Heba were there, but no other members of the cast, it seemed. Then I saw Julie Dreyfus. God, she's beautiful! So elegant. So sweet. I talked with Lawrence for quite a while, and then drifted over to give my respects to Sonny Chiba and his daughter, Yoko. Sonny loves me as much as I love him. We made a deal to do a picture together: something like *Red Sun,* I said, which had been written for me by Denne Petitclerc, and which I lost to Charles Bronson. Sonny said they should have had him in it. I didn't quibble about Sonny versus Toshiro Mifune. I just told him he was too young, then. He said, well, he wasn't now. We shook hands on it.

I finished off the party with a little conversation with Quentin, just joking around. Quentin moves so fast that any little moment you get with him feels like privilege. I noticed that James was just staring at him wide-eyed. He'd never seen Quentin in action before. He's quite a trip. I rode home in the Lincoln, feeling relatively fulfilled. It was strange, though, banging around in the empty house.

Wednesday, September 3, 9:22 P.M.

James called with the information that Miramax has upped their budget for promotion, a good sign. They want to do a photo shoot—as though they don't have enough pictures of us. Well, they want to get the whole cast in a single shot. That we don't have. With all the makeup and wardrobe intact, just as though we were in the movie together. Where are they going to find a Chinese temple in L.A.? Am I kidding? There isn't anything you can't find in L.A. There are probably five Chinese temples.

Then, James wanted to know how many tickets I need for the premiere, which is set for September 29. He said he could get me sixteen. After some calculations, Annie and I came up with twenty-nine, as the figure that would not be a slap in the face to anyone. I have a large family. I told Jim to tell Miramax they're dealing with a dynasty. Actually, it's several dynasties. We settled on trying for twenty-five. Though I told him that would mean leaving out the Barrymores and the Fondas. The Plimptons are all on the East Coast, so they can wait for the New York opening. But, what about the Keaches and the Quaids, who are like family, and the Derns?

Got the twenty-five tickets. Then a week later, the folks at Miramax called to say they had to cut the figure in half. Everybody in town wants to come. This was after I'd invited everybody—my closest friends, and everyone in the family who's old enough to be allowed in. James Selman, though he's British, got his Irish up, and became absolutely apoplectic at them, flatly refusing to force me to slap everybody in the face. They backed down, which means I'll have two rows of the Chinese Theater devoted to Carradines and their supporters. It should make for a good claque.

Sunday, October 12

I'm way behind here. Since I last wrote in this journal, I've been to the premiere in New York. That was pure fun, a lot more so than the one in L.A. The audience was super: pure Manhattan. Nobody sat on their hands. People talked back to the screen. "You tell 'em baby!" Stuff like that. Jim Selman told me I had thirteen tickets to give out. I don't know thirteen people in New York. I sent e-mails inviting my old New York agent, Marv Josephson, who, as a guy who rides his big motorcycle to work every day, would probably dig the flick; my old friends Fred and Jan Yager, a husband-and-wife writing team; and a reporter who once wrote a great review of my band in concert. Then I called my beautiful and over-talented niece, Martha Plimpton, and asked her to bring a slew of her crazy friends. Fred and Jan were out of town. So I was still left with a couple of empty seats. I got Jim to find Georgina Walken, whom I had lunch with once, thinking she might bring her husband, Christopher. Martha showed up with three young, hip people, Marv came on his bike, and Georgina was a no-show.

I kept looking over at Martha. She was really digging the movie. After the after-party, we had our own little celebration at Elaine's, where I had celebrated my first night on Broadway, thirty-nine years ago. I was twenty-six, fresh out of the Army. I remember Emmett Jarrett, my old Army buddy, asking me, "Does this mean you're part of the establishment now?" Martha's late uncle George Plimpton's white plaster bust looked down on us from his perch on a shelf, like the Raven. He looked as though he approved. As for my being part of the establishment: "Nevermore," as the Raven would have said.

It turns out everyone loves this picture, including people whom you'd think wouldn't. Oh, yeah, it got a couple of tepid reviews: You can't please everybody. Well, those critics must be feeling lonely. Last weekend Volume One opened to packed houses, and everybody says they can't wait for Volume Two. Suddenly Miramax is asking me to do a lot of publicity. That might have something to do with the fact that my nemesis in the PR department quit her job and moved to Hawaii.

Yesterday, I spent the day in a tiny TV studio, where I did twenty radio interviews and as many TV hookups, one after the other, without moving out of the one chair. Last night, I was on the Craig Kilborn's show. Lots of fun. He had me taking swings at a watermelon with my samurai sword.

Today, I'll leave for London, where I'll be doing an appearance at an autograph convention, on a cruise ship without an engine which was built purely as a movable hotel; they've got it tied to the docks in London. Then I'm off to Spain for the Valencia Film Festival, where they're showing the movie I made there, just before this whole thing began: *Bala Perdida,* or *Lost Bullet,* a movie within a movie about a company making a spaghetti Western. That's when I got my fast draw back together, which I would need for *Kill Bill.* Everything always seems to have more purpose than what appears on the surface.

I guess I've finally come full circle. Then, it's back to London to do a cameo in a movie Michael Madsen is doing there. No pay to speak of: just for the fun, and because I love Michael. I don't know what the part is, or even the name of the movie.

Wednesday, December 10

I've been doing interviews and photo shoots and writing pieces for trendy magazines nonstop since I got back from London. In the meantime, stuff that I did months ago is starting to surface: covers of both *Black Belt* and *Inside Kung Fu* in the same month; that's the martial arts equivalent of being on the covers of *Time* and *Newsweek* the same week. *Smoke* magazine ran a silly picture of me on its cover, smoking a big cigar. I wrote a piece for *Flaunt*, and one for *Jane*, the female version of *Maxim*, for which I also did a piece. I talked for an hour on the phone to Scotland for the English film magazine *Uncut*. Then there were the standards: *Entertainment Weekly, Premiere, Variety, The Hollywood Reporter.* This is all great, and, I'm sure, good for my "profile," but it's all icing. I'm itchy to get back in front of a movie camera.

That's where the cake is.

Tuesday, December 23

Been going crazy for the last week or so, preparing for a big party we're having tomorrow. Annie put the idea together. The point of it was to gather my extended family in one place for a big reunion. It's been a while since a whole lot of us have been in the same room—two years ago on my birthday, I think.

Annie's cooking a turkey. She's repainted half the house and planted flowers all around. Rented two big propane heaters for the backyard. Moved all the furniture around. Thrown out a bunch of stuff. We have the tallest Christmas tree of my experience—ever. It was a bitch to decorate. We should have some fun, and it will be a blast for the kids, but it will be a long time before I'm eager to throw another party.

I got some news a few days ago: The February release date for Volume Two is scratched. The picture is now set to open in April. That changes all my plans enormously. Well, not a problem. We've waited this long, we can wait a little longer.

¡Attention!
All Ye

-You and your favorite person(s)-
Are cordially invited
To spend a festive afternoon on Christmas Eve Day
(Or is that an oxymoron?)
With the Carradines and the Biermans at their home
Many of our friends, as well as family, will be there
People you may know and some you don't
- Folks from all walks of life -
Mainly movie people, of course
As well as Artists and Musicians.
A Magician, a Healer, Witches and Warlocks
A Lawyer, perhaps an Accountant
At least one Sea Captain and one Bad-Ass Biker
Plus one or two Creatures from other Planets
Several languages will be spoken
There will be intellectual stimulation, music
And, of course, food
No "Drink" unless you bring it yourself
That's just the way we are
You are, in an effort to produce variety,
Encouraged to bring something to Eat or Drink or Play
No Presents. Your Presence is present enough
We're expecting about thirty celebrants
Could be More (The Merrier)

Celebrate Christmas, Hanukkah or the Winter Solstice
- Or Just Celebrate -

Friday, January 23, 2004

I'ts almost two years since I got that call from Quentin. All that time has flown by, and crawled snail-like at the same time. Right now, I'm in a hotel suite in New York City, where I came to do a TV appearance on the *Morning Show*. A nice bonus being that I got to see the trailer for Volume Two for the first time. It's a very subtle pitch: provocative and mysterious, consisting mostly of a shot of Uma driving a convertible and talking to herself about how she's out to kill Bill; a couple of quick cuts of Michael Madsen and me; and a few seconds of martial arts action.

The release date has finally been officially set: April 16. That's Easter week. Spring break. Perfect scheduling. All the high school and college students who dote over Quentin's stuff (and mine) will be out of school, with nothing to do except party, get drunk, stoned,and laid, and buy tickets to Volume Two. My granddaughter, Mariah, who works in a video store, has told me that the number one reserve item right now is *Kill Bill, Volume One*. Lookin' good.

The Oscars are again just around the corner. I saw *The Last Samurai* a couple of days ago. Great movie; nothing at all like our film. Nothing at all. The only real similarity is the samurai sword. Tom Cruise is wonderful in it, as is everyone else. Saw another movie I really liked: *Big Fish*. Watched it with my daughter Kansas, who is back from her vision quest. We both cried a lot. The character that Albert Finney plays—a father who was never around, who told tall stories that always turned out to be more-or-less true, who didn't seem to care about much beside himself, but whom you couldn't help but love—is exactly like I remember my father, and for Kansas is exactly like *her* father (me). We sat in the car in my driveway and laughed and cried for about an hour. When a movie can do that to you, you're talking about a rare one.

These days are very slow, just waiting for the year to start humming. Several things are about to click into place. In a month or two I won't have much free time, perhaps for quite a while. Well, that's the way I like it.

When I get back to L.A., I have a court date with one of my ex-wives. This one should put all that to rest for good. Finally! Annie pointed out to me that, though I can't seem to stay married, I hold the record for extended divorces. Nine years in and out of court for this one. Very Kafkaesque.

Wednesday, March 10

⎯⎯⎯⎯

I settled down to read the rave review that Harry Knowles had posted on his insane Web site, aintitcool.com (check it out; it clears the head, like a whiff of smelling salts, or a slap in the face), of the first more or less secret screening of *Kill Bill, Volume Two*.

KILL BILL VOLUME 2 REVIEW

You ever have a day where you just need a great film?

That was me today. Last Friday I received a phone call inviting my father and I to Tarantino's first theatrical screening of KILL BILL VOLUME 2 anywhere in the world, and it happened that it would be taking place here in Austin. That happened last night. I was, of course, overjoyed. What film geek wouldn't be truly excited beyond words to see the first theatrical screening of an uncut Tarantino film? Not I.

As Quentin took his seat and the theater went dark . . . a hushed buzz went through the crowd. This was clearly an audience that "wanted" to see KILL BILL VOLUME 2.

The end result? As the final Q&U hit the screen and the projector turned off, the audience rose to its collective feet, turned to face Quentin and went on to applaud for 5 minutes. It was so overwhelming, that Harvey did not have the Research Firm conducting the screening pass out cards, clearly . . . Their work here was done.

The film is perfect as I could have ever hoped for. On my way out of the theater, Quentin asked me what my favorite moment of the film was. It was near the very end, as Uma and David are sitting at a table and well, the end is pretty certain. It is an incredibly emotional scene. Specifically—over the course of this film, you are struck with such an incredible amount of affection for David Carradine's bastard Bill . . . as well as for Uma's Kiddo that this exchange is wrenching it out of you. And Bill says a line to her that has an incredibly rude phrase at the end of it and I found myself at that moment, honestly crying and laughing at the exact same moment, and not for crass manipulative reasons, but for earned tears and laughs. Specifically—that is such a hard thing to elicit from me in a theater . . . To have honest tears and laughs simultaneously is the very definition of the idealized version of entertainment for me. Something that touches you deeply and makes you laugh and enjoy yourself . . . That's entertainment!

Michael Madsen is so fucking cool in this. If you've seen Charles Bronson in MAGNIFICENT SEVEN telling those kids about the strength of their fathers . . . or even Jon Voight in RUNAWAY TRAIN, when he tells a reckless Eric Roberts that if he gets free, if he would get down on his knees and scrub the tiniest stain off the floor with a toothbrush and follow orders and get the sort of job a con can get, he should be thankful . . . Well, Madsen is that man. He's a man that has such sins that he has given up that life, finding no warmth in it. Instead, he lives in a tiny trailer in front of a magnificent view . . . and at night he works as a bouncer at a shithole strip club being treated like crap by people he could snap like his fingers . . . but he takes it. He takes it and he goes home and he plays his records and chews his tobacco knowing this is the best he can ever hope for . . . and wow. He's great.

David Carradine is going to amaze people. Nobody anywhere has seen him this good. When I saw him onstage with Tarantino at Quentin's last film festival—I knew there was the potential for magic. If you've seen his Cole Younger in THE LONG RIDERS—then you know that it wasn't just stunt casting, that there was a purpose behind it. If you remember and like CIRCLE OF IRON—there are some elements here that are just taken to such a higher level . . . that it just isn't even funny. Quentin does wonders with David in this film. In fact, David has several of the best monologues you've seen in a Quentin film here . . . His Peter & The Wolf style story of Pei Mei is a classic . . . His "Superman" monologue is also classic. I'm also particularly fond of the bit at Two Pines between him and "The Bride," as well as the "Fish" story. David is, I imagine, the perfect portrayal of Satan in many ways. He's charismatic as can be, eloquent, deceitful, manipulative, smooth and treacherously deadly. He's a bastard and he knows he's a bastard and he's fine with that. That you will mourn his passing is a testament to Quentin's direction and to David's performance.

Uma Thurman is amazing. The phrase, "Hell hath no fury like a woman scorned," has never been more true than when talking of her Beatrix Kiddo. She is amazing. The day she goes through beginning with her encounter with Madsen's Budd till the end of the next chapter . . . WHEW! This is great stuff! Her time with Pei Mei . . . surprisingly affecting. In particular the relationship between Uma and Gordon Liu on screen is truly outstanding. I was surprised by the "tough love" and "respect" between the two of them. The payoffs on these scenes will elicit shrieking applause if you're audience is anything like the one last night. Watching Uma and David together is magic. This isn't nearly the action film of the first part, this is really getting down to the meat of the characters and their relationships.

Gordon Liu . . . WOW. Pei Mei is a cinematic god. For anyone that ever even briefly flirted with love for Shaw Brother's classics . . . You will be blown away. So much of it is in his eyes, his gestures and yeah . . . even the subtitles. Pei Mei is funny as hell, cruel, but with an incredibly powerful sense of purpose. The rice eating scene as Uma is attempting to use chopsticks with broken hands is particularly affecting. Great work.

Daryl Hannah is such a great fucking bitch in this thing. Elle is horrible, but because she would always be second. Her patent leather shiny eyepatch is cool as hell and man is she mean. She took on all the worst qualities of Bill—this is the Loki to Uma's Thor. Two Nordic Goddesses fathered by Bill's Odin. When they fight . . . imagine if you will the fight scene between Sean Connery and Robert Shaw in the closed quarters of that train in FROM RUSSIA WITH LOVE . . . Now, give them the spacious environment of a white trash trailer smack dab in the desert outside Barstow—and you'll begin to get it. This thing is an epic smack down. Right up there with Wayne and Victor MacLagen in THE QUIET MAN—this is a rumble that can be felt over seven states and when it ends . . . I dare you not to clap. No fancy smanchy wirework here. This fight hurts deep tissue.

The music is wonderful. At the moment, I'm a bit dazed . . . trying to recall it all, but like the music of the first film, this thing will spend considerable time being played in your world most likely.

What is missing? Well—you won't see Bill's fight with Michael Jai White which I described in detail from my China trip . . . I didn't ask Quentin why he cut it out, instead, I understood. In this film it was more important that the audience like Bill, than fear his skill. Because it was more important how you feel about the end of the fight, than the anticipation of that fight. To that, it is a testament to how well Quentin understood what was truly important to the story. THAT BEING SAID, I can't fucking wait to see that fight on the extras on a DVD!

Ok, for now, I'll call it quits on this review. This is my favorite film of Tarantino's . . . Can I say that with all my experiences with this film to the side? No, not really. I was the only person in that theater that had climbed the cruel steps of Pei Mei, so sure I'm sure that colors my view of things . . . but then, I was the only person in the theater that wasn't standing and applauding for five minutes straight when it was done, but then . . . I was in a wheelchair.

Well, taking out the fight with Michael Jai White is a blow, but I'm sure Quentin knows what he's doing. Judging from this review, and what I've heard from Lawrence, its absence won't hurt me, and as Harry said, it'll be on the DVD, like Ray Bolger's solo dance routine in *The Wizard of Oz*; only in this case, we won't have to wait sixty years to see it. Actually, the first thought that came to me after I got over the shock was: Great—I'm going to be judged pretty strictly as an actor, not as a kung fu artist, and that's what I want. After all, I knew in advance that was what Quentin hired me for. Tough for Michael, though. A fight between us two icons on the big screen would do a lot for his image, not that that giant of a man really needs it.

After some thought, I could understand what Quentin's problem with the scene was: It was originally meant as Bill's introduction. Then, Quentin wrote that wonderful scene outside the wedding chapel. He couldn't very well introduce Bill twice. But he liked the fight a lot. He'd been watching us rehearse it for three months. So, he decided to shoot it anyway, writing a new scene for it and figuring he'd drop it in somewhere. Then I guess when he got down to it, there was just no place for it.

Well, I've thought about it a lot, and the only spot I could imagine him fitting it in would be while Uma is buried alive, on the way to her reminiscence of her teaching by Pai Mei. And any digression at that point from the reason for the flashback—how her training prepared her for this moment—just wouldn't be right. Quentin told me he'd thought about putting it in while Uma is in Mexico, driving to our ultimate meeting. And then her voice-over would say, "And that's the first time I ever saw Bill kill." It's cute, and it makes sense: seeing Bill and The Bride in happier times. And it would work.

As we walked together, all but hand in hand, through the back streets of China, we looked like honeymooners; it would tug at your heart. And then, we come around the corner, and there's Michael Jai White, with his four ninjas, and that great fight ensues. But no; it's too late for it. We don't need any detours at that point; we're rushing to judgment. Maybe the scene will be in the Japanese version. I could hope for that. Over there, they don't care if it belongs in the picture; they just want to see another fight!

The other thing that happened today was receiving a tentative schedule of my obligations to Miramax for the promotion of Volume Two. I'm going all over the world with this thing: to Europe, Asia, Australia, and, of course, to all the great and not-so-great towns in the U.S.A. One day in each burg, except for New York, which is two days.

I'm going to be busy.

Saturday, March 13

I've SEEN the movie. Quentin had another one of his director's screenings, and I was invited. There were, just as with Volume One, no other actors there. I pleaded for Annie to get to go. Quentin's watchdog Pilar said, "Hey, no problem." Well, she's grown to love Annie, as everyone in the company has. Annie would have been heartbroken otherwise, and I would have had no one to talk frankly with about it.

No need for that. Because the movie is, frankly, wonderful. As I thought it would be. Better than the first one in some ways. More like what we expect from Quentin. Lots of story, lots of character, and lots of Quentin's peculiar dialogue, most of it from me. I do go on. And that's the point, I guess. Quentin didn't hire me because I know kung fu. He likes to listen to me talk. I think some people call that "acting."

As I had learned from reading Harry Knowles' review, my fight scene with Michael Jai White was missing. Some juicy bits of dialogue were gone too. I missed the tiny chunks that were removed from my scene with Michael Madsen, as my brother. When we did the scene, there was a sense of endless time, and that's gone now. But Quentin is in a hurry here; he has a lot of material to get through. Not that the film wouldn't hold, no matter how long it was—it's that good—but Quentin wants it short. And, at two hours and nine minutes, it's right on the edge of being long.

The only real comment I had was with the black-and-white stuff at the beginning of the film. I get what Quentin is doing, and, yes, it works. But, I was there when we shot it, using color stock, and the light on Uma was so great that I would gladly throw out the whole black-and-white idea just so I could feast my eyes on that day, the way it was. I really dig color.

A funny thing. All through my career, I've always been able to see my performances crystal clearly. I could look at, say, *Bound for Glory,* and think, Yeah, I'm great. Or at some exploitation thing that was shot in two weeks, and say to myself, Uhh, not so great. With this Bill thing, though, for the first time ever, I can't read it. I can see I'm getting away with it, but is it great? I just don't know. Everybody slapped me on the back, with words like "awesome," "fantastic," and so on. But I can't see it.

And then they start talking about how good I look. Annie tells me it got her hot for me. I can't see that either. It looks to me like the guy I see in the bathroom mirror on slightly-below-average mornings. This is new for me. Quentin has apparently taken me somewhere I've never been. I think it's a good thing. At least it's new. I need "new" right now.

Daryl is kind of phenomenal. No one has ever seen her like this. And her fight with Uma actually beats out the one with Vivica for sheer brutality. I didn't think that would be possible. If I had to put money on someone, though, it would be Michael Madsen. He just took me and shook me. Every second dripping with some emotion or another. And he got better as he went along. It was like watching a bull fight: You know the bull is going to lose, but the majesty and power of the beast makes you sort of wish the odds were different.

When he went down, it was hard. You could almost believe half a dozen bites from a black mamba weren't going to be enough to put that bull down. Quentin obviously knows all this. He gave Michael more close-ups than anyone, except maybe Uma. Now, she is something else. No matter how dirty or fucked-over Quentin has her looking, her beauty shines through it all, and her performance just moves straight ahead, never dipping even once. And Michael Parks! One of the most arresting examples of absolute chameleon acting in the history of film. I've talked to dozens of people, some of whom actually know Michael, who never picked up on the fact that the old Mexican pimp who has just got to be some old guy they picked up south of the border is the same actor as the redneck sheriff in Volume One; and *that* isn't Michael, either.

The thing that's going to surprise everyone is the tears that come to their eyes. Uh-huh: tears! One does not expect Quentin Tarantino to make you cry; that's not what he's famous for. Laugh, yes—and this movie does that, too. But in the end, without your even noticing it's happening, you are seriously moved. You leave the theater feeling good, though. That's one of the things about Quentin's movies: They put you through hell, and then you walk away happy.

Monday, March 15

Today the publicity blitz got its real start. Not that I haven't been doing stuff all along, but today was the official start of the big Miramax push. I can see this is going to be a lot of work. I was picked up at 9 A.M. and taken to a subway (actually elevated) platform in Chinatown which has an Oriental theme. There I met with Jim Selman, who stood by while an artful photographer took arty pictures of me wearing a Hugo Boss suit and leaning on a samurai sword, while apparently waiting for a train. This was for a London magazine. It had the feel of a Magritte painting—you know, the guy who always has a dude wearing a bowler hat in the picture. The most famous one has an apple in his mouth. Everyone who saw the remake of *The Thomas Crown Affair* knows that painting.

After a couple of hours of this, I was driven (through thick, very slow traffic) to the Four Seasons Hotel in Beverly Hills, where I had my picture taken in three different setups, by a Japanese lady, reminding me of Bill Murray's scenes in *Lost in Translation.* Then I spent several hours being interviewed by Japanese journalists, mostly giggling young ladies, through an interpreter, which made me feel even more like Bill Murray. I was all prepared to tell them what a great movie this is, but it turned out they'd all seen it; so, it was back to the old stupid grind of answering the same largely self-evident questions over and over again.

Without Jim beside me to share an occasional sidelong glance with, this would have been unbearable. Toward the end, Jim arranged to have the interviewers brought by in pairs to get it over with. Then, the last reporter swaggered in: a man with a Toshiro Mifune macho-style low voice, and not quite the same questions. We even managed to share a couple of laughs together. Finally, Jim and I went downstairs to the posh restaurant to talk with a British journalist over dinner. Jim warned me that this dude worked for a rag and would be looking for dirt. He told me to watch myself and get out fast. We found a table in the garden where I could smoke and, after a little introduction, Jim left me with him. It turned out to be a very long interview.

At about eleven o'clock, I got a message on my cell phone from Jim telling me to get the hell out of there before I said something I shouldn't. Of course, the gent had just asked me how I'd happened to be in a jail in South Africa. I told him about my evening with Tina Turner: We were trying to have a drink at a classy bar in Johannesburg. Mixed couples were a definite no-no in the apartheid-crazy '80s. A security guard decided to push Tina around a little, so I bounced him off a wall. The evening turned out beautifully, in the end. We had a great time together at an even classier place, and I got Tina home safely. But the bouncer I'd bounced off the wall turned out to be an off-duty cop. I didn't see the end of it for a while. I guess the reporter thought it was a juicy bit, but it probably wasn't what he was hoping for.

I stepped out of the hotel just as Jim came rolling up in a Range Rover to rescue me before I blew it. Too late, of course. I'd spilled the beans.

Since Miramax is using me for its main runway model in the push for Volume Two, I can expect a lot of this. I've seen a partial itinerary. James and I will take off for a regional tour to San Francisco (an interesting place these days), Chicago, and Toronto, arriving in each town at night, sleeping in, doing the press all the next day, and then flying out that night. Then we're back in L.A. for several days of another marathon like the one I did today, only on radio and satellite TV. I'll attend the premiere, and then we're off again to Philly and the Big Apple, where I get to languish for a weekend before doing a two-day blitz there. Annie will fly in for that (she loves New York) and stick with us as we go straight from there to a tour of Europe, including a couple of premieres, then I'm off on my own to Australia to open the picture in Sydney.

After that, we would have a few days at home in L.A. before we'd need to head for Cannes for the festival, where they're screening the picture out of competition—necessarily, I guess, since Quentin is the president of the jury this year. This sounds like an exhausting run, but it can't be much worse than getting a root canal, and it's for a good cause: *me!*

April 5, 2004

Okay. Today is D-Day for *Kill Bill* and me. The premiere is tonight, and there is simply no doubt that we're going to take that beach by storm, with very few casualties. Probably the only serious wounds will be sustained by the few sad and lonely detractors.

Some of the reviews have come out, and they're all raves, for the movie and for me. Several of the critics and dozens of the reporters seem to think I should get some kind of a statue for this. Well, that would certainly be nice, but it's best, I think, not to get carried away about that. I tried to tell everyone that the guy to put your money on is Michael Madsen. He just knocks me out in this movie. Now that things are looking so up for me, he is going to have to take my place as the most underrated actor in Hollywood.

Monday, April 12

Well, I'm bursting to write about the premiere. It was entirely over the top. I haven't had a moment to sit down and get into it until today.

I've been doing press for the movie nonstop. Everybody wants to talk to me. Lawrence told me at the premiere after-party that I stole the picture. My brother Bobby, who was standing beside me, said, "No. Dave just took it, fair and square." Quentin, though, deserves most of the credit, or the blame: for hiring the right guy, I guess; for writing a great part for me; and for walking me through it like an Indian scout, keeping me clear of the rattlers and the quicksand pits along the way.

Jim Selman talked Miramax into giving me thirty tickets, a miracle, since they were as coveted as Super Bowl seats. Present were most of my family, as many as I could wrangle, plus some representatives of several walks of life. George Christy, the president of the Ojai California chapter of the Hell's Angels, who's in line to replace Sonny Barger whenever he steps down. A very sweet guy, he showed up in his colors. That was cool. Then there was Gayle, my manager, who was ecstatic; my agent, Scott, who was equally stoked; Alberto Mariscal, the great Mexican director; Rich and Doug Holmes, two brothers who are respectively my business manager and my attorney; and Patrick Culliton and his ten-year-old kid, Kirin, who flipped over the movie. That's naming just a few.

The after-party was immense and intense. I made a deal with Snoop Dogg to appear in his next video. While I was outside grabbing a smoke, some guy told me he was a reporter for *Variety,* but assured me he was off-duty. He told me my performance was awesome. I said, "Well, it's just my usual shit." And right away he pulled out his notebook, saying, "I gotta write that down."

So, about the movie. I've decided I'm going to spread the idea that you have to think about Volumes One and Two as one three-and-a-half-hour epic to appreciate what a masterwork it is. And it is.

It's all there, an hour and a half of Quentin showing us what he can do in all different genres, plus his own personal, high-class take on movies as Art; and then, like going down a rabbit hole, or like that first breathless descent at Pirates of the Caribbean (the ride at Disneyland, not the movie) when you hit the water, everything changes. You're left breathless, and you've entered a whole new world where girls are as tall as houses and caterpillars smoke hookahs. It's definitely the best movie I've ever been part of.

That's saying a lot, what with stints with Ingmar Bergman, Marty Scorsese, Walter Hill, and Hal Ashby, bless his heart and God rest his restless soul. With Ingmar, you don't give your performance; you give *his*. It works for him, but I don't thrive under that kind of discipline. I never even discovered what I might have come up with if I'd been given my head. I don't think I got Marty's best shot. It was at the very beginning of his career, and he was still feeling his way. But Marty could never be so much fucking fun as Quentin. It's just not his nature to fuck around. Walter was my favorite director for years; mainly, I have to admit, because Hal was no longer alive. Walter was real easy to get along with, and there was always a twinkle in his eye. Hal was like looking in a mirror. He would stand next to the camera and go through everything I was going through. And I could see by his expression that he thought I was great, which made me great.

This Quentin dude, though, is so complex, and the movie expresses so many levels. Quentin did his homework. He studied all the great directors, and he's standing on those guys' shoulders. There's this one other thing, and I think maybe it's the most important part of his ability to get special things out of actors: He cares about us. Wants to continue to know us, and help us along our way. And he confides in me some of his innermost feelings. And quite seriously asks my advice—and then takes it! All this makes me work harder for him than it ever occurred to me to labor for anyone.

Hey, fuck it! I'm not going to talk about it anymore. If you've seen the picture, there's no point. If you haven't, go do that. Catch them both. They will absolutely zap your parameters.

So, today, I'm preparing to go on Craig Kilborn's show again, this time without the samurai melon-slicing act. They want me to play the Silent Flute. That's cool. They'll probably show a clip as well. After that I meet up with Annie and we go to the Playboy Mansion for the party to introduce the DVD of Volume One. That should be okay. I've never liked the mansion much. The grounds are beautiful and I love Hef, but the guests at his place are mostly guys who have a fondness for plastic, and then there are, of course, the ladies who exhibit it (plastic). Not my scene. There's usually a good band, though.

Tomorrow, I leave for the extended press tour, three U.S. cities, four European premieres, an Australian convention, the Mexico City opening, and then, at long last, Le Festival de Cannes. Quentin is president of the jury. That should be a hoot. They'll show the movie in the Grand Palais— not in competition, of course; that would be a little suspicious. Still, we'll get to stand up beside Quentin and accept the applause of the French film crowd. They'll all be as in love with us as the rest of the world, I'm certain. Come to think of it, the rest of the world will be represented there too. Cannes is an international wingding. I'll hang out with the big boys, accept the compliments, party a little, and that should put this movie finally to rest.

Wednesday, May 5

Just got back last night from the ten-city junket: seven time zones and four continents, the last being Australia, which was pretty cool, totally down-home compared to the elegance of Europe

The rest of the tour was very sweet. *Bill 2* opened huge everywhere. James and I did the American leg, and we were treated royally in Toronto, Chicago, and New York, where Annie joined us.

Every city we went to we were treated like, well, royalty: huge beautiful suites, cars to take us everywhere. And all expenses paid.

We piled up some great reviews. *The Toronto Star* gave it five stars. The only tepid review was in the *New York Daily News*. This was strange. *The News* is a real rag, with headlines like "APE ESCAPES FROM ZOO" and "MILKMAN MURDERS TWO." You'd think they'd flip over Quentin's stuff. On the other hand, *The Wall Street Journal,* maybe the stuffiest daily paper in the country, treated it as an artistic tour de force. Well, they're right. It is. Maybe that's the explanation. Artistic tour de forces may be over the heads of the boys at *The News.* Sometimes I find it easy to forget that journalism is a literary profession.

As we prepared to set out for the Emerald Isle on the first leg of our European adventure, we had a slight delay at JFK, because of a bomb scare. They emptied out the entire international terminal. About two thousand people were stretched out along the access roads for a couple of hours. Fortunately, we'd just finished checking our baggage, or we would have been saddled with lugging it around. Imagine: all the stuff for four premieres, press things, parties and all, in five different countries. That's a lot of stuff to be dragging around. No one knew exactly what was going on. No one seemed scared, though. We took a footbridge to another terminal and sipped tea until the all-clear came through.

We were treated even more royally in Dublin, London, Munich, and Rome. We were moved about in a private jet: a Falcon 900, set up like a floating living room. It was great skipping the whole security hassle, and we could smoke on board. Daryl and Uma were along, with their entourages, and Michael Madsen with his wife, who got along famously with Annie. And, well, Michael and I are almost blood brothers by now. I love that guy. We just partied across the continent, six miles up. No napping to speak of; we were all having too much fun.

Each city was a completely different experience. Dublin was wonderful: very homey, and low-key compared to all the rest. The hotel was right in the heart of the city, and when you're talking about Ireland, "heart" is where it's at. For the inevitable round of interviews, I took each reporter for a walk. We strolled along, smoking cigarettes. (Ireland had just instituted a California-style ban on smoking in public places two weeks before. I'm surprised the Gaels went for that.)

I was invited to a dinner with the Irish director Neil Jordan. That was very cool. We stepped outside for a smoke at one point. He borrowed an English Oval from me and we got to know each other. He asked me to shake hands with him and then, as he was gripping my hand, he told me, "This hand has shaken the hand of Elliot Goldenthal, who was taught by Aaron Copland. Elliot shook the hand of Aaron Copland, who shook the hand of Camille Saint-Saëns, who shook the hand of Franz Liszt, who shook the hand of Schubert, who shook the hand of Beethoven, who shook the hand of Mozart. So you have just shaken hands with Mozart." We definitely clicked. I hope I get a chance to work with him. He's published a couple of novels, and just finished a third. He gave me a copy. I'm reading it. It's narrated by a ghost. Neil is a real poet, I think. Well, that's obvious from his work: *End of the Affair, Interview with the Vampire, The Crying Game,* to name a few. And *Michael Collins,* a truly fine movie, maybe Liam Neeson's best performance, which is saying a lot.

At the premiere I was introduced by the president of the festival with a Supércool glowing critique of my performance, and treated to a veritable hail of accolades, so I had to give a speech. This gave me a hint of what I would be likely to do on stage at the Kodak Theater if I ever got one of those gold statues from the Academy. I cried, for one thing. Told them how I'd been waiting for something like this all my life, and just hadn't expected that I'd be on social security when it happened. That got a big laugh. And I thanked my mother. I think I might have called her "My Sainted Mother." Well, I really do feel that way, and this *was* the Emerald Isle, and you talk like that there, if you've got any Irish blood in you at all, and I do.

London just went ape for us, and the accommodations at the Dorchester weren't just royal, they were more like imperial. James had set up Armani and Hugo Boss to give me clothes. I scored two pinstripe suits, which was great; I've always wanted one of those. And a tuxedo. That makes five I have now, I think. Silly, I suppose. Tuxedos last forever, and they never go out of style. But, why say no?

Munich was, surprisingly, the most romantic interlude. The drill at the premieres was as follows: We got dressed up—and groomed, yet—then walked the red carpet for the photographers and the TV cameras. We'd be presented to the audience, and then, when the lights went down, whisked

When in Rome *JAMES SELMAN*

The Angel and the Badman *JAMES SELMAN*

off to a state dinner. After that we'd go to the after-party. Annie, Michael, De Anna, and I would watch some of the movie before we split, just to see ourselves dubbed into German and Italian. I think maybe I actually act better in Italian. What with the spaghetti Western aspect of the movie, it fits perfectly. I can't say the same for the German version. It just didn't seem quite right seeing Quentin's characters speaking German. Except for Uma. She was perfect as Marlene Dietrich. And, of course, Daryl's one-eyed dominatrix was right on.

Rome is a great city. The four of us, the Carradines and Madsens, peeled off from the group and did our own thing. The Coliseum, Vatican City, the Via del Corso, and that fountain where you throw the coins in and wish for things. Then dinner at some cool restaurant and up to the top of one of the seven hills for the view. All this with each family in separate chauffeured Mercedeses provided by Miramax.

Annie had heard about a little bar where all the celebrities go, up there at the top of the town. She suggested we go there. Michael said, "Hey, I have a bottle in the car!" Well, that's not the point, we explained. So we finished up the evening at that place. As far as I could figure, we were the only celebrities there.

The next day, they all, including Annie, went back to L.A. I had to hang for another day before my flight left for down under. I walked around a little through the streets, never straying far from the hotel. It was strange, being alone in Rome with absolutely no one I knew.

Then I boarded the flight, twenty-four hours(!) including a two-hour layover in Hong Kong, where at least I could grab a smoke. I picked up a few magazines there to fill the time on the next leg, and when I opened *Entertainment Weekly* was greeted with a full-page picture of me. *Bill* is everywhere. This is a definite hit-hit; you know, like a win-win. Well, not quite. There are a few rats in the woodwork. *The National Enquirer* published a piece likening my relationships with the women in *Kill Bill* to those with a couple of my ex-wives. But, hey, *The Enquirer* only writes about people who sell papers. They haven't cared much about me in a few years.

An interesting side effect to all this is that as a result of Quentin's talking about it on television as "the best autobiography I've ever read," a whole new group of people are starting to read *Endless Highway*. Jesse Vint, an old acting buddy of mine, and a very wise and cool dude, sent me a long critique after he finished reading it. He calls the writing "Part Mark Twain, part Jack London, and part Jack Kerouac!" Not bad! Makes me think I'd better snap up a bunch of copies off the Web before the price goes up. He went on . . . and on: "I think it's phenomenal!" he said. "It should be required reading in every high school and college in the country."

Then he said, and this is rich, "Anyway, I think you're going to see a change in all your acquaintances from now on. Two things . . . two things: They will become generous, and very profound. You know why? Because they want to be immortalized in your next book, *Endless Highway II,* in a *very nice* way."

Well, Jesse, there you are: your generosity and profundity immortalized, right here in *The Kill Bill Diary*. And, well, because you never know: If I ever need someone to talk to a judge or a parole officer about my value as a human being, I'm definitely going to call you up, Jesse.

Wednesday, May 19

This morning, I'm in the mountains above Saint Tropez, at a palatial villa owned by a famous art collector, Enrico Navarra. I'm beside one of the three swimming pools. The sun is blazingly bright, but the day is cool. I awoke before anyone else and raided the refrigerator for some peach-flavored Lipton ice tea, which I heated up in the microwave. The hard part was finding a cup. I had my first cigarette and sipped the tea.

It is so quiet here that my fingers on the keys of my Mac are the loudest sound. I decided to bring my laptop with me to Cannes (a first for me) so I could document things as they happened. I never had a chance until now; there were no free minutes during the days, and the nights were just as full.

Okay. There is now some peace in the world—my world—again. The madness of Miramax's push at the festival is over. The film has shown in the Grand Palais, to a huge, happy crowd, acting more like the bunch on Forty-second Street than you'd expect from the collection of gowns and tuxedos at the top of that red carpet. By the end of the credits, they were clapping in unison to the music. And they all stayed to the end, to see the cheerful outtake of Uma snatching out Daryl's eye. When the lights came up, no shit, there were tears in my eyes.

Then we did our obligatory round of parties, sometimes with Quentin, sometimes with Lawrence, sometimes with Michael Madsen, sometimes just Annie and me. Mick Jagger made a pass at Annie, and then when he found out she was with me, he just ran. Funny. Every time he hits on a woman, she turns out to belong to me. And then he flies. Hey, I'm not a jealous guy, but I guess Mick remembers when I was courting my second wife, Linda, how I chased off her ex-husband Roger McGuinn. He was giving her a hard time, and I told him he was history, and to stop fucking with her, or else, more or less. But, my God, that was over a quarter of a century ago, and I didn't hurt the dude, just made him go away.

We came here to this beautiful place yesterday afternoon. The plan was to arrive by helicopter, but we couldn't get ready in time, so instead our driver Jamal drove us in the Mercedes, with two motorcycle cops riding escort. It was great. We went as fast as the car could go, weaving through traffic, driving on the wrong side of the road, the cops waving cars aside, pushing even fire engines out of the way for us.

Annie just stepped out of our room into the sunlight. She's wearing a sun yellow bikini that Celine gave her, whoever that is; some famous designer, I suppose. The outfit, which has little gold chains dangling here and there that catch the sunlight like twinkling daytime stars, came with a pareu, which she has draped around her hips. I have not seen anything this pretty since I was in Tahiti, way back in '79; maybe not even then. I am so fucking lucky.

Today, we'll go back to Cannes, to our new hotel, the old Savoy, which has been refurbished and renamed the "3.14." I don't know what that means, but it's supposed to be the newest, hippest scene on the Croisette—away from the Miramax people, but still in the thick of things.

And, so, now, a whole new stage of the madness will begin—not for *Kill Bill;* we've pretty much said good-bye to that long story for the moment—but just for ourselves, and for the rest of it all: the other movies, and the town itself. Finding an out-of-the-way place for a romantic dinner, stuff like that. And I need to start to figure out what I'm going to be doing for the next couple of decades or so.

Yes, there is life after Tarantino.

Saturday, May 22

Last night we walked the red carpet again with Bobby for the premiere of the newly reconstructed version of Sam Fuller's *The Big Red One*. It was pretty cool. About fifty minutes of material has been put back in, stuff that never saw the light of release when it first came out in 1980. It's a little long, at about three hours, but it holds. Bobby is great in it. He almost steals the show from Lee Marvin, no mean feat. And I'm being conservative when I say "almost."

Sam's take on war is definitely strictly his own. He doesn't seem to have any special attitude about the German enemy, except that we're supposed to kill them. Well, he was there. I think he's probably just telling it like it was.

I talked to Bobby about the way these restorations come about. Some brilliant director makes a film; the distributor cuts the heart out of it. Then, twenty years later or so, the movie gets the reputation of being a masterpiece, and someone puts it back together. The amazing thing to me is that these studio bosses never seem to learn. They do this over and over again. Chop something up and then have to look for the pieces a few years later. Bobby said it's because Hollywood never remembers and never forgets. He says it's a quote from me.

It was great hanging out with Bobby.

All that's left now is sitting through Volumes One and Two, the Japanese versions, bolted together for a special Sunday night screening. Then it's home for us. It's been great, but I'll be glad to see it end. That's not the finish to the *Kill Bill* phenomenon, though. We still have Moscow and Madrid to get through. Then it should be over for us, and on to something else, whatever the next rabbit hole may turn out to be.

Sunday, May 23

Actually, it's Monday, but very early. Sunday night was the closing ceremonies, which include the giving out of the prizes; we figured we should
be there, since Quentin is the president of the jury. Annie called up Paula
at Miramax to arrange tickets, and Paula said, "Oh, my God! It's impossible! Everyone wants to go. I'm having trouble getting tickets for Harvey!"

Well, no problem; that's Miramax. A couple of phone calls from our
friends and we were in, with an official car and all the extras. So, up the red
carpet again, with Annie in yet another fabulous gown from Sterling
Capricio and her pick of jewelry by Chopard. By now they'd seen how
much photo coverage they get when Annie wears their stuff. Some big-
time designers wanted to dress her as well, but Annie remained faithful to
Sterling. The photographers, as usual, went crazy.

We had great seats, and it was wonderful to watch Quentin standing
up there and announcing the winners, with great pride. When it got
around to the Golden Palm, he was positively ecstatic to be able to hand
it to Michael Moore for *Fahrenheit 9/11,* his documentary condemning the
Bush administration for their actions. Well, we all know that story. Annie
and I were invited to the screening a couple of days before, but had opted
for Naomi Campbell's party on the beach at Saint Tropez instead.

Anyway, as they announced Quentin, the background decor changed
to a collage made of huge close-up artwork of the anime face of the little
Japanese girl who would grow up to be Lucy Liu, and they started playing
the music from *Kill Bill.* The applause on his entrance was pretty huge,
and I stood up for him, with Annie right beside me.

This might be the best time I've ever had at the Cannes festival. That's saying a lot. I have, after all, many glorious memories of visits there, sometimes with movies in the main competition—*Bound for Glory, The Long Riders*—and twice with my own directorial efforts. And then, of course, there was my very first visit in 1975, when I came on my own as a sort of hobo, with the clothes on my back and my guitar over my shoulder. I saw some great movies, hung out with Carlo Ponti, and made love to a beautiful girl I had just met on the beach in the moonlight.

Tuesday, June 15

Getting on a plane, with Quentin and Lawrence and our ladies, for Russia, where we're to present *Kill Bill, Volume Two* at the Moscow Film Festival. After which, we'll all go to Spain to open the picture there. This should be a lot of fun, and will bring the whole saga to a close.

Wednesday, June 16

We're laying over for a couple of hours in Frankfurt, waiting for our plane to Moscow. Somewhere over the Atlantic, Quentin came back and fucking knelt beside me to tell me how much he loved his copy of the first draft of this book, which I had sent to him, to give him the chance to object to anything that struck him wrong. He had two small things, very delicate and correct, which he thought might hurt someone's feelings. He mentioned that the book has a great leading lady: That's Annie. Quentin is cool. Then he leaned in close to give me some advice as to how to make certain I made full use of the huge boost in my career that being the title character in a Tarantino film was going to give me. I hate that word, "career." It doesn't fit the lifestyle of anyone who's trying to be an artist. You don't talk about the "career" of van Gogh or Beethoven or Rodin. I guess it comes from calling it show *business,* which I also don't care for. The other phrase that I cringe at when actors use it is when they talk about "the work" in highbrow, artsy tones. We don't work, we play. It's called "entertainment," for Christ's sake. Have some perspective, guys. We're clowns!

Quentin cautioned me especially to avoid turning down something great because there wasn't enough money involved. He gave me a couple of examples of people who had blown it by doing that. I had to laugh. I don't think I've ever had that luxury. I've never had much of a chance to pick and choose projects. I just took what was offered to me. I guess things could change now, though; so I'll keep his advice in mind.

Friday, June 18

So, we're in Moscow. Quentin, Harvey, Lawrence, his incredibly beautiful paramour Leasi (I hope I'm spelling her name right), Annie, and myself. Harvey showed up with a young actress in whom he is showing an interest. A discovery, I guess. We have a wonderful girl named Anna (easy for me to remember) who is supposed to be our interpreter. There's not much need for that, but she is very helpful with other things and she's great to have around. We have also been assigned a bodyguard, a giant named Rushan, who is omnipresent. It's impossible to lose him. If we step into an elevator and leave him behind, when the door opens on another floor, there he is. Bodyguards are usually a joke for me, but his main use here is to clear the way for us as we move about through the enormous throngs that appear everywhere we go.

Quentin is huge here. Something about his films has ignited the youth of Russia. The way Quentin explains it, when the Russian Mafia took over the country, they became interested in American gangster movies—not *The Godfather*, and not Marty Scorsese's take on the subject, but *Reservoir Dogs*. Well, these people aren't Italian. Anyway, those other movies are all about history, and Quentin is very much right now.

I didn't know what to expect here in the "New Russia." Well, in a lot of ways it's very like any other city in Europe—with some peculiarities, certainly, but only a trace left over of the old Iron Curtain mentality. Most of that disappeared by the time we got out of the airport. We didn't have to clear customs. Some kind of noblesse oblige thing. I remarked to Quentin that this kind of special treatment was possible only in a corrupt country. I'd experienced similar stuff in Marcos' Philippines. If you were classy

Rushan, our "bodyguard." That huge edifice behind him is a shopping mall! *ANNIE BIERMAN*

enough, or had enough money to burn, you could get away with just about anything there.

We weren't even required to pick up our own luggage. We were all ushered into a lounge, the kind of place usually available only on departure, not arrival, and they plied us with drinks while we waited. Lufthansa had misplaced some of our bags. There's always some kind of glitch. Annie had to spend the whole day in her traveling clothes; not her style at all, though she was cute in her designer jeans and her sexy top, and she always had the option of slipping into her black leather trench coat and looking like an exotic Russian spy.

One nice thing about Russia: There are very few places where you can't smoke. And even in those few theoretically forbidden enclaves, I just went ahead and lit up, and no one said a word. That noblesse oblige thing again, I guess. Privilege can be fun. A Russian producer passing by expressed admiration for my acting, but mainly he liked the fact that I always have a cigarette in my hand. We both agreed that the worldwide antismoking obsession is simply uncivilized. And, you know, I recently read a comment from the female leader of some third-world country, as she vetoed the enactment of a law prohibiting smoking in public, even on the street! She said, "The poor people have very few pleasures, and they consider smoking to be one of them." Yeah, and "poor me," too. This producer went on to say I was great in the film, and that I should do some Chekhov. I told him to make me an offer.

Red Square and us *ANNA*

Quentin made a visit to the Moscow Art Theater Museum. He was able to sit at Stanislavsky's makeup table and finger all the stuff there: tubes of grease paint, a wig, a false nose. I asked him if he tried on the nose. He said no, he thought that would be pushing it. I think if I'd been there I wouldn't have been able to resist the impulse.

Quentin endeared himself to everyone with his encyclopedic knowledge of Russian film. At the press conference, because of his prodding, I made some friends myself due to my familiarity with Boleslavsky, the other director of the Moscow Art Theater. I was able to tell them that my dad's seventy-fourth movie had been directed by him. Boleslavsky gave Dad a signed copy of his book, *Acting: The First Six Lessons.* The inscription read, "To John Carradine, a good actor." I always carry a copy of it around with me. I buy them by the half dozen, because I give them away all the time. It's a simple little book, but it tells you everything you need to know. Quentin wants me to give him a copy.

The people here are very friendly. They are hospitable to a fault. Every time we turn around, they're plying us with food—and vodka . . . lots of vodka. And everything goes on till very late. It's very near the summer solstice, and at this latitude, it doesn't get dark until around midnight. No one wants to go to bed.

The premiere was huge, and very positive. This was the biggest screen I'd ever seen the picture on, and we were seated close to the front. It's overwhelming to watch it that way. The close-ups are awesome; and when Uma squashes Daryl's baby blue eyeball between her toes, the eyeball—and the toes—are three or four feet high.

They had put together a brilliant film collage of all of Uma's work for the occasion, after which the president of the festival gave a long, adoring speech about Quentin and Uma—and me! I whispered to Quentin, who was sitting beside me, grinning all the time: "You know, a decade or so ago, these people wanted to destroy us, and now look at them—they love us!" Thank you, Ronald Reagan (who died just a few days ago). The most positive thing I remember about Ronnie was when he went to East Berlin and said, "Mr. Gorbachev, tear down this wall." I think the only other time he impressed me was when he cracked a joke right after he was shot. Well, he always wanted to be John Wayne, and that was a very Duke-like moment; and it was for real! But ending the cold war without a shot being fired is the thing that will assure his place in history. Oh, I know that Poland and Bulgaria and the whole of NATO, not to mention the obvious failure, economically and philosophically, of the "Communist Experiment," had a lot to do with the fall of the curtain, but "The Gipper" will get a lot of the credit.

Harvey showed up this afternoon, and I sat with Quentin and him in the hotel restaurant, all of us smoking Cuban cigars. Harvey abruptly asked me, "So, who is it that made the one-point-five million offer?" I guess Quentin had told him about a movie I'd been offered—working title: *His Name Is Grasshopper.* But I had to say, "It's one-million-two. I *wish*

The new Rusian army? *ANNIE BIERMAN*

it were one-point-five," and went on to tell them about it. It's kind of like *Sea Biscuit,* only about a greyhound instead of a racehorse. I'd be playing the trainer who comes out of retirement to help an orphan boy bring the dog into the winner's circle. It's a real tear jerker, and a great part for me. Quentin opined that it was a perfect character for me to play right now. After *Kill Bill,* where I was an international assassin, a gruff but kindly good guy would be just right. And I think I've proved I'm great with kids. Harvey loved the fact that the offer was made by Warner Brothers, who've treated me so shabbily over the years, while I was making them hundreds of millions of dollars.

He and Quentin talked about the upcoming Elmore Leonard story they're working on, Harvey seductively mentioning that there were many parts I could play in it. Then the two of them had an exchange talking in code. They spoke about some role, perhaps in that movie, or maybe in something else. Harvey said, "David could get away with it. De Niro they might not take it from, but David could pull it off." Quentin turned to me and said, "We're talking in riddles—deliberately." Then, his signature laugh. I guess I'll find out what that was about somewhere down the line. I'd sure like to know what it is that Robert De Niro can't get away with that I can.

Sunday, June 20

Spain. A very nostalgic place for Annie and me. Our romance really gelled in Valencia and Alicante when we were there to make *Baela Perdida*. That, you might remember, was two and a half years ago, just before I got the call from Quentin. Now we're back here to put an end to it. (The movie, not the romance. *Definitely* not the romance!) A perfect circle.

The hotel definitely rates six stars, if only for the lobby. And there's a Schimmel grand piano in the gorgeous garden restaurant. I've been playing it every night. Annie and I have had nothing to do for a whole day and two nights. We started out with a romantic midnight supper in that garden. Then we slept in till about two, when we took off with Quentin to a little restaurant down a narrow street for lunch. That was delicious: both the food and the company. Quentin and I talked about all kinds of shit,

and Annie was at her best. After that, we took a car to the Botanical Gardens. We walked around for an hour among the trees and flowers. Somewhere in the distance, a South American band was playing.

The evening ended with a paella feast for the whole *Kill Bill* crowd. Quentin was in great form, telling lots of stories, and every-

The Botanical Gardens in Madrid

body had a lot of fun. At a certain point, I started to flag. I couldn't keep my eyes open. I didn't want to fall asleep with my face in the flan, so I went outside for some air. Then I decided to call the driver. I sent him in to tell Annie I was in the car, and fell asleep in the back while I waited for her to come out. She appeared very quickly, a glorious vision to wake up to in her flowered print dress.

Monday, June 21

Today is the big day. Lots of press, and then the final premiere. Both volumes back to back. We're not required for the showing of the first one at seven-thirty; we'll attend a cocktail party at the hotel while that's going on. I'll put on my Francesco Smalto tuxedo again (a gift from Cannes) for the last time for this film, unless of course I have to walk down the aisle at the Oscars. (Don't laugh. It could happen.) Annie will slide into her incredibly sexy Sterling Capricio gown (floor-length, red) and get her long hair done up in some fabulous way. Then the cars will pick us all up at nine-thirty for the red carpet and the presentation.

Then, Volume Two, in three theaters: one in English, with subtitles, and two in Spanish. No way can Annie and I sit still through the whole movie again right now, but we both want to watch some of it in Spanish: her because it's her second language, and me because I want to hear what Bill sounds like in Castilian Spanish. The voice I'll hear is the guy who has dubbed all my movies into Spanish for the last forty years. Then we'll attend the after-party. Maybe we'll dance. Who knows? And that will be it for *Bill*.

Tuesday, June 22

The whole evening was pretty cool. We all met in the lobby of the hotel. Sofia Coppola had arrived. She's Quentin's new flame. They had kindled their romance in Paris. Quentin is like a teenager with her. It's very sweet. We all went out to the garden where about forty photographers snapped our pictures in front of a huge *Kill Bill* poster. After that, I got Quentin and Lawrence to get into one of those team handholds with me, and said, "Here's to our last walk up the red carpet," then added, "Until the Kodak Theater." Quentin said, "Yeah!" And Lawrence grinned.

When we arrived at the red carpet, Quentin had just shown with Sofia, and the crowd was going a little more than wild. They are a weird and lovely couple. Quentin is a very big guy, and Sofia is a delicate little thing. It's really cute. We all had our pictures taken together, Annie looking spectacular, in her red Sterling Capricio gown with the long train trailing down the stairs behind her and her hair loose and wild. She looked like a runway model, only without the frown those chicks always wear. Then we went inside for the ceremonies. I got a big cheer as I ran up to the stage. Well, the Spanish are crazy for Westerns, and I've done a lot of them. As soon as the lights started to dim, Annie and I headed for the back door. I said to Quentin, so that he wouldn't think we were deserting him, "We're going to watch it in Spanish." He said, "Cool," and off we went. The Spanish version was great. The dubbing was right on. The audience was great, too. They actually got jokes that the Americans always miss. Annie was getting a huge kick out of it. We watched until Michael Bowen put the Johnny Cash record on. Annie said, "I've had my fill." Fine, so had I. It was fun watching us in Spanish, but not understanding a word gets old after a while. I was having to provide subtitles from memory.

We left our seats and were immediately swept away to a dinner that had been set up for us at a fancy club which had been made over from a casino. Lawrence was already at the table, with Leasi and Paula, who is always there for us. The food was fascinating, little bits of stuff that always looked like one thing and tasted like another.

When we'd finished our strange but delicious dinner, we were squired back to the theater to pretend we had always been there. Then we went off to the after-party. That wasn't much. Kind of a bland place, with a table at the back for us and the rest of the place cordoned off to keep the fans away. Quentin was pissed because they told him they couldn't make a margarita. "You have tequila?" "Yes." "So, what's the problem?" Finally, they figured out that all a margarita amounts to is tequila and lemonade. They brought him one which he could tolerate, though they missed the salt on the rim.

I told Quentin that the original idea for a margarita was to make a cocktail that the ladies could handle out of the old tequila-lime-and-salt trick. He liked that. So, I went on to tell about how I was introduced to the ritual in Old Tucson, while making a Western with Glenn Ford called *Heaven With a Gun*. At the end of the first day's shoot, I followed all the cowboys into the bar. I wasn't much of a drinker then, but it had been a really hot, dusty day's work, plus I wanted to hang out with the guys. The bartender asked me what I wanted, and I just blurted out what I thought was an appropriate cowboy order. I knew how to do it. You shake a little salt onto the back of your hand, shoot the tequila, suck the lime, and then lick the salt off your hand. Or maybe I've got it backward; I can't remember. Probably my brain cells have been diminished by too much tequila, lime, and salt. Anyway, I loved it. It fit me. Or maybe it just fit the character of the rough, tough cowboy I was playing in the movie. I had two more and then dove into the pool. Since then, I've drunk enough tequila to swim laps in.

We were all really high on this, our last premiere. Quentin told some great stories, and Sofia kept sneaking glances at me. Annie told me Sofia was taking pictures of me with her digital mini-camera when I wasn't looking. Maybe she'll put me in her next movie. I could dig that.

Even so, the experience at this place was wearing on us all, with the fans straining at the ropes and tons of noise. Quentin abruptly decided we should split and go see some flamenco dancing. Sounded hot to me.

The plan was to meet at a bar and figure out where to go from there. We piled into our separate limos and started out. Then, down the road a piece, the plan changed to reconnoitering at the hotel and going from there, which was cool for Annie and me, as we were running out of cigarettes. Annie caught Sofia snapping pictures of me again out the car window. Maybe I *will* get to be in her next movie.

When we got to the hotel, we sped up to our suite, grabbed some cigarettes, and changed out of our formal finery to dancing clothes.

We met up with the rest of the bunch in the garden. The flamenco idea was a bust, as Monday nights they're dark. We sat around drinking champagne and mellowed out the rest of the evening. Quiet, but definitely sweet, and the feeling of the garden was super, with trees and flowers, and a little bit of moon.

Friday, June 25

We're back in L.A. now. It's good to be home. Foreign countries can get to be tiresome. And I've done fourteen cities, I think it is, in eight time zones, on three and a half continents (Russia is not exactly Europe) in a little over a month. Yes, home is good right now. We're just barely over our jet lag, if that's what it was. Total exhaustion, in any case. I think more a reaction from the whole two and a half years than from this little junket. We've done a lot of sleeping. We're both fat as Russian bears and Spanish bulls from all the hospitality, plus the constant feeding that goes on in transoceanic flights. We're going to have to do some serious working out to get back to normal.

When we got home, the house was turned a little more than upside down. Max had thrown a can of paint down the stairs (he didn't like the color) and the steps looked as though Jackson Pollock had been to visit. Then Madeleine had thrown a monopoly game at Maria, our Inca nanny. Maddie is a very poor loser. Maria was having an anxiety attack. She was in her room in tears, being comforted by Theresa, our day-maid, whom Maria had called over to give a hand. We found out later that she had almost called 911. Sure glad she didn't; that could have started a never-ending story. Once the authorities show up, they can't just walk away. Johnny Barrymore once said to me, "There is no situation so dismal or so hopeless that it can't be made worse by the arrival of a policeman." The result would have been tons of paperwork and social service employees snooping around. I've been there. Social workers are like mice: They get into everything and you can't get rid of them.

It didn't take long to get things back to normal. Annie was amazingly calm about the whole thing, considering the shape of the stairway. She told Madeleine she was banned from Monopoly. I would have said that Max ought to pay for the repairs out of his allowance, except he doesn't *get* an allowance. Annie said she preferred to downplay the whole thing, and anyway, this is a piece of cake compared to the last time we went out of town, when Maria was ready to quit. So Annie calmed Maria down, prescribed a program of calcium and magnesium supplements to help her deal with her anxiety, and we all went to bed.

Today, the painters are here to repair the damage to the walls and banister, and we're measuring the stair carpet for replacement. It was pretty seedy, anyway.

That doggy picture that Warner Brothers was going to make has become a little iffy. Apparently, WB passed on it, which brings up the question: Why did these people come on as though it was a done deal? Well, as my friend Kenny Hatley said, "People don't always say what they mean, and they don't always mean what they say." It's okay. I've got a couple of other irons in the old fire.

Anyway, the main thing for me right now is: I'm glad to be home. I hope I can stay here for a while. I'm very weary of airports, limousines, and even six-star hotels.

You can get tired of anything if you're fed enough of it.

Saturday, June 26, 2004

Well, this is it. One last word and I'm out of here.

You remember that Quentin, when I talked to him at the *Jackie Brown* cast-and-crew party, said we needed to work together, but it had to be a home run? Those were his words. I think he didn't want to just *use* me in a film, he wanted it to be proving something: about me, and about his good judgment. It had to blow people's minds or it wasn't worth it to him. Well, it wasn't just a home run, it was a grand slam. Bases loaded and out of the park. Bottom of the ninth. Everybody gets to go home a winner. No child is left behind. All that shit.

Quentin hadn't made a movie in six years, then there was the bad aftertaste of how the critics treated him in his Broadway stint. I saw him in that on some trip to New York or another, and he wasn't bad. He was strange, but that's Quentin, and that's also the part. But, as Lawrence once said to me, they love Quentin, but they're also ready to trash him if they get a chance. He needed a blockbuster hit, I think, to restore his belief in himself. So he wrote this magnum opus, and he gathered a cast and crew that he could take to the top. All of us, particularly myself, Uma, and Michael Madsen, actually collaborated with him. There was really almost no way he could fail with us in his camp. Any one of us would have stopped a bullet for him. And he returned the favor, extracting performances from all of us that were beyond anything we had done before. The result was not just a great movie—he'd done that before—but a fucking masterpiece. And I was lucky, and honored, to be a big part of it.

My life will probably never be the same. Actually, my life is sort of starting over. This isn't the first time this has happened to me. I've walked over some kind of bridge and burned it behind me, never looking back, several times in the past. But this is the biggest jump ever.

When I played the emperor of the Incas on Broadway, way back in '65, I really pushed the envelope. I remember a conversation with my agent, Jane Oliver. God, she was great! She made it her mission to discover brilliant young actors, off-Broadway or in regional theater, and send them to Hollywood to be movie stars. Jon Voight, Sylvester Stallone, George Peppard, Dustin Hoffman: guys like that. And me! Thanks, Jane. Rest your soul, Honey.

Anyway, after the first preview of *The Royal Hunt of the Sun,* I was in some kind of funk. She asked me, "Now, what's wrong?" I said, "I'll tell you what. This is probably the best performance I'll ever give, and it's coming right at the beginning of my career. It's all gonna be downhill from here." She said, "Well, look at it this way: You'll never have to audition again." Not true, of course. I auditioned for something three weeks ago. Didn't get it, either.

Then a few years later, *Kung Fu* came along. And I wasn't just a TV star—I was more like a rock star, a phenomenon; Bobby called me "A *Thing* on the Planet." *Bound for Glory,* the movie about Woody Guthrie, was almost a religious experience to make. And it generated awards for me. That was nice. Still, that opening on Broadway took the cake.

But with *Bill,* I seem to have finally achieved escape velocity. After this, I'll be in orbit, or maybe on the moon. It took a creature from another planet—that's Quentin—like Superman, set down here among us mortals, with a mission to serve and protect us. It took that kind of superhuman critter to get me out there.

Sounds weird, right? Well, it is, but, you know, I'm as weird as Quentin is, and I'm pretty sure that I, too, am a creature from another planet. I have very few human problems. We're both outsiders, ugly ducklings who grow up to be beautiful swans . . . if we get that far. That's the rub. Most guys like us don't take the whole trip. We bog down early on. Finish it off with dope or booze, or go down in a plane, and never realize our potential. Quentin, though, figured out, empirically, how to beat the game. He made a science out of it. Me, I'm just lucky. I stumble around bumping into walls, but miraculously I've always landed on my feet.

I figured out a long time ago that we are all living in a little box. We think it's the world, but it's just a box. If we work at it really hard, super-humanly hard, we break out of that box, and find ourselves in a truly big, wide world. But if we continue to evolve, we'll eventually discover that this New World is nothing but a bigger box. And then, maybe, we'll break out of that one into, yes, yet another much bigger box. The process may be endless. I don't know. I may not live long enough to find that out. And, if there is no end to it, it doesn't matter how long I live, or how many times I reinvent myself, I'll never come to an ending to the journey.

Someone once asked Einstein if the universe was infinite. And he said, "No. But it's *almost* infinite." Albert was one of the greatest stand-up comics of all time; I mean, look at his hair. He had to know that was funny. I'm sure he did it that way on purpose. And I think the mustache was camouflage, to hide the secret smile.

Anyway, back to the subject. I've gotta get this stuff out. This book and this whole trip are both almost over, and I've got to put it all in some kind of larger perspective before I write "The End."

I told a reporter for *Entertainment Weekly* the other day about a dream I had a few decades go. I was in a shipwreck, and almost drowned. But, as the ship went down, I managed to get out and swim up to the surface, like the folks in *Titanic*. I made it, just before my lungs were gonna burst, and, treading water while I tried to catch my breath, I looked around. There were no other people, not even any bits of wreckage. I was the sole survivor. But, way off in the distance, I saw the bobbing head of the survivor of another shipwreck. We swam toward each other, and met other survivors of other wrecks, and we became a new society of survivors, all our former friends and neighbors gone, working together on the island we were swept onto to create a new order of civilization, like Noah after the flood. This would work until the next shipwreck or similar catastrophe. Then the process would repeat itself all over again. Well, that's how my life has worked. Me the last man standing and meeting up with another little bunch of survivors like myself. I don't know anyone from my childhood, or from the Army, or from my stage actor life, or even from the old *Kung Fu*. I just go on, ever climbing; and here I am, at sixty-seven, still trying to make a name for myself, and being fucking reborn.

It's amazing.

Everyone is telling me that I'm wonderful in this movie. And they want to know how much Quentin had to do with that. Hey, he had everything to do with it—except, of course, the part that I contributed. I really bloomed under his gardening.

You know, film critics are always going on about how Quentin borrows everything from other movies. Somebody said to me somewhere in these travels that Quentin is like a great chef. He takes a big pile of ordinary things that you can find in anybody's garden, and out of them whips up a magnificent feast. Yes, he starts out with common ingredients, but the result is unique, and really tasty.

See you in the movies.